Jung as a Writer

Jung as a Writer traces a relationship between Jung and literature by analysing his key texts using literary criticism. An experimental writer whose radical and daring works have not yet been fully appreciated, Jung addresses the modern world darkened by weapons of mass destruction and global environmental crisis. Susan Rowland's exploration of his works illuminates the literary nature of Jung's writing in order to shed new light on his psychology and its relationship with literature as a cultural practice. The book maps Jung's unique blend of artistry and ideas, imagination and ethics, speculative fantasy and cultural analysis – an 'aesthetic science' which aims to overcome the divisions between art, religion and science. Jung's textual creativity provides new ways of being at home in modernity, by writing the psyche *whole*.

From early spiritualism in his doctoral thesis to the late autobiography, *Jung as a Writer* explores Jung's stunningly ambitious cultural project by looking at his writing through core themes of myth, gender, modernity, authority, argument, nature, history, discourse god(dess) and culture. Through studies of individual works such as *Anima and Animus, Trickster, On the Nature of the Psyche, Psychology and Alchemy, Aion* and *Synchronicity*, Jung's literary techniques are revealed as integral to his ideas. The book demonstrates Jung's contribution to literary and cultural theory in autobiography, gender studies, postmodernism, deconstruction, ecocriticism and postcolonialism, and concludes by offering a new, culturally orientated Jungian criticism.

Jung as a Writer traces the outline of a Jungian theory of discourse that bridges psyche, history and culture and provides a new and unique perspective on Jungian psychology that will be of interest to anyone involved in the study of Jung and psychoanalysis, as well as literary and cultural studies.

Susan Rowland is Reader in English and Jungian Studies at the University of Greenwich, UK. She is also a Fellow in the Centre for Psychoanalytic Studies, University of Essex, and the first Chair of the International Association for Jungian Studies. Her research takes Jung into literary studies and cultural theory.

Jung as a Writer

Susan Rowland

Routledge
Taylor & Francis Group

LONDON AND NEW YORK

First published 2005 by Routledge
27 Church Road, Hove, East Sussex, BN3 2FA

Simultaneously published in the USA and Canada
by Routledge
270 Madison Avenue, New York, NY 10016

Routledge is an imprint of the Taylor & Francis Group

© 2005 Susan Rowland

Typeset in Times by Garfield Morgan, Rhayader, Powys
Printed and bound in Great Britain by MPG Books Ltd, Bodmin
Paperback cover design by Sandra Heath

This publication has been produced with paper manufactured to strict
environmental standards and with pulp derived from sustainable forests.

British Library Cataloguing in Publication Data
A catalogue record for this book is available from the British Library

Library of Congress Cataloging in Publication Data

Rowland, Susan, 1962–
    Jung as a writer / by Susan Rowland.– 1st ed.
        p. cm.
    Includes bibliographical references and index.
    ISBN 1-58391-901-5 (hardcover) – ISBN 1-58391-902-3 (pbk.) 1. Jung,
C. G. (Carl Gustav), 1875–1961–Literary art. 2. Psychoanalysts as authors.
I. Title.

    BF109.J8R69 2005
    150.19'54'092–dc22

                                                        2004027215

ISBN 1-58391-901-5 (hbk)
ISBN 1-58391-902-3 (pbk)

For the philosopher, Gerard Livingstone, with love.

Contents

Preface

Jung and Freud could never agree about religion. What was for Freud an illusion with no future, remained for Jung a way of getting in touch with, and so regulating, unconscious energies. Secular modernity's loss of faith was, to him, a psychological disaster that could easily become an ethical collapse if there was no alternative found that could *treat* humanity's dark potential seriously. For Jung, the so-called advanced nations were in danger of substituting a literal narrative of apocalypse for a religious one. He regarded religion as the best type of discourse capable of taming the materialization of our unconscious destructiveness in weapons of mass destruction. All his works after the Second World War are devoted to finding a form of psychic healing that would avert the acting out of apocalyptic myth. So he experimented with the kinds of writing in which the word has the power to heal through appeal to more than rational understanding. For it was the privilege of rational cognition over any other kind of psychic endeavour, he believed, that has caused irrationality and unconsciousness to be repressed so far that it has become dark matter.

Jung and Freud once had a conversation about dark matter, meaning the religious heritage of modernity that had been pushed to one side. Freud wanted Jung to hold onto the sexual theory of psychic energy as a 'bulwark. . . [a]gainst the black tide of mud. . . of occultism' (Jung 1963/1983: 173). I think that this conversation has unwittingly found a home in twentieth-century humanities, and in its cultural theory in particular. For the centrality of Freudian principles (ironically in theorizing claiming so eloquently to seek out the margins) has often worked to banish religious thinking and, significantly, what it represents in terms of sheer imaginative exuberance informing ethics, metaphysics, psychology, art and, crucially, politics. Cultural theory became determinedly secular, and thereby lies some of its own contemporary marginality in a twenty-first century that desperately needs to understand the mechanisms of faith and power.

One development in the humanities is suggestive of the avoidance of religion and of Jung, as a metonym for it. Literary studies, with the insecurity of a relatively new subject in higher education, is deeply attached to canons of 'authorized' works. During the last century it replaced a canon of great literary authors with one of great theorists. While there is nothing inherently reprehensible in agreeing a core curriculum of superior texts, the problem lies in the (ironically) 'theological' reading of them that restricts their revolutionary implications. Just as canonical Shakespeare was not read in the 1950s for his criticism of racial politics, so Michel Foucault was not read in the 1980s as one who would expose the structures of exclusion that make up the secularizing discourse of literary studies and cultural theory.

My argument on a large scale is that endemic marginalization in the humanities needs to be examined if they are to be able to respond to a world of environmental crisis and global terror. On a small scale, Jung's omission from cultural theory is so profound as to be more than can be accounted for by his real political and personal defects, which have been extensively researched (Samuels 1993; Bair 2004). Jung not only is not read, he is misread while being unread. What many scholars in the humanities regard as 'Jungian' is often a distortion of what he actually wrote. The taboo surrounding his role in cultural theory ought itself to arouse suspicion in those who are expert on exclusion.

A conservative with revolutionary ideas, Jung's works deconstruct the divide between art and science. He does so knowingly because he held that only by uniting the imagination germane to both could the modern world be restored to health. As the critic and novelist Terry Eagleton has demonstrated, cultural theory today is emaciated and lacking with respect to some of the most urgent political and ethical challenges:

> Cultural theory. . . fails to deliver. It has been shamefaced about morality and metaphysics, embarrassed about love, biology, religion and revolution, largely silent about evil, reticent about death and suffering, dogmatic about essences, universals and foundations, and superficial about truth, objectivity and disinterestedness. . . It is. . . a rather awkward moment in history to find oneself with little or nothing to say about such fundamental questions.
>
> (Eagleton 2003: 101–2)

I am not going to argue that Jung is always right, or is even the most helpful on all the pressing issues above. However, he does address such fundamental questions in ways that could help our culture understand itself. *Jung as a Writer* reads Jung for the twenty-first century as a thinker for an era of global crisis. He analysed a world built on structures of exclusion and knew it was sick for that reason. Here is his heartfelt attempt to write it aesthetically and scientifically, as whole.

Susan Rowland
February 2005

Acknowledgements

Completion of this project was made possible by funding from the Arts and Humanities Research Board (AHRB) Research Leave Scheme, for which I am very grateful.

arts and humanities research board

The AHRB funds postgraduate training and research in the arts and humanities, from archaeology and English literature to design and dance. The quality and range of research supported not only provides social and cultural benefits but also contributes to the economic success of the UK. For further information on the AHRB, please see their website www.ahrb.ac.uk.

I would especially like to thank Andrew Samuels for all his generous help during the writing of this book, including inspiring the epilogue. *Jung as a Writer* has benefited enormously from his support. I have also gained so much from email conversations with David Tacey, and from all the other members of the first committee of the International Association for Jungian Studies (www.jungianstudies.org), Raya Jones, Renos Papadopoulos, Andrew Samuels, Don Fredericksen, Lucy Huskinson, Ien Hazebroek-Buijs, Alberto Pereira Lima Filho, and Leslie Gardner. In addition Roderick Main went out of his way to help by discussing synchronicity with me. Responsibility for all opinions and any errors is, of course, mine, but I would like to express my gratitude to the following for sharing their insights into Jung: Sue Austin, Luke Hockley, Chris Hauke, Robert Segal, Terence Dawson, Frances Gray and Phil Goss. I would also like to thank staff and students at the Centre for Psychoanalytic Studies, University of Essex, where I have the honour to be a Fellow. In particular, Liz Evans's work on Jung and ecology was of great assistance.

Judie Newman and Avril Horner supported this project when I applied to the AHRB for funding and I am very grateful to them.

Three research students at my institution, the University of Greenwich, have contributed a lot to my thinking about Jung and writing. Thank you, David Weaver, James Barrett and Debbie Phung. My kind colleagues, in particular Pippa Guard, Jenny Bavidge, John Williams, Peter Humm, John Dunne and Gareth Jenkins, have strengthened my resolve and provided consolation. The sensitive sympathy of friends such as Wendy Pank, Christine Saunders, Edmund Cusick, Claire Dyson, Ailsa Camm, Juliet John, Alice Jenkins, Margaret Erskine and Wendy Young has been wonderful. I am also truly lucky to have an understanding family in John, Cathy and Mary Rowland. The support of Gerard Livingstone in helping me write this book is more than I can say.

An earlier version of Chapter 2 appeared as, 'Myth, Biography and Jung', *Harvest: International Journal for Jungian Studies*, 2003, vol. 49, no. 1, pp. 22–39.

Grateful acknowledgement is made for permission to reprint from the following previously published material:

Jung, C. G., *Collected Works*, vol. 1, *Psychiatric Studies*, G. Adler and R. F. C. Hull (eds and trans) 1957, published by Taylor & Francis.

Jung, C. G., *The Collected Works of C.G. Jung*, vol. 1, *Psychiatric Studies*, G. Adler and R. F. C. Hull (eds and trans). Copyright 1957 by Princeton University Press. Reprinted by permission of Princeton University Press.

Jung, C. G., *Collected Works*, vol. 7, *Two Essays on Analytical Psychology*, 2nd ed, G. Adler and R. F. C. Hull (eds and trans) 1966, published by Taylor & Francis.

Jung, C. G., *The Collected Works of C.G. Jung*, vol. 7, *Two Essays on Analytical Psychology*, 2nd ed, G. Adler and R. F. C. Hull (eds and trans). Copyright 1966, by Princeton University Press. Reprinted by permission of Princeton University Press.

Jung, C. G., *Collected Works*, vol. 8, *The Structure and Dynamics of the Psyche*, 2nd ed, G. Adler and R. F. C. Hull (eds and trans) 1969, published by Taylor & Francis.

Jung, C. G., *The Collected Works of C.G. Jung*, vol. 8, *The Structure and Dynamics of the Psyche*, 2nd ed, G. Adler and R. F. C. Hull (eds and trans). Copyright 1969 by Princeton University Press. Reprinted by permission of Princeton University Press.

Jung, C. G., *Collected Works*, vol. 9i, *The Archetypes and the Collective Unconscious*, G. Adler and R. F. C. Hull (eds and trans) 1959, published by Taylor & Francis.

Jung, C. G., *The Collected Works of C.G. Jung*, vol. 9i, *The Archetypes and the Collective Unconscious*, G. Adler and R. F. C. Hull (eds and trans). Copyright 1959 by Princeton University Press. Reprinted by permission of Princeton University Press.

Jung, C. G., *Collected Works*, vol. 9ii, *Aion: Researches into the Phenomenology of the Self*, G. Adler and R. F. C. Hull (eds and trans) 1951, published by Taylor & Francis.

Jung, C. G., *The Collected Works of C.G. Jung*, vol. 9ii, *Aion: Researches into the Phenomenology of the Self*, G. Adler and R. F. C. Hull (eds and trans). Copyright 1959 by Princeton University Press. Reprinted by permission of Princeton University Press.

Jung, C. G., *Collected Works*, vol. 11, *Psychology and Religion: West and East*, 2nd ed, G. Adler and R. F. C. Hull (eds and trans) 1969, published by Taylor & Francis.

Jung, C. G., *The Collected Works of C.G. Jung*, vol. 11, *Psychology and Religion: West and East*, 2nd ed, G. Adler and R. F. C. Hull (eds and trans). Copyright 1969 by Princeton University Press. Reprinted by permission of Princeton University Press.

Jung, C. G., *Collected Works*, vol. 12, *Psychology and Alchemy*, 2nd ed, G. Adler and R. F. C. Hull (eds and trans) 1968, published by Taylor & Francis.

Jung, C. G., *The Collected Works of C.G. Jung*, vol. 12, *Psychology and Alchemy*, 2nd ed, G. Adler and R. F. C. Hull (eds and trans). Copyright 1968 by Princeton University Press. Reprinted by permission of Princeton University Press.

Jung, C. G., *Collected Works*, vol. 15, *The Spirit in Man, Art, and Literature*, G. Adler and R. F. C. Hull (eds and trans) 1966, published by Taylor & Francis.

Jung, C.G., *The Collected Works of C.G. Jung*, vol. 15, *The Spirit in Man, Art, and Literature*, G. Adler and R. F. C. Hull (eds and trans). Copyright 1968 by Princeton University Press. Reprinted by permission of Princeton University Press.

Jung, C. G., *Collected Works*, vol. 17, *The Development of Personality*, 2nd ed, G. Adler and R. F. C. Hull (eds and trans) 1964, published by Taylor & Francis.

Jung, C.G., *The Collected Works of C.G. Jung*, vol. 17, *The Development of Personality*, 2nd ed, G. Adler and R. F. C. Hull (eds and trans). Copyright 1964 by Princeton University Press. Reprinted by permission of Princeton University Press.

Jung, C. G., *Collected Works*, vol. 18, *Miscellany*, G. Adler and R. F. C. Hull (eds and trans) 1977, published by Taylor & Francis.

Jung, C. G., *The Collected Works of C.G. Jung*, vol. 18, *Miscellany*, G. Adler and R. F. C. Hull (eds and trans) Copyright 1977 Princeton University Press. Reprinted by permission of Princeton University Press.

Chapter 1

Introduction: Jung and literature
'Poetry' CW15, 'Psychology and Literature' CW15, 'Ulysses' CW15

> If it were possible to personify the unconscious, we might think of it as a collective human being. . . having at his command a human experience of one or two million years, practically immortal.
>
> (Jung 1931/1960, CW8: para. 673)

> The collective unconscious, moreover, seems to be not a person, but something like an unceasing stream or perhaps an ocean of images and figures which drift into consciousness in our dreams or in abnormal states of mind.
>
> (Jung 1931/1960, CW8: para. 674)

> Therein lies the social significance of art: it is constantly a work educating the spirit of the age, conjuring up the forms in which the age is most lacking.
>
> (Jung 1922/1966, CW15: para. 130)

Introduction

Introducing this book

In this book I aim to explore the works of C. G. Jung by looking at how he wrote them. Why devote such attention to Jung's writing style? Of course every writer who has something to say will find it affected by his or her means of saying it. So given Jung's profound impact on psychology, the history of ideas and culture, it is important to consider the kinds of expression that convey his unique perspective. However, it is the contention of this book that there is something special, and hitherto neglected, in the need to examine Jung's prose.

For Jung believed *and wrote as though he believed* that the thinking and discriminating mind – conventionally used to produce non-fictional argument – was situated within a sea of unconscious creativity. To him this inner world of unfathomable and inexhaustible creativity is one of the most important aspects of the human mind. So it is not enough just to write about it in a rational, logical manner. Jung thought that psychology writing should aspire to the greatest authenticity by including unconscious psychic creativity *within* writing, not limit it to outside, to what psychology is *about*. Truly, Jung's works aim for a fidelity to psyche-logos, words that respond to the *whole* of the mind and not just its well-mapped territories.

My metaphor of the mind as a landscape, and psychology as a form of mapping the unknown, is indicative of the kinds of thinking this book will look at. For Jung proves to be persistently fascinated with the psyche as a form of space and time. First of all, however, I will introduce some of the basic approaches I will be using and offer those readers new to Jung a guide to the most significant Jungian ideas.

Jung has often been criticized for his writing style. At times given to what appears as self-indulgent digressions, many of his essays seem to constitute an excursion around his topic rather than the crisp, tightly focused abstract prose modern culture has been conditioned to call 'science'. Indeed, the struggle to define 'scientific writing' when addressed to the vagaries of the human psyche is the subject of much of Jung's unique style. Roderick Main has comprehensively analysed Jung's attitude to science, especially in relation to religion (Main 2000, 2004). It will be one of the tasks of this book to look at how 'science' is used as problematic textual terrain; how it becomes a literary domain constructed and, often, deconstructed in the works.

Jung as a Writer uses methodologies devised in the discipline of literary studies in order to explore Jung's writing. My purpose is to show that literary techniques can provide a valuable perspective on Jung because the notion of creativity was fundamental to his conception of the psyche. In writing, Jung is not just describing the creativity of the psyche, his words also enact and perform it. It is possible that here we have a clue to Jung's constant revision to his texts. For perhaps, for Jung, a piece of writing was only truly valid if it retained a trace of the spontaneity that he believed to be integral to psychic functioning.

Take, for example, the first two quotations at the head of this chapter. Situated close together in an essay that purports to be introductory, they would appear to be going in different directions. If I wished to summarize them, I could say: on the one hand, the collective unconscious is like a mythical ageless being; on the other hand, it is not like a being, it is like an ocean, a flow of images. Readers new to Jung could be forgiven for finding such – essentially literary playing with metaphors – unhelpful. Why tell stories of the collective unconscious instead of offering a neat definition? What *is* the collective unconscious? What is it really like?

Fortunately for Jung's durability in the psychological community, he did provide 'proper' definitions and offer firm 'concepts'. Shortly I am going to make use of this kind of writing and give an outline of the key ideas for those unfamiliar with his work. However, the juxtaposition of these two quotations illustrates something very important: Jung put the expressive, creative nature of the psyche *first*. The ability of anyone, including himself, to produce a comprehensive science of the psyche, even to describe psychic processes accurately in words, comes second to the innate property of the human mind to be mysterious. Ultimately, the psyche confounds the essentially cultural divisions of science and art, will reveal them to be culture. The unconscious is like a mythical being; no, the unconscious is like an ocean of flowing images. It is an attempt to evoke in writing what cannot be entirely grasped: the fleeting momentary presence of something that forever mutates and reaches beyond the ego's inadequate understanding.

Such a form of writing cannot help being, in part, literary. This is not to allege that Jung was, or considered himself to be, the author of fiction. Rather, his psychology needs to be understood in terms of its aesthetic qualities. And these qualities, in the Jungian approach, do not detract from its identity as 'psychology'; they are basic to it.

Just a quick note about the structure of this book. The following chapters concentrate on large topics such as 'Gender', 'Myth', 'Nature', 'Culture' and 'Argument' by focusing on major Jungian works. These chapters often fall into two parts because I am doing two things. First of all I will be drawing out the implications of Jung's way of writing on a subject; constructing an argument about *what* is presented. Second, I will examine the organization of Jung's text directly, the *how* it is written. Of course it is integral to my project that there can be no real separation between content and form. Therefore the chapters constitute an attempt to realize a whole, by a discussion of parts that belong together in an aesthetic entity.

So while the overall scope of the book is to understand the extent and consequences of the combination of aesthetic and scientific writing, individual chapters will pursue discrete but related themes. After introducing Jung's core ideas, the rest of Chapter 1 will examine his role as a literary critic. Chapter 2 takes 'myth' as its subject since it is a form of representation that Jung wanted at the heart of his psychology. Naturally, myth is a key expression of the tension in Jung between narrative and conceptual expression. Therefore Chapter 3 looks at this dichotomy as one between dialectical or oppositional thinking, and storytelling, in the complex area of gender. Desire and control come together in the fascination with the feminine as spectral.

As a result of this study, the perspective of Chapter 4 on Jung's form of 'argument' is able to explore his use of rhetorical versus logical methods. This chapter also uncovers the key role played by textual criticism or hermeneutics, in the building of the psychology. So later, Chapter 5 on 'nature' develops Jung's textual sense with the help of theories of ecocriticism (devoted to rethinking the relation of 'man and nature'). Now able to show Jung as a dialogical thinker and author, I explore how Jung's writing reaches out to the ecosystem in ways that could excite (post)modernity.

Chapter 6 turns to history and the writing of the self as the discourses of the imagination. *Jung as a Writer* develops by analysing Jung's imagination as progressively more plural and spatial, as the tension between literature and science drives him into experimental and fantasy modes. Always he seeks to enlarge the psychic home of modernity, so in Chapter 7, I look at his understanding of culture and ethics in the context of science, gender and religion. Ultimately, Jung's struggle with writing is with a modernity historically framed by exclusion. In Chapter 7, the critique of modern culture is polarized between issues of visibility and intelligibility. The book ends with a reversal, in that the art of Jung's writing provides a Jungian approach to art. The Epilogue gives a new Jungian criticism of Shakespeare's *Hamlet* in order to demonstrate Jung's writing as a reading of the psyche as an organ of meaning in space and time.

Jung for literary studies?

Literary studies or the discipline of 'English' has neglected Jung to its own detriment. On the one hand, a form of Jungian literary criticism exists that draws upon the conceptual Jung; the one that offers definitions abstracted *from* the writings and applied *to* fictional texts. Such criticism often ignores the aesthetic quality of Jung's own prose. On the other hand, the explosion of literary theory in the latter part of the twentieth century has drawn almost exclusively upon Freudian and Lacanian psychic principles.

In an era of philosophical and ethical approaches to literature, it seems perverse to exclude Jung, as the 'other'. Jungian literary criticism needs to be brought into modern literary theory and literary theory needs to look at what and how Jung actually wrote. Not least because Jung's specific essays on literature reveal him to be deeply concerned with literature as cultural production, as the third quotation at the start of the chapter demonstrates.

The rest of Chapter 1 will provide a guide to the key concepts, an analysis of the essays on literature, and then will look at Jung's surprising and fantastic act of cultural criticism of *Ulysses* by James Joyce (Joyce 1922). Readers familiar with Jung might like to skip the next section and move on to the works on literature and art.

Introducing Jung: A guide to key concepts

In addition to this brief introduction to Jung, I would recommend the novice to consult Andrew Samuels's ground breaking *Jung and the Post-Jungians* (1985), and *A Critical Dictionary of Jungian Analysis* (Samuels *et al.* 1986).

To begin with the founding principle of Jung's psychology is to realize that the unconscious is superior to the capacity of the ego to comprehend it. The unconscious is characteristically spontaneous and creative. It often acts independently of cognitive structures brought to bear by the ego and it is 'collective' because it contains structuring principles inherited collectively by mankind. These elements Jung came to call 'archetypes'.

A common misconception is that archetypes are inherited images, inherited *content*. They are not. Archetypes are inherited principles for certain kinds of generic meanings. Those meanings actually generated, or images produced in dreams, will depend to a great extent on the culture and personal history of the dreamer.

In addition to the superior spontaneity of the unconscious, Jung believed that the psyche was developing forwards towards some goal; it is teleological. The reason that the collective unconscious is so playfully active is that it is leading the more limited ego – that part of myself that I know and can control – into greater forms of consciousness possible through relationship with the unconscious. The notion of a teleological goal-oriented psyche is a fundamental difference between the theories of Sigmund Freud and Jung. Freud believed that the unconscious was dominated by the repression of infantile sexual fantasy.

Jung largely accepted Freud's pioneering concept of the Oedipus complex in which the child structures its ego-unconscious relationship through repressing forbidden incestuous desires. However he regarded the unconscious so produced – looking backwards into the archaic vestiges of infancy – as a less significant 'personal unconscious'. It is the task of adult subjectivity to realize ever more of the collective inheritance of archetypes that drive the psyche forwards.

The name Jung gave to the lifelong, complex relationship between ego and archetypal energies is 'individuation'. A person individuates, becomes more individual and less conventional, because archetypes *compensate* for the biases of the ego, whether they be cultural or personal obsessions. The collective unconscious of archetypes is devoted to opposing and compensating rigid opinions, tendencies and modes of functioning in the ego. Therefore the psyche is a dynamic, self-regulating mechanism. By drawing upon its own 'other', it aims to heal itself of one-sidedness.

Jung held that ideally the ego's role is to become a satellite of the most enigmatic and numinous archetype, which he called the 'self'. Therefore it is very important to understand that the word 'self' has a totally different emphasis in Jungian language than in everyday use. The self is one's identity as mystery. It is a state of being transcendent of, but not disconnected from, cultural forms. The second and sixth chapters of this book deal with some of Jung's radical and experimental attempts to write about the self.

The ego's goal is connection with the self yet other archetypal factors also play a powerful role in the individuating psyche. For compensation of the ego's personality may begin with opposition. Jung gave the generic name of the 'shadow' to those psychic images of the opposite qualities that the ego rejects as its conscious identity. Hence the shadow's capacity to generate images of horrifying and morally reprehensible modes of behaviour with seemingly annihilating potency. The shadow is that which the ego has no wish to be; the darkness in the soul it has no wish to live out. It is therefore that which the ego must understand as its own potential, its own 'other' side. Too often the inner psychic shadow is projected 'outside' onto another person, race, culture or history. Only by recognizing the shadow as a figure *within* the psyche is the danger of demonizing the other avoidable.

A less potentially catastrophic form of psychic compensation is that of gender. On the one hand, Jung was essentialist on gender in believing that sexual identity bestows an unproblematic gender identity. Such a position leads him to state sporadically that women have less rational characteristics than men (see Chapter 3). On the other hand, the starkness of this position is problematized by the role of the founding principle of the creative psyche. For by producing radically different psychic gender images, individuation constantly undermines conscious gender identity. Archetypes are androgynous. They are as capable of manifesting feminine as masculine forms. The logic of individuation through compensation entails that men need to be in dialogue with feminine images in their psyche, women with masculine images. Jung called the feminine image within the psyche of a man, the 'anima'; the corresponding male figure in the psyche of a woman, the 'animus'.

It is important to remember that the unconscious is the leading partner in individuation. Women and men are required to come to terms with their inner bisexuality and to respect the other, both within and without, in the form of the other gender. In *Jung: A Feminist Revision* I extensively analysed Jung's radical and naive treatment of gender (Rowland 2002). Here it forms the subject of Chapter 3. Gender provides one of the greatest points of tension within Jung's writings as it often becomes the structuring pivot between the desire to pin down the psyche in rational statements, and the need to acknowledge the limitations inherent in that very desire.

Indeed it is this tension between the desire to know something definitely and completely and the requirement to keep the creativity of the psyche as part of the act of cognition that underpins all of Jung's writing. It is time to see what he made of 'creative writing' unconstrained by the label 'psychology'; his treatment of literature and art.

'On the Relation of Analytical Psychology to Poetry' (Jung 1922/1966, CW15)

This dynamic essay critically focuses upon the whole notion of literature in relation to culture and intellectual disciplines. Too little attention has been paid to Jung's serious investigation of his own context in looking at something wholly outside his professional domain. What is at stake when using the lens of psychology to investigate avowedly aesthetic writing?

'On the Relation of Analytical Psychology to Poetry' falls into four movements in which four stages of argument roughly correspond to the progression of the text. There is a linear spine to both the essays on literature discussed here, despite a tendency to a circling recapitulation of themes, which we will discover to be even more pronounced in the larger works. The four movements are: first, the essay's exploration of disciplinary frameworks; second, the autonomy of art *vis-à-vis* the artist, together with the iconography of artistic symbols and signs; third, Jung offers a surprisingly trenchant critique of 'scientific language'; fourth, that the role of some art is to compensate the prevailing culture. Literature can either veer towards being an expression of the ideals of its epoch or, conversely, it may subvert its norms.

In a disciplinary frame

> Art by its very nature is not science, and science by its very nature is not art.
>
> (Jung 1922/1966, CW15: para. 99)

Jung begins by writing explicitly as a scientist and opening 'On the Relation of Analytical Psychology to Poetry' by insisting upon disciplinary contexts. To assume straightforwardly that a psychology can explain all art or even religion would constitute a 'violation' of their 'essential nature' (ibid.: para. 98). Art and religion can never become subdivisions of psychology. Any attempt on the part of psychology to expand its framework to encompass such territories betrays an underlying assumption: that there is some fundamental 'unifying principle' that would justify such disciplinary imperialism (ibid.: para. 99). One discipline may subsume another only if there is some underlying truth that unites them.

Crucially, Jung finds no grounds for such a unifying principle from cultural history. 'Primitives', he says grandly, do mingle psychology, art and religion, but in an 'undifferentiated chaos' (ibid.: para. 99). I shall be looking at the endemic colonialism of this notion of 'primitives' in the following chapter. Here it is important to stress that Jung *resists* condensing art, psychology and religion into one drive or principle in cultural history, and in the individual's development from childhood. The plurality of differentiated states pertaining to these separable entities should not be falsely homogenized.

For the consequences of such a reduction to 'oneness' would be to project a favourite mechanism of the 'scientific attitude', that of causality, where it has no business. Jung argues that it is illegitimate to condense the chaotic, undifferentiated infant psyche into one structural psychological principle that would then determine or 'cause' artistic and religious expression. Here,

Jung's prime candidate for the error of making infantile psychology subsume all cultural production makes an appearance: Sigmund Freud.

To Freud, insists Jung, art and literature are reducible to infantile
neuroses. Through this 'corrosive' method, the work of art is reduced to
the all too familiar dynamics of sexual repression and Oedipal agonies. So
from the imposition of a unifying principle, psychology itself becomes an
aggrandizing monster that presumes to a superior explanatory power over
art. Jung is quick to elaborate on the weaknesses of what he has set up as
the Freudian method. Since all poets share the common human predicament of a father and mother complex, the compulsion to make all art
submit to Oedipal explanations risks saying the same thing over and over
again. It turns art into a neurotic search for symptoms.

Signs, symbols and detaching art from the artist

Jung is undoubtedly unfair to Freud, given the other's capacity for a
nuanced response to literature. Yet, the argument about causality and
Jung's desire to resist it is important for art criticism. In particular, Jung
alleges that Freud treats artistic expression as a series of signs standing for
symptoms. As he goes on to explain, the work of art as sign points to what
is already known or knowable (usually personal or Oedipal anxieties). To
counter such a reductive reading practice, Jung offers the notion of the
'symbol' in which the work or image is an emblem of the unknown or
unknowable. Such art principally speaks a language foreign to the ego of its
author; its significance surpasses traces of the formation of the ego. Such art
is autonomous of the author because it is rooted in the *collective* unconscious, not reliant upon the author's *personal* life, but rather his *impersonal*
one. For symbolic art, the author is not a guide to the work.

To illustrate the idea of the work of art possessing symbolic inde-
pendence from its author, Jung describes it as a plant that uses the human
scribe merely as a 'nutrient medium' (ibid.: para. 108). This portrayal of the
artist as a kind of 'zombie' suggests all sorts of science fiction possibilities.
It is reinforced by his repeated use of 'alien' and 'alien will' to indicate that
the hapless artist 'may be taken captive by his work' (ibid.: paras. 108–14).

One of the interesting aspects of this language of mutation is the way that
'nature' and 'plant' as words for art rooted in the collective unconscious,
become reframed as alien. For such works the reader is unable to interpret
the work in the sense of comprehending it fully, however many times it is
read and studied. Reading a symbolic work is to experience – in a phrase
redolent of a territorial mapping of the mind – 'bridges thrown out towards
an unseen shore' (ibid.: para. 116). However, despite this conjuring of
'alien' symbolic art, Jung concedes that many works do correspond to what
is known, conscious and intended by the author.

The later essay 'Psychology and Literature' will develop and name this division into intentional and symbolic works as 'psychological' and 'visionary' (Jung 1930/1950/1966, CW15: para. 139). It is worth mentioning here that Jung is fully aware of the problems of positing absolute categories. He notes that the intentional poet is capable of unleashing the alien will, just as a symbolic author may lapse into daylight conventions. More suggestively still, a culture may misread a work. It may fail to experience its true symbolic value until a later evolution of consciousness enlarges public understanding.

The problem of scientific language

When speculating about art and meaning, Jung regards himself to be in the sphere of art. Now he turns to address the issue of writing about art from the perspective of psychology *as a problem*. Psychology and science require cognitive analysis. This kind of writing is itself a construction made from splitting off rationality from irrationality. Rational language is the voice of an ego that rejects the functioning of the unconscious. Significantly, Jung's description of rational language as the proper mode of science problematizes the division from the unconscious, but does not directly challenge it. Science requires that irrational unconscious experience be broken down and fashioned into concepts:

> We have to break down life and events, which are self-contained processes, into meanings, images, concepts, well knowing that in doing so we are getting further away from the living mystery. As long as we ourselves are caught up in the process of creation, we neither see nor understand; indeed we ought not to understand, for nothing is more injurious to immediate experience than cognition. But for the purposes of cognitive understanding we must detach ourselves from the creative process and look at it from the outside. . . In this way we meet the demands of science.
>
> (Jung 1922/1966, CW15: para. 121)

So science 'frames' meaning in more than one respect. For science is a framework that *produces* scientific meaning; it does not merely transmit it from pre-existing reality. Science is a mode of thinking and writing that transforms psychic products. It is the making of rational meaning by discarding or reworking the irrational aspects of the mind. The activity of being scientific, in applying psychological concepts to unruly psychic texts, *constitutes* its own knowledge out of material that to some extent will forever escape such 'rational' working.

Jung is talking about critical distance, integral to both science and literary criticism, as a loss of *authenticity*. There is a gap between the experience of literature as an intervention in subjectivity and the ability to rationally 'frame' it.

After incorporating such a profound challenge to his own practice, and by extension to that of literary criticism, Jung makes a circular movement back to refine the categories that he put in place earlier. It is to risk the sin of simplistic causality to identify literary characteristics – in an artist and/or his art – with a psychological complex. However, art manifesting symptoms rather than symbols can be relegated to Freud's harshly described 'purgative methods' (ibid.: para. 125).

Such a concession is not really a rapprochement with Freud even though it is limited to symptom-led works considered of secondary interest. For Freudian criticism is now also transplanted to the framing discourse of science, about which Jung has just expressed reservations. The circling movement of the essay, back to the 'unsatisfactory' nature of Freudian psychoanalysis, has the clever effect of both exposing the limitations of the assumption of a unifying principle that subsumes art into psychology, while later revealing the problems of not possessing such an argument in the inauthenticity of critical distance.

Freud's ideas are inadequate, on the one hand, because they sink what is special about art into the common Oedipal story. On the other hand, their 'scientific' credentials for examining art are shaken by the argument that psychology creates itself out of psychic experience in a way that inevitably falsifies some of the psyche's native 'wildness'. A unifying principle, would, in fact, support psychology as exposing the 'true' interior forces within art. Freud cannot win: he obscures the art by his overmastering theory because *his* unifying principle sinks the unique qualities of the artifact. Yet without it, any attempt to speak of art in the language of science would be merely a rational screen unable to detect art's irrational properties. Doubly chastened, the Oedipal pathologizing of art resurfaces under two modes of erasure.

Another and better way of dealing with the problem of 'critical distance' is provided by Jung's notion of the 'collective' as pertinent to symbolic art. Without a principle of the 'collective' nature of symbols (which is Jung's way of asserting the social nature of human beings as fundamental), the rational apparatus of science could have no dialogue with the creative psyche. So it is unsurprising that the rest of the essay shows Jung interested in the relation of literature and culture as a mainstay of his scientific 'frame'.

Literature is cultural

To Jung all art is profoundly cultural. Intentional art, employing signs rather than symbols, is *expressive* of the cultural consciousness, of the surface preoccupations of the age. Symbolic art is compensatory: what is ignored or repressed in a culture is shaped by archetypal energies into something strange yet mysteriously necessary to the culture as much as to the individual. It is the archetypal symbol that animates the most powerful national allegories: the passion for 'mother' country or 'fatherland'. In educating the spirit of the age, art is socially transformative. Art is a means by which the collective unconscious informs collective society. Jung even brings to mind the way cultures operate by exclusion. In a resonant social metaphor he describes the symbolic artist as bringing to consciousness material consigned to 'the back streets' (ibid.: para. 131).

Finally, symbolic art has a cultural function more dynamically therapeutic than merely bringing to consciousness what has been excluded or missed out. Such art represents the healing self-regulation of the psyche amplified into the cultural dimension. Just as the collective unconscious provides a teleological drive for the individual psyche, so symbolic art structurally transforms collective culture in ways that amount to an internal self-regulating mechanism. Jung is quite explicit about this:

> Thus, just as the one-sidedness of the individual's conscious attitude is corrected by reactions from the unconscious, so art represents a process of self-regulation in the life of nations and epochs.
>
> (ibid.: para. 131)

Jung is here an early contributor to cultural studies. Suggestively, the essay ends with a twist. In a final flourish Jung calls for his audience to devise their own literary examples that would serve as flesh and blood to 'my abstract intellectual frame' (ibid.: para. 132). There would appear to be a lingering anxiety about disciplinary frameworks with their fatal ability to reduce mysterious psychic phenomena to inauthenticity. In Jung's language of the alien will battening upon the hapless artist as a nutrient medium there is more than a hint of the uncanny. Jung's own art in this essay exposes the way Enlightenment rationality ('my abstract intellectual frame') emerges out of that psychic hinterland, and then fails to contain it.

'Psychology and Literature' (Jung 1930/1950/1966, CW15)

In 'Psychology and Literature' Jung returns to the preoccupations of 'On Analytical Psychology in Relation to Poetry' with a heightened sense of the personal, philosophical and epoch-making role of art. In four movements again, Jung takes a Romantic sensibility into anxieties about modernity and popular culture. Yet his language also betrays a fear of the Romantic possibilities of art, as potential harbingers of chaos. First of all, he places his collective unconscious in pursuit of Romantic notions of literature aspiring to realize what can be thought of, yet not adequately represented.

In other words, Jung is more consciously interested in art of the sublime. Second, the argument about disciplinary frameworks is imaginatively recast in spatial and even territorial terms. The essay is framed as Jung's 'quest' beyond the bounds of 'science' to the door, the veil, the painted curtain blowing eerily over the abyss. Third, what was a far-reaching notion of the cultural function of art has intensified into Jung's own myth of the psychic perils of modernity. Science and reason are modern constructs designed to conceal more irrationally infused modes of consciousness from cultural recognition. Fourth and last, Jung has intimations about popular culture that are more evident to an age of mass media technology than to his own. To what extent does the hypnotic and addictive quality of popular art trouble the seemingly neat categories of 'psychological' and 'visionary'?

Jung in the Romantic sublime and beautiful

In this essay Jung officially divides literature into the 'psychological' mode of the known, collective consciousness and the 'visionary' category of works drawing more upon the collective unconscious (ibid.: para. 139). Jung's awed fascination for the 'greater' of his two categories, the visionary hints at an affiliation with Romantic theories of art. Approximating to the Romantic philosopher Edmund Burke's description of art as either 'beautiful' or 'sublime', the psychological and the visionary provide something of a Romantic psychology (Burke 1757). Like the 'beautiful', 'psychological' literature satisfies conventional aesthetic categories. Indeed its label derives from the fact that psychological art is its own psychologist: it inhabits the consciousness of author, reader and culture very comfortably. Psychological art may be subtle, but its artifice is fully present to its audience.

There is almost something suspicious about a class of literature that troubles no disciplinary framework, being transparent to both the aesthetician and the psychologist. Far more deeply disturbing is 'visionary' art that challenges structures of all kinds from the traditional disciplines to the very notion of 'human':

> Sublime. . . it arises from timeless depths; glamorous, daemonic, and grotesque, it bursts asunder our human standards of values and aesthetic form.
>
> (ibid.: para. 141)

'Abstract frameworks' quail before this red-blooded language.

A quest through disciplinary fields

At this point it is important to look closer at the essay's treatment of disciplinary categories. In an introduction published posthumously, Jung begins the essay by granting psychology itself some of the explosive qualities of his visionary art: it has 'burst the framework assigned to it by the universities' (Jung 1967/1984: 84). The implications of such a dramatic development of an area of intellectual enquiry are mitigated by the assertion that Jung claims no grand narrative. His psychology is not an overarching structure of knowledge. No one psychological approach can promote itself as orthodox dogma. As a psychologist, Jung is merely building hypotheses upon his own partly subjective premises (Jung 1967/ 1984: 84–5).

Jung uses spatial metaphors to suggest that psychology can expand into other areas without dominating them or violating their 'differences'. In effect he is starting to answer some of the problems about psychology mastering art criticism set up in the earlier essay on poetry. The figure he uses to suggest range without aggressive invasion is that of the psychology as a quest for truth into foreign realms. He 'must abandon his thickly walled specialist fortress and set out on the quest for truth' (ibid.: 85).

A quest suggests that the 'truth' sought for will be hard-won, its seizure will be fraught with dangers, and both the questor and the treasure itself may be transformed by the adventure. Of course, the quest is also the narrative genre of the hero myth. It carries overtones of the masculine ego seeking validation through appropriating the 'other' (truth) rather than making peace with it. Still, the insistence on leaving the 'thickly walled specialist fortress' is indicative of the risks to both the knower and the known (the ego and 'his' desire for rational cognition) that Jung is prepared to take.

He makes it clear that this quest should not be an 'encroachment' on the territory of the literary critic. Just as he cannot provide a complete theory of the psyche, so he will not attempt a comprehensive account of literature. In order to make the distinction between a psychology that would colonize art and his own designs, Jung metonymically displaces psychology, his avowed profession, into science. 'Science' here is that body which would characteristically impose causal explanations for art. Science would make diagnoses and the art would disappear into pathological symptoms. Only aesthetics is distinguished by the principle that 'a psychic product can be regarded as existing in and for itself' (Jung 1930/1950/1966, CW15: para. 135).

Jung is indeed on a quest, but in describing himself as having left the fortress of his specialism *as science*, he proves to have brought with him something innate to his *psychology*. For here he describes as fundamental to aesthetics the position we know to be his own on symbolic art from the earlier essay; a position he will soon allot in this text to visionary art. Far bolder than before, Jung is prepared to venture outside the fortress of psychology as science in order to secure aesthetics as *within* his psychology; its foreign heart stands for the unknown collective unconscious.

In fact, the extent and depth of Jung's quest identity in this essay only becomes truly apparent at the sublime spectre of the visionary. For the territorial spatial metaphor of different disciplines abutting each other is radically overthrown by the eruption of height and depth. The visionary is the *matter* of endless heights and unfathomable abysses. It metaphorically *undermines* Jung's landscape of quest through the fields of knowledge, by summoning a chaos that overwhelms direction, even and especially, the direction of Jung's argument. Then, at the moment of greatest peril, there is a touch of the domestic. Visionary art is suffused with archetypal energies that tear aside the curtain upon which ordinary reality is imaged:

> But the primordial experiences rend from top to bottom the curtain upon which is painted the picture of an ordered world, and allow a glimpse into the unfathomable abyss of the unborn and of things yet to be.
>
> (ibid.: para. 141)

It is as if on one level we are reminded that domesticity as a core of civilization is fragile, and therefore a suitable metaphor for the domestic architecture of the ego. This is an essay about not being at home in the psyche. Whereas the tone of the 'Poetry' text was sanguine about symbolically charged art, its 'blood' vital and coursing, later Jung seems more aware of the daemonic possibilities of the defeat of reason.

Jung's myth of modernity

Such tremendous intuitions lead Jung to develop a fully fledged myth of modernity. The post-Enlightenment west is characterized by a turning away from the recognition of the limitless potentials of the psyche. It has erected a 'shield of science and reason' to screen out uncomfortable manifestations of the unconscious (ibid.: para. 148). Whereas premodern peoples possessed a technology for collectively regulating the psyche in magic and propitiatory rituals, modernity is pitifully unaware of the probable consequences of ignoring the human hunger for the irrational.

Jung again identifies the scientific approach to literature with Freudian attempts at causal explanations, while arguing that such a scheme is wholly inadequate to account for visionary art (ibid.: para. 144). Now for visionary art, the emphasis has shifted from 'On Analytical Psychology in Relation to Poetry'. There the inadequacies of scientific language were explored, yet its very lack was seen as creating a necessary critical distance. Here Jung seems to be finding it more difficult to respond to daemonic unfathomability in the language of reason. So he turns deliberately to myth. The sublime visionary is of itself unrepresentable because it is the defeat of all cultural codes of understanding. Myth is a necessary resource because it preserves something of the numinous collective nature of the visionary, while at the same time managing its dangerous volatility by transmuting it into something less devastating to the ego. It is the proper role of the psychologist to bring myth – in multiple and comparative modes – to try to shape what can never be wholly accounted for in rational speech:

> [I]t is so dark and amorphous that it requires the related mythological imagery to give it form. In itself it is wordless and imageless, for. . . it is nothing but a tremendous intuition striving for expression.
>
> (ibid.: para. 151)

Still convinced that visionary art plays a vital compensatory role in culture, what comes to the fore in this essay is a gnawing anxiety about the vulnerability of modernity. Art, like dreams, has the power to heal by taking the compensatory function of dreams into collective consciousness. Jung even gives rare examples of how archetypal intuitions might take on 'modern dress' in contemporary dreams. Aircraft might be the equivalent of a mythological eagle, Pluto may lurk in a careless chauffeur, a woman selling vegetables is an earth mother while a railway crash may stand for the fight with a dragon (ibid.: para. 152).

There is a palpable sense of relief in Jung's turn to myth in this essay. It even provides a way back to science, on his own terms. What is needed is a science based on myth that refuses to replicate the errors of over-rational modernity. Integral to mythical language is the refusal to reduce the impersonality of the collective unconscious to the personality of the artist. The visionary work of art is like a child leaving the body of its artist-mother, giving the creative process a 'feminine quality. . . from the realm of the mothers' (ibid.: para. 159).

Again, in the progress of the visionary artist, Jung's writing enacts what he is describing. Embarked upon a quest into the psychic sources of art, Jung lost his bearings and suffered terrifying intimations of conceptual and mental chaos. In suggesting that only a 'science' of myth can both stabilize and map the annihilation of critical distance in the artist and his audience, he produces his own myth of modernity. 'Psychology and Literature' is a process of mythmaking laid bare: it is itself a creative work that transforms the mythological qualities of the psyche in art into a larger myth of the modern world. For the fortress of 'scientific psychology' has come to function as a constricting metonym for modernity itself.

Popular mythmaking beyond Jung's division into psychological/visionary

Consequently, it is not surprising that the retention of the binary frame in the division of art into 'psychological' and 'visionary' proves problematic.

Visionary art answers the thirst of the age. It is the compensatory dream of the collective culture. However, Jung acknowledges, not only is visionary art sometimes mistaken for psychological and vice versa, its cultural location cannot be securely pinpointed. 'High' or culturally valued art may be visionary or psychological and so may be popular or 'low' art forms. It is notable that Jung includes the creator of Sherlock Holmes, Conan Doyle, and the whole genre of the detective story, as well as the imperial fantasies of Rider Haggard in the category of the visionary (ibid.: para. 137).

Interestingly, both Haggard and Conan Doyle could be accused of popularizing genres strongly allied to powerful myths of modernity: that of the triumph of scientific reason in Holmesian detection and of western colonialism for Haggard. It could be argued that such writers bring into overt cultural consumption obscured mythical structures. Such elements are both supportive of contemporary cultural practices and contain – in the plural possibilities of myth – a counter-argument exposing darkness, failure and cruelty. In 'Psychology and Literature', Jung's quest leads him to adopt some of the customs of other realms. Like the artist, he becomes a myth-maker for his age; perhaps even anticipating the erosion of the division between 'high' and popular art in postmodernity. I will now look at Jung's literary criticism of a seminal modern work, *Ulysses* by James Joyce.

'Ulysses: A monologue' (Jung 1932/1966, CW15)

Jung's 'Ulysses' is an account of the act of reading James Joyce's long experimental novel of that title. It is an astonishing encounter with the literary text as 'other', in which Jung suffers in body and soul. Confounded, bored, repeatedly sent to sleep, he cannot cope with the novel as a conventional reader. In desperation he embarks upon his only other option: to adopt his therapeutic methods for himself and for the novel. What he gives *his* reader is a dramatic staging of reading as a traumatic event. Again, disciplinary frameworks are invoked with sensitivity to the possibility of doing violence to the integrity of the other.

The essay progresses through five movements. In the first stage, he argues that the bodily paralysis he experiences, is matched by the bodily non-cerebral quality of the novel. He calls *Ulysses* a tapeworm epic. Second, somatic distress leads Jung to reach for his professional identity as the only way of rousing his intellect and psyche. A third movement expresses the need, in an evocative image, to 'find a scaffold' for a meaningful response (ibid.: para. 169). Marking a fourth stage is the astounding conclusion that so profound is the novel's rendering of consciousness in multiple voices that it has become the mysterious Jungian 'self'. Finally and very seriously, Jung links this piece of modernist art to the weakened condition of the modern European. The essay ends with a provocative flourish: 'I am now getting on pretty well with my reading of *Ulysses* – forward!' (ibid.: para. 203).

Whatever the essay does for Jung's reader, writing it seems to have liberated his own psyche.

Reading the body and the tapeworm epic

One idiosyncratic step on Jung's part is only apparent later in his text. Where most readers identify the character Leopold Bloom, meandering around the Dublin of 1904, with the mythical traveller, Ulysses or Odysseus, Jung does not. He takes the novel title literally. For him, Ulysses is the many narrative voices and linguistic styles that make up the whole novel. You could say that Ulysses is the novel *Ulysses* as a 'being' if not accurately a 'personality'.

Therefore Jung opens by citing the passivity of Ulysses-narrator; he is a non-unified perceiving consciousness, a series of fragmented bodily stimuli. This Ulysses is almost a machine in the identification with physical senses; it is modern man as merged with technology:

> Joyce's Ulysses. . . is a passive, merely perceiving consciousness, a mere eye, ear, nose, and mouth, a sensory nerve exposed with choice or check to the roaring chaotic, lunatic cataract of psychic and physical happenings, and registering all this with almost photographic accuracy.
>
> (ibid.: para. 163)

As a result of the obsessive concentration on the senses, the book itself is 'senseless'. The reader is therefore forced into *becoming* Ulysses; a wanderer from one meaningless event to the next. Such emptiness has a psychological counterpart of horror and despair. Jung records falling asleep twice on the way to page 135 (ibid.: para. 165). He argues that the novel reveals the Joycean mind as cold-blooded and the text the offspring of 'visceral thinking' (ibid.: para. 166). In an image uniting the mental characteristics of the act of creation and the work, the novel is a worm written by a wormlike brainless organ:

> If worms were gifted with literary powers they would write with the sympathetic nervous system for lack of a brain.
>
> (ibid.: para. 166)

Moreover this species of worm literature is not confined to a portrayal of the outer skin of the world. *Ulysses* mingles subjective and objective so that the worm image begins to suggest inner and even cosmic qualities (ibid.: para. 166). It is a neat demonstration of Jung's contention that body and psyche are united, with neither one able to subordinate the representation of the other. Jung flourishes the 'fabulously procreative' tapeworm as a cosmos breeding endless Joycean chapters (ibid.: para. 166).

A sense of the novel as energetically generative is not accompanied by joyful comprehension. On the contrary, Jung the intrepid reader is depressed and feels fooled by the absence of recognizable meaning. It occurs to him that perhaps the novel is not even trying to 'represent' anything at all in its mindless sensory physicality (ibid.: para. 167).

Doctoring the text

Frustrated and forced to feel inferior, Jung, in some desperation, tries to recover his intellectual confidence by resorting to his professional role. Significantly, his attention is directed not to the book – an instance of his distrust of clinical diagnoses of works of art – but to himself as the receiving psyche. He starts to examine his own baffled irritated reactions (ibid.: para. 168).

Freed up by the switch of approach, Jung's meditation on the human body as source and subject begins to expand spatially and temporally. As a conversation with the intestines, the novel is saurian – pre-human, evoking figures of stone and the terrifying unconscious 'otherness' of nature. In this underworld there is no distinction between ego and other; the monstrous authorial being is everywhere and everything:

> From this stony underworld there rises up the vision of the tapeworm. . .
> In every segment of the book, however small, Joyce himself is the sole
> content of the segment. . . It is the boredom of nature.
>
> (ibid.: para. 169)

The novel is not a human character or a personality: it is a being. Perhaps the saurian reference suggests pre-Oedipal (and so pre-human) unconsciousness prior to the construction of the ego in early infancy. Consequently, *Ulysses* is 'art in reverse, a backside of art' (ibid.: para. 178). It turns what Jung has described as visionary art with its intimations of transcendence, into bodily abjection. Or as Jung puts it, '[e]schatology becomes scatology', in this response to modernity (ibid.: para. 195).

Finding a scaffold

However, a condition of the therapeutic framework is that it is inevitably interested in process and teleology. Where is the novel going? Or more accurately, where is the impact of the novel upon the reader's psyche going? What is the effect of the reduction, which is perhaps also a regression, of humanity to a wormlike condition? Jung's teleological psyche means that we can only truly know the present by including the perspective of the future: for culture as well as for the individual. So he diagnoses that the coldness and unrelenting sensory observation of Ulysses is the apotheosis of modern consciousness, so persistently attuned to matter. Jung suggests that the goal of the work is to *embody* a detachment of consciousness; the whole novel is a great moonlike eye. It is a union of body with psyche so complete that it ignores those inner demons that threaten to overmaster consciousness: 'in thrall neither to the gods nor to sensuality' (ibid.: para. 186). The reader becomes the many narrative eyes of Ulysses in a fusion of bodily sense with consciousness:

> This, surely, is its real secret, the secret of a new cosmic consciousness; and it is revealed not to him who has conscientiously waded through the seven hundred and thirty five pages, but to him who has gazed at his world and his own mind for seven hundred and thirty five days with the eyes of Ulysses.
>
> (ibid.: para. 186)

Ulysses is a novel that *enacts* the triumph of western consciousness. It is a performance rather than a representation. It structures a mask of consciousness in the act of reading.

For these reasons the novel proves resistant to most of the conceptual tools at Jung, the psychologist's, disposal. There is something schizophrenic about its alienation yet it does not display the lack of control of the illness.

Much more worrying for the Jungian literary critic, is that the archetypal armoury is also not up to the job. So wedded to consciousness is the novel that it cannot be described as either psychological or visionary. Far from the intelligibility of the 'psychological' novel, *Ulysses* also fails to be visionary in pointing to the unknown. It is not a dream (ibid.: para. 185). Similarly, when Jung casts around for an archetypal background and comes up with Molly Bloom as an anima figure, he has to concede that that is not really what the book is about as its true subject is objective consciousness (ibid.: para. 185). By the end of the essay, only Jung's belief that a work of art is profoundly cultural, as either compensatory or revelatory of collective consciousness, will enable him to draw conclusions. To do this Jung needs to explore further the nature of *Ulysses*'s modern consciousness and its function for its writer.

Ulysses the novel resists causal explanations. Jung distrusts them anyway as they too easily become 'scientific' reductions of the power of art to confound and disturb the psyche. He also resists biographical criticism while conceding that Joyce's Irish Catholic background is the conduit for the medieval concentration on the desouled body. It is not, however, the sufficient explanation for it. Very subtly, Jung produces the figure of 'scaffolding' for the narrative understanding of a work of art. 'Themes are unavoidable, they are the scaffolding for all psychic happenings', he pronounces (ibid.: para. 169). He thereby detaches a critical narrative from a causal 'explanation'.

Scaffolding is not an integral part of a building. It is an addition, a *supplement*, erected temporarily to contain a crisis for the purpose of repairs. Indeed scaffolding is a liminal structure between the outside and the inside. Jung suggests that the reader both detects and erects themes just as a scaffolding respects, yet is an addition to, a pre-existing work. A narrative understanding of art does not need to dismantle it, nor to excavate a causal explanation by digging up the foundations to have a look. Such 'scientific' causal approaches are both destructive of the work and ignore the aesthetic appreciation of the building. 'Scaffolding' may be a necessary intervention for a work that has induced trauma in the reader. It enables the reader to stabilize her mental environment without violating the essential integrity or 'otherness' of the work. It is literary criticism drawing upon insights from other disciplines as temporary aids, not as a bulldozer.

Of course, hidden within the word 'scaffolding' is 'scaffold', a public structure from which criminals were once hanged. Jung suggests that for powerful works of art the reader needs to 'add' something out of her own psychic processing of the text; something that will erect a structure to contain the trauma. Yet what is erected could itself prove the means of augmenting its lethal potency. Literary criticism need not be safe and recuperative, as Jung goes on to show in finding in *Ulysses* an indictment of western modernity.

As a work of creative destruction, *Ulysses* is part of Joyce's forward looking search for unity of personality within the fragmented consciousness of modernity. If considered causally related to the author, then Joyce would appear as a mere victim of his repressive Catholic origins. On the other hand, if granted the scaffolding of a teleological perspective, he is a reformer, who is currently enacting the stage of nullifying the corrupt heritage (ibid.: para. 183). Joyce is even a prophet as his soulless, heartless novel implicitly denounces the 'hideous sentimentality' of his epoch (ibid.: para. 183).

Ulysses as Jungian self

Focused by the (scaffolding) theme of cultural reform, *Ulysses* is a spiritual exercise in consciousness; it functions as an 'eye' for perceiving the world. That does not mean, as Jung goes on to specify, that the novel is all ego. On the contrary, the ego, with its organizing, lucid properties, has dissolved into multiplicity. *Ulysses* is so complete that it amounts to a cosmos, yet so multifarious that it subsumes any centre of ego understanding. Joyce is everywhere in the novel and is everything: there is no self–other dynamic in the work. Quite unlike many conventional Jungian approaches, the novel is not symbolically pointing to the unknown in a structure that presupposes an observing self-conscious ego. Rather, the heaving visceral life of the

Ulysses narrator *is the self*. Against the vastness of this novel self, the author, Joyce, is merely an ego complex:

> The ego of the creator of these figures. . . had dissolved into the countless figures of *Ulysses*. And yet, or rather for that very reason, all and everything. . . is Joyce himself. . . not the ego but the self. For the self alone embraces the ego and the non-ego.
>
> (ibid.: para. 188)

Ulysses is the self as creator-god, the higher being who can return home only when he has achieved detachment from both mind and matter (ibid.: para. 192). In this sense only is the many voiced Ulysses what Jung calls a symbol. He is a symbol of the self as totality. Here the novel works as a symbol in the mind of the reader by *enacting* totality: it can never be completely *represented* for it includes the irrepresentible 'other'. In the reader's psyche the novel is sublime, pointing to what is not yet, and can never be wholly, known.

In this most imaginative act of Jungian literary criticism, Jung here explores the implications of this narrator as self. 'He' is a being of extreme plurality. 'His' expansiveness subsumes personality and gender since 'he' is not only all the characters in the novel, but is also a monstrous being composed of all the houses, pubs, activities, the drama, the weather, food, drink; *everything* made into consciousness (ibid.: para. 198). The only trace of an individuation narrative within Jung's account is his perception of the novel's ending. In the final moments, there appears to be an evolution within the self of masculine creativity into feminine acquiescence. And existence beyond extreme consciousness takes Jung's reading further into topos of the reformer, the cultural critic.

The critique of the western subject

Jung's essay ends with a profound sense of the novel as a dynamic cultural artifact. *Ulysses* is a meditation on western material consciousness that seeks to be part of its transformation. This literary work goes so deep into the western obsession with matter that it achieves a detached consciousness. Consequently, it performs a spiritual exercise for its culture; it is a catalyst of a new consciousness, an escape from blind entanglement in matter:

> O *Ulysses*, you are truly a devotional book for the object-besotted, object-ridden white man! You are a spiritual exercise, an ascetic discipline, an agonising ritual.
>
> (ibid.: para. 201)

When Jung addresses the novel, O *Ulysses*, it is a sign, literally an acting out, of distance. Beginning the essay in blind, paralysing immersion in the text, Jung shows how his self-analysis of its effects has enabled the 'critical distance' of a critic *without the resort to the conceptual language of the scientist* that he identified as problematic in the 'Poetry' essay. Jung, the literary critic has achieved a response to art in which his professional identity as psychologist is liminal to his aesthetic sense.

The early stages of Jung, irritated, falling asleep over his reading, are his entanglement in matter. He is possessed by the other; his ego is swamped, and, at first, he is in danger of being reduced to mindless bodily responses in sleep. The scaffolding that can free his ego from the other, the text, is initially only available through the desperate resort of assuming his doctor persona. At his disposal are therapeutic techniques and the belief that both psyche and cultures have a teleological drive to remake consciousness. It is this tenet that provides the scaffolding to make a narrative that is both an aesthetic act of criticism *and* one of self-therapy: as long as the 'other' is respected as other, then the two activities can become a mutual dialogue.

Jung's criticism of *Ulysses* demonstrates an act of individuation (through reading) with the other that is the novel. The spiritual exercise for white western man that he evokes at the end of his essay has already taken place in the essay itself. The essay is no record: it acts out individuation as a cultural and psychic event. We witness the very immersion, struggle for meaning, and then detachment from the dream-image/text/event/person, etc., with a changed consciousness that is the habitual path of individuation. Here literary criticism *is* individuation because the achievement of critical distance, the ability to say something meaningful about the novel, *is* the hard-won struggle of the ego to separate from, and simultaneously maintain a connection to, the other.

Perhaps Jung's 'Ulysses' essay provides a deeper clue as to why literary studies has found the Freudian psychoanalytic tradition more congenial. Literary history, by its nature, looks back. It understands a model that looks back to psychic origins in satisfactorily comprehensive ways. Jung can do this too, for example, in discussing the medieval Catholic heritage of Joyce as exerting a peculiar psychic pressure on the text.

Yet principally, Jung sees works of art as both compensatory and forward looking. In particular, visionary or symbolic art, channels the energies of the collective unconscious as an 'objective' cultural phenomenon. *Ulysses* compensates the hideous sentimentality of post-Victorian modernity and offers a spiritual journey towards a detachment from western materialism. Ultimately, to Jung, we are all Ulysses. His final remark betrays his own acknowledgement that he may reach Ithaca, arrive 'home' remade. The fragmented alienated modern consciousness registering only sensation at the start of the 'Ulysses' essay, may finally have a vision of home in modernity:

Concluding remark: I am now getting on pretty well with my reading of
Ulysses – forward!

(ibid.: para. 203)

Although the wanderer is heading home, he is not doing so by retracing his
steps. No looking back.

Conclusion

It goes without saying that in the two essays on literature and in the act of
criticism, Jung is primarily interested in the relations between consciousness
and unconsciousness. What is less obvious is his focus on 'knowledge' or
'theory' as problematic. Anything derived merely from rationality risks
being profoundly inauthentic unless it also bears witness to the destabilizing
presence of unconsciousness. To encounter a work of art is to be in the
presence of something not derived from one's own known psyche: it is to
encounter the other. Jung's concern not to make one discipline master
another is of a piece with his insight that what the ego brings to understanding the other should be regarded as only one aspect of art criticism.

The three essays analysed here show Jung working through the problems
of 'psychology' commenting on 'literature'. In the end he provides a model
for a Jungian literary criticism that blends the modes of different disciplines
without reducing art to symptoms or 'evidence' for another cultural activity. These texts show Jung eroding the division between science and art and
figuring a liminal space between them for his psychology. Later chapters of
this book will examine this attitude further.

Revealing a penchant for spatial metaphors, which will prove characteristic, Jung portrays disciplines as the cultivated pastures of the ego. Where
literature and art point to the as yet unknown and unknowable, the ego's
ground must be remade. Jung is even willing to question his own formulations to indicate the provisional quality of his theorizing. For *Ulysses*
surely is both a visionary and psychological novel. Apparently a creature
of soulless consciousness, *Ulysses* is a psychological novel so intensely
expressive of the known world that it makes consciousness mysterious.
Perhaps it is 'psychological' with respect to its author and 'visionary' to the
culture (for which it provides an archetypal, collective transformation). In
identifying this work with an image of the self for western modernity, Jung
brings together the collective culture with the cosmos. No literary critic
could be more ambitious, or more provocative.

Chapter 2

Myth: Representing the self in auto/biography

Memories, Dreams, Reflections 1963/1983 and 'Answer to Job', CW11

> But then what is your myth – the myth in which you do live?
>
> (Jung 1963/1983: 195)

> [T]he self, which is man's totality, consisting on the one hand of that which is conscious to him, and on the other hand of the contents of the unconscious.
>
> (Jung 1952/1958, CW11: para. 755)

Introduction

Memories, Dreams, Reflections, an autobiography published posthumously, and 'Answer to Job', a work of biblical commentary, are both writings devoted to Jung's notion of the self. Jung's self is both conceptual and narrative: it is frequently subject to a kind of dictionary definition, *and* somehow mysteriously escapes the capacity of rational language to represent it. Conceptually, the self refers both to the totality of the psyche, conscious and unconscious, and to the most powerful centring archetype of the collective unconscious, the goal of individuation. These definitions pull in different directions: self stands for everything, or alternatively, for a particular numinous focus for the process of individuation. My analysis of *Memories, Dreams, Reflections* (hereafter *Memories*) and of 'Answer to Job' (hereafter 'Job') will explore this apparent dichotomy. As definitions they are examples of one type of writing about the self; an attempt at 'objective' description. Narrative and mythical writing in these two works constitute the project to represent the self as enactment or performance.

So in this chapter I will be looking at myth and its relationship to genres of autobiography and biography in Jung's self-representation. Later, Chapter 6 will consider Jung's self as god-image and as an historical construction of time and space. *Memories* reads as an autobiography, yet builds its narrative upon notions of a 'personal myth'. 'Job' is a biography of the

Judaeo-Christian God, or a reading of sacred scriptures in the language of Jung's own psychology that in *Memories* he calls a kind of 'myth'.

At first glance, myth and biography would seem to be unlikely allies in self-representation, Jungian or otherwise. Whereas biography and autobiography focuses upon the individual, seeking out historical particularity in the lived life, myth is essentially a collective and cultural story. Myths provide for cultures narratives that are not limited to historical events. They connect the human world to the non-human, to nature and/or the divine.

Robert Segal has examined Jung's treatment of myth as a reaction (along with Freud) to the nineteenth-century accounts of it as invalidated by the triumph of material science (Segal, 1998, 2003). For Jung as for Freud, myth refers to the inner world of the mind and is to be read symbolically. Where Jung differs from Freud is in regarding myth positively as a means of encountering the unconscious and so contributing to self-realization. So there is no contradiction between Jung's discussion of collective myths and his devising of an individual 'personal myth':

> Far from an inferior alternative to a group myth, under which would fall all religious myths, a personal myth for Jung is the ideal, for it alone is geared to the unique contour of one's personality. A personal myth seeks to nurture unrealized aspects of one's personality.
>
> (Segal 2003: 612)

In my previous study of *Memories* I argued that Jung's 'personal myth' has even more radical implications (Rowland 2002). It is used to describe first of all, Jung's sense of an inherent shape to his own most intimate experiences. Second, 'personal myth' acts as a bridging term from the 'personal' to the conceptual. It comes to signify his psychological ideas, and therefore becomes a means of representing his inner life and his work as united. 'Personal myth' becomes analytical psychology in a confession of a crucial weighting of the theories as a *life's* work. So I am going even further than Segal in suggesting that, for Jung, myth *is a kind of writing that is part of his psychology writing*, not only that which is redefined by his psychology as a science of the mind. In this chapter I plan to show how myth works as a kind of psychology writing with particular emphasis on the self, and auto/biographical genres.

I also posited previously that Jung's writings are characterized by an entwined dual impulse in which an acknowledgement of the roots of his ideas in his individual experience (personal myth) works with, and against, a drive to universalize and construct a comprehensive psychological scheme (Rowland 2002). This I termed a mode of writing as 'grand theory' in that it makes large claims for the ability to account for psyche and culture. Personal myth mutates into grand theory where the sense of the provisional and subjective intrinsic to the 'personal' becomes lost in the pursuit of broad cultural analyses. An example of these two tendencies would be my point earlier about Jungian ideas such as the self existing both as concepts subject to dictionary definitions (constituents of grand theory) and simultaneously as never completed narratives (the subjective apprehensions of personal myth).

Therefore I propose in this reading of *Memories* and 'Job' to explore how myth, personal or otherwise, becomes so implicated in texts with a strong biographical element. What is the nature and status of this 'personal' myth? How exactly do these works connect myth and biography? And finally, what then are the implications for Jung's representation of the self? I shall be making direct use of recent work on autobiography, biography and myth, in particular Laura Marcus's excellent study *Auto/biographical Discourses* (1994) and Lawrence Coupe's invaluable *Myth* (1997). Additionally, Christopher Hauke (2000) in his pioneering *Jung and the Postmodern* reclaims Jung for twenty-first century cultural theory. In the context of such research, I will show how the mythical texture of Jung's writing is directed to the psychology underpinning urgent contemporary anxieties, in particular war and weapons of mass destruction.

For as well as sharing the use of myth and biography, both *Memories* and 'Job' are experimental readings of modernity. By staging the issues germane to the writing of the self, these works offer themselves as healing narratives for the modern psyche afflicted by violence. Indeed, I will suggest that the texts provide a sequence, that *Memories* works peculiarly as a sequel to 'Job' in a myth that is at the same time personal, cultural, postmodern and cosmic. This is despite the fact that *Memories* is a highly problematic text.

Authorship, authority and the problem of Memories, Dreams, Reflections (Jung 1963/1983)

Memories is an account of Jung's life written in the first person. It has been variously described as an autobiography and a biography. In a powerful essay, 'Memories, Dreams, Omissions', Sonu Shamdasani argues that *Memories* is 'by no means' Jung's autobiography (Shamdasani 1999: 33). His research highlights drastic editing and decisive input by others (Shamdasani 2003: 22–4). Shamdasani concludes that it is important to remove the term 'autobiography' from any consideration of this enigmatic work. Other scholars have placed the emphasis differently. Alan C. Elms reassesses the evidence for Jung's own suppression or distortion of material and suggests the re-emergence of a split within this so-called author (Elms 1994). *Memories* itself described a division within the narrator between a conventional No. 1 persona dwarfed by a mysterious, unconscious hidden self, No. 2. Elms makes a good case for Jung's hesitations amounting to a dual inner urge to reveal and conceal.

F. X. Charet in his article on biographies of Jung finds Elms's conclusion 'psychologically suggestive' (Charet 2000: 210). He discerns a unifying myth in *Memories*, but whose myth is it? Is it a foreign imposition on Jung's biography or the heart of his 'message'? Is the 'personal myth' actually Jung's or is it contaminated by the personal myths of others?

I would like to suggest two possible reactions to the problem of authorship in *Memories, Dreams, Reflections*. One reaction is practical and methodological. *Memories* refers repeatedly to 'Answer to Job', a work whose authorship is undisputed. If the myth of *Memories* and the myth of 'Job' offer intertextual correspondences then that indicates that the relationship between these two works should continue to be fruitful. It does not suggest or 'prove' that the essentials of *Memories* come undiluted from the mind of Jung. Indeed, what is particularly resonant about Elms's argument is that even Jung himself could be regarded as a sort of collective author.

In matters of the psyche, Jung was concerned to play down straightforward causality in favour of forward driving teleology. In reading *Memories* with 'Job', I wish to play down any suppositions about what it 'proves' about the origin of *Memories* in favour of what it indicates about myth and selfhood for the Jungian canon. My method, like Jung's, will be to displace causality in order to privilege meaning.

Such an attitude brings me to my second reaction to the problem of authorship in *Memories*: what is at stake in a work when the author is disputed? Clearly, by cultural consensus the author is the guarantor of the meaning of the work. In effect, authorial intention becomes the principle by which the reader interprets the work. What did Jung really mean by describing God as a symbol of the self?

Reading for authorial intention is so culturally pervasive that it has become 'natural'. It is barely noticed that such a theory of reading is explicitly hierarchical. The principle of authorial intention is a principle of authority. The author represents the ultimate authority to which all textual disputes must be referred. What Jung really means by this is. . . . Ultimately this is a theological model with the author as the god of the text; the only source, the sponsor, the controller of all meaning.

An effort to read differently from such an authorizing inferred 'presence' can best be summed up by Roland Barthes's resonant phrase, 'the death of the author' (Barthes 2001). The author is dead, not just because Jung can no longer be called upon to explain his work, but primarily because the author as supreme authority, as the god of the text, need no longer be the defining principle of interpretation.

Perhaps what is almost uncanny about *Memories* for the modern reader is that recent archival research seems to self-consciously prohibit the 'natural' practice of reading for Jung's authorizing presence. There is no single author: the current English text is contingent and was produced collectively through a tangle of conflicting desires and interests.

What I find most intriguing in the whole project of switching a reading of *Memories* and 'Job' away from an emphasis on origins, to one of resonance, purpose and correspondence, is the way that it mimics Jung's own suspicion of mechanistic causality and his preference for symbolic amplification. Jung did not ignore causality; he chose to de-emphasize it. Similarly, I will still be using a rhetoric of authorial intention while stressing the vital connections that these texts infer between myth, biographical writing and reading. Within such literary structures are to be found the potent mysteries of Jung's self.

Genres of auto/biography and selfhood

In Laura Marcus's history of auto/biography she elegantly describes a genre at the heart of debates about modernity, the self, history and representation (Marcus 1994). If the post-Enlightenment era is dominated by reason and scientific objectivity, then autobiography in particular promised to heal the split between the self and the world. At its very core autobiography contains a recurrent tension about the status of language. Can language connect consciousness to the world beyond the inner life? Does auto/biographical 'truth' lie in a positivist notion of correspondence in which language truly reflects physical events 'in the world'? Alternatively, is an idealist conception of language more correct in which the only truth of auto/biography is to be found in its internal textual coherence. An auto/biography is 'true' insofar as it provides a coherent story, an aesthetic wholeness enacted in the writing. So the construction of an aesthetic object takes precedence over fidelity to the historical events of a life.

Such a division within auto/biography, between faithful representation of the events of a life and a faithful construction of coherence and wholeness in writing, is variously staged throughout the long history of the genre as a tension between history and literature, between science and literature, and between history and myth. Broadly, are biography and autobiography essentially literary forms for which the facts of a life are of secondary importance to the creation of an aesthetically pleasing narrative? Or can the focus on the unique position of the autobiographer as both author and subject offer substance to those collective forms of knowledge (history and science) that rely upon a correspondence between words and things?

One aspect of the history–literature tension inheres in the status of the self. Is autobiography, for instance, the representation of a pre-existing self, or is it the *construction* of a self through writing? Does the self (in the everyday sense of a consistent, knowable identity) exist apart from acts of self-expression? Is the self 'transcendent'? Or, conversely, is the modern self contingent upon discourses such as the very making of autobiography that call it into being?

Biographical critics have tended to rely either upon stabilizing the genre or on stabilizing its human subject. Both possibilities have been radically undermined by the theoretical approach known as deconstruction, pioneered by Jacques Derrida (Derrida 1977, 1978). For in deconstruction there is neither an essential self pre-existing language, nor has language the resources to construct it. Deconstruction undermined both attempts to 'ground' auto/biography in a self by challenging the efficacy of language to correspond to external facts, and also its previously assumed competence to create internally coherent works.

In effect, deconstruction argues that the slippery nature of language reveals that the self is a continual contingent performance. It does not exist outside, and prior to, language. There is no 'outside' of language because meaning and significance are always caught up in a process; a system of relations that is language itself. Unfortunately for those desirous of a true essential self, transcendent of cultural corruption, meaning is uncontrollable. Words are slippery; they disseminate rather than secure meaning and so there is no sure system by which words can correspond to the world, or even correspond to each other.

In such a worldview, writing an auto/biography is an endless exercise in revealing the illusions of presence. Meaning is not 'present' in words and so there is no present self in the writing of autobiography, nor true self 'out there' in the biographical subject. If such a true self did exist (transcendent of the system of language that creates slippery significance – not meaning), then it would be beyond the powers of language to represent it. As it is, in denying truth in language and refuting being outside it, deconstruction proclaims the death of the subject.

Given such acute assaults on auto/biography, it is time to look at whether myth has anything to offer the crisis of self-representation.

Myth as allegory and radical typology

Lawrence Coupe's illuminating study of myth describes a recurrent dual impulse within the form (Coupe 1997: 100–15). From the time of the ancient Greeks, mythos or story has tended to be bracketed off from logos or forms of truth including science or history. However, the division between mythos and logos is never as absolute as different ages like to pretend. Aristotle was the first to perceive that certain kinds of knowledge are intrinsically narrative. For him, mythos meant emplotment, the story, and it structured history as much as the religious stories of his culture (ibid.: 38).

Modernity, according to Coupe, relies upon a paradoxical post-Enlightenment myth of mythlessness: the idea that humanity has outgrown its need for shaping stories and can now live in the pure forms of empirical science and reason (ibid.: 9–13). This works so long as the theoretical underpinnings of science and reason are not themselves subject to mythical scrutiny. Postmodern critics have pointed out that modernity's mythlessness is essentially narrative: grand narratives of the progress of science and of human emancipation are its necessary 'foundations'. Consequently, it is correct to speak of a myth of mythlessness rather than just an absence of myth. Such an idea relies upon an Aristotelian sense of myth-in-history – a shaping narrative within history that makes it intelligible. History and myth are not, in this sense, opposed.

Of course, the perception of logos as depending upon a backbone of mythos does not eliminate the differences between the idea of truth as separable from narrative (logos) and the notion of narrative as fundamental (myth). Such differences are not absolute for logos turns out to rely upon an underpinning of mythos (see Chapter 6 for Jung's own intuition of this), and mythos itself has too often been culturally wrenched into a form of logos.

For myth can be a dangerous narrative method if it entails closure, leaving some 'outside' or 'other' body (ibid.: 153–5). Closure is a consequence of the drive to perfection, which converts innately narrative mythos into abstract 'truth' or logos. A prime example is the way biblical narrative has been interpreted by churches as incarnating absolute precepts, truths or logos. Such a practice always excludes some person or group. A scapegoat results. Interestingly, Jung makes a distinction between completion and perfection in his mythography, to which I will return.

Myth regarded as antithetical to the particularities of history is peculiarly susceptible to being abstracted into some exclusive dogma. Myth saturated with history, not divorced from it, is a myth of disclosure rather than closure. Coupe identifies two main forms of reading myth (which become ways of writing myth) that illustrate the continuing struggle between logos and mythos: these are allegory and radical typology (ibid.: 100–15). Allegory is the means by which myths lose their narrative quality and become reconfigured as logos. Truths are condensed from a mythological narrative and are *set above* as the higher, governing element. For example, Marxist doctrine is abstracted from the Marxist myth of deliverance just as the Enlightenment is, in essence, an allegory of reason. Allegory is the tendency to reduce narrative to tenets or 'truth'.

As a contrast, radical typology is Coupe's term for the possibility of amplifying myth into ever new narratives (ibid.: 106–15). Typology was the medieval method of reading the Old Testament of the Bible as a foreshadowing of the new. Adam becomes an early 'type' of Christ and so on. In effect, this typology is another form of allegory since all narrative motifs lead to the highest truth of Christianity. Coupe coins 'radical typology' as the recreation of myth without foundational pretensions. Myth unites with history in an endless recapitulation of narratives without closure. Although this corresponds to the condition of myths in postmodernism, it is not exclusively a contemporary phenomena. Radical typology is also contained in the shamanistic view of myth as the intersection of sacred and profane time that can never be stabilized or reduced to a dogma. It is myth-in-history as not divisible from it; the practice of mystical writers such as the poet William Blake.

Indeed, radical typology is a form that includes a sense of the 'other' in its endless denial of closure and exclusion. It is therefore potentially an ethical form of writing since acknowledging the other forever beyond its horizons *is* the unappeasable drive of its never satiated creativity. Radical typology becomes writing that spans modernity's rational/irrational divide (ibid.: 122–4). History is no less history for being built around recurrent themes. Rather, radical typology history recalls Aristotle's position that history is 'plotted' and not some revelation of a 'true' causality that has nothing to do with a culture's recurrent stories of itself. Allegory is the tendency to create non-narrative truths out of narrative; radical typology regards truth *as* narrative. It is time to turn to Jung for his insights into 'personal' myth.

Memories, Dreams, Reflections (Jung 1963/1983)

At first glance, *Memories* appears to obey the conventional expectation of auto/biography that it will tell a life story in a linear sequence from earliest memories until close to the end. However, the chapter titles reveal a chronological structure giving way to a thematic one. After six sections working through the early life, succeeding chapters are entitled 'The Work', 'The Tower', 'Visions', 'On Life After Death', 'Late Thoughts', and a final brief section, 'Retrospect'.

What we have in the existing English published edition is a life story in which chronology surrenders to thematic organization. Just by looking at these contingent chapter arrangements, it is possible to perceive an ambivalence in the work between life history in *linear* time and the desire to shape that history in order to construct an *argument*. Is *Memories* primarily the individual history of Jung (whether written by him or by others), or is it an argument for his unique psychological perceptions? Of course it is both and the text generates the term 'personal myth' as a kind of pivot or transforming catalyst (as described earlier) from one form of writing to another.

Symptomatically the chronological life story is easily summarized. This is partly because much of the energy of *Memories* remains elsewhere than in recording events and is also the result of the vigorous editing (Shamdasani 1999). Born in 1875 to a clergyman father and a mother subject to mental disturbances, Jung as a child suffered overwhelming psychic experiences. These he tended to define religiously while gradually and firmly departing from the orthodoxy of his father. Early perceiving a dual self in his mother,

Jung became convinced that he too had a No. 1 personality adapting to society, and a mysterious, unfathomable inner self or No. 2.

Success as a student and in his medical career requires him to live as No. 1, yet at crucial moments No. 2 makes a decisive contribution, such as a dream influencing his choice of study. Marriage and children are barely mentioned. By contrast the conflicted relationship with Freud fills a whole chapter. After the traumatic severing of the friendship, Jung suffers a breakdown, heroically portrayed as a 'confrontation with the unconscious'. From these troubled years comes the 'first inkling of my personal myth' (Jung 1963/1983: 224). This chapter ends with a statement that definitively separates significance from chronology. The inner history of these years became the *matter* for the life work:

> The years when I was pursuing my inner images were the most important in my life. . . It all began then; the later details are only supplements and clarifications of the material.
>
> (ibid.: 225)

The next three chapters act like spokes radiating out from this statement. 'The Work', 'The Tower' and 'Travels' describe Jung's mid-career as defined by scholarly study of alchemy in 'The Work', as a bodily exploration of the unconscious through building in 'The Tower', and by visiting non-European cultures in 'Travels'.

Final chapters concentrate on post-1945 Jung. In particular, they explore the effects of his nearly fatal illness in 1944. Jung recalls a series of visions and a near-death experience in which he is reluctantly forced back into his life on earth (ibid.: 321–7). These glorious narratives, together with the dreams that punctuate the whole book, provide the basis for his final speculations on the possibility of psychic life outside time and the limitations of the human body.

If there is a tension in *Memories* between the recording of life events as a sequence and the attempt to read the life history for meaning rather than rational causality, then that is the key condition of the personal myth. One of the effects of the omission of many of the historical figures in Jung's life is that there is a reduced sense of a myth-in-history, the weaving of historical particularity together with narrative mythical shaping. So it is very important that *Memories* never uses the term 'personal myth' in a way that suggests that it is abstractable from this particular life story. The work achieves this sense of an indissoluble bond between Jung's story as history and Jung's story as myth-becoming-psychology, principally by disrupting linear forms of writing. It is this disruption from history as a causal sequence to history as mythically structured, as personal myth, to which I shall now turn.

Memories, Dreams, Reflections *as a non-linear narrative*

I would like to suggest that there are eight key methods where the circularity that was reduced by the editing of *Memories* can still be traced in the work. The methods are: thematic organization, repetition and substitution, metaphor, spatiality, ritual, monumentality, reading, and myth. I am going to indicate how these methods operate before exploring the implications of linear chronology and non-linear literary forms. To what extent is *Memories*' personal myth a non-linear history and what does this imply for the portrayal of the Jungian self?

The thematic organization of *Memories* has already been discussed in this chapter. It is, I would suggest, the overarching structure by which more submerged non-chronological literary devices surface and disrupt linearity within the auto/biography. Repetition and substitution is far more intrinsic to the substance of the work's 'I'. For example, the use of dreams to both interrupt and contribute to the flow of outer events is itself a formal repetition of a narrative device in which linear time and logical causality are suspended. A dream is an interruption to a life regarded as structured in time because dream narratives flout linear causal relations. Yet a dream in *Memories* frequently allows the linear life to *carry on*, allows the flow of events in time to flourish by re-energizing or refocusing the 'I', the narrator figure. Again and again dreams return to repeated themes, to houses, architectural forms, figures representing the past, dreams Jung associates with alchemy, and his parents.

Repetition becomes the basis of a mode of interpretation. Repeated dreams citing circular motifs are read as the tendency for the psyche to produce centring signs. *Memories* reads dreams *allegorically* in two ways. Repeated images in dream narratives are the foundations for Jung's psychological ideas such as circular mandala representations indicating the structural principles of the self. Dreams are presented as the basis of ideas that may become substantial as concepts: narrative (mythos) *is the basis of* concepts (logos).

Secondarily and contrary to Jung's explicit statements about treating dreams as meaningful in themselves and not reducing them to the (ego) preoccupations of the dreamer as either personal, causal or historical, *Memories* frequently uses dreams to advance the linear sequential narrative. Dreams become devices that advance the *story* of Jung's outer life. A dream may enable Jung to know what to do next, as in the decision to study medicine, or it may reveal some attitude that needs discarding, or it may be diagnosed as contributing to the personal myth.

A famous instance is his dream of Liverpool, which describes a journey through depressing rainy streets to a central square containing a pool and an island where stands a magnolia tree shedding red blooms (ibid.: 223–4). *Memories* takes this beautiful resonant story and interprets it as a revelation within the personal myth that unites Jung's life with Jung's psychology. It is presented as demonstrating that Jung's 'psychology' – his own psychic disposition, is the ground of his 'psychology' – as a system of ideas:

> Through this dream I understood that the self is the principle and archetype of orientation and meaning.

(ibid.: 224)

Personal myth stands for a mythical structure to the life story and that same mythical structure is indissolubly embedded in the psychology.

Substitution is another form of repetition in which structurally similar elements take each other's place in ways that disrupt their historical particularity. Most noticeable to me is the way that *Memories* is full of substitute parents. In a strategic displacement of the 'paternal' authority of Sigmund Freud, *Memories* rather astoundingly suggests that positions of father and son are *substitutable* between Freud and Jung. Freud is said to have interpreted a dream of Jung's as a fantasy of father murder against him. However, when Jung picks up the fainting elder man he exclaims that 'he looked at me as if I were his father' (ibid.: 180).

Jung's refusal to stabilize the paternal metaphor with regard to Freud is itself a repetition of his refusal to respect the (religious) authority of his actual father, Paul Jung. Both paternal figures are portrayed as misreading a jealous god: Paul Jung's faith is strangled by conventional Christianity; Freud's Jehovah is disguised as his sexual theory in another of *Memories*' resonant substitutions (ibid.: 192). Of course, a refusal to respect the role of the son by Jung is more than just a challenge to the superiority of the 'father'. In Freud's case, remaining the 'son' means remaining in Freud's theories, in the Oedipus complex with its implications of a causal origin to trauma back in infantile history.

Persistent repetition and substitution within *Memories* is a prime ingredient of its predilection for metaphor. Not only people and images, but also uncanny events and 'things' like stones, all work metaphorically across the text. Metaphor entails the substitution of one element for another. It presupposes an accretion of meaning from the repetition-with-a-difference that is metaphoric substitution. Metaphor associates elements that are not linked causally; it perceives likenesses, not answers. For example, at university Jung describes a fellow student as a 'lone wolf' with a 'monomaniacal ambition' who later became a schizophrenic (ibid.: 131). Here Jung discerns not his double but his parallel. The anecdote offers a metaphoric substitution stressing likeness *and* difference in which the young man represents a narrative possibility for Jung, not an 'answer' or definitive statement.

The devotion of a chapter to travel indicates the importance of space as a topic to *Memories*. Spatiality is both the inner space of the creative psyche and the 'outer' space of travels over the earth's surface. It is also the moment in which *Memories'* indulgence in metaphoric substitution becomes problematic. When Jung argues that the unconscious psyche stands for the mythic land of the dead, he is transforming both psyche and time into space (ibid.: 216). *Memories'* dreams and visions are essentially spatial. The inner world is an inner *landscape* of nature and cities, castles and even travel beyond the earth. To journey into the psyche is to wander in space and time beyond the usual boundaries, since a crusader knight may haunt a modern city or a dead father be visited in his new abode (ibid.: 188, 239–41).

Unfortunately, this profoundly non-linear intersection of space, time and psyche can become naive and colonial when 'space' signifies existing other cultures. Travelling in the psyche may condense history into space, but to assert that travels in Africa, India and North America similarly compress time relies upon the assumption that western cultural difference consists of being 'further ahead' in the colonial narrative of 'progress'.

As evidence of Jung's own naivety, he equates the non-westerner with the 'primitive' or 'child' (ibid.: 272). It is an error by Jung that what is a narrative device to frustrate rational causality in the writing of the psyche so often decays into a colonial assumption of western linear and hierarchical 'progress' in Jung's encounter with the other as other cultures.

On the other hand, throughout the 'Travels' chapter, an accretion of correspondences *across cultures* begins to complicate colonial attitudes. Jung starts understand himself as implicated in his own colonial thinking. Famously Jung in Africa dreams of an African-American barber and interprets it as a fear of 'going black under the skin' (ibid.: 273). Despite the continuing atmosphere of inferiority about the discussion of the other race, the metaphoric substitution of the western located African *American* for the truly alien situation of Africa suggests a closeness to the idea of blackness within Jung, and a sense of cultural difference being made. No longer simply denoting the European past as the 'infancy' perceptible in other cultures, travel starts to engender a psychic otherness *within* that is the sense of an outside to his own cultural presuppositions. This 'outside' becomes a standpoint, a vantage position from which to 'view', to perceive anew western modernity. Michael Vannoy Adams, in his important book *The Multicultural Imagination*, provides a comprehensive analysis of Jung and race, and of this episode in particular (Adams 1996).

Eventually Jung records the opinion of a Native American, that the sharp faced white people are all mad (ibid.: 277). Jung is then inspired to a meditation upon colonialism that produces a striking visual image: white 'civilization' as a bird of prey (ibid.: 277). At last Jung's evocation of time, space and history is suggests a dawning of a political consciousness.

What is colonial in the 'Travels' chapter is the extension of metaphoric substitution (from the psyche's condensation of time into space) onto other cultures; an extension that maps *Memories* onto the whole cultural enterprise of colonial fantasies. Paradoxically, a literary device designed to frustrate linear causality in the psyche surfaces as the support for a political linear colonial narrative. On the other hand, Jung never lets go of the personal myth as personal, and *Memories* use of substitution is potentially endless. The sense of cultural otherness accretes through the repetition of narrative excursions until it becomes a lens that reflects back the underside of the Enlightenment claim to reason and progress. The result is a revelation of blind exploitation of the other. This time, instead of substitution acting as an invasion and renaming of the territory of the other, the voice is treated as a mirror. It reflects back something in Jung's own cultural and western identity. *Memories* discovers postcolonial cultural criticism without acknowledging its participation in the colonial imagination.

Like spatiality, ritual and monumentality are also narrative means of shifting from linear chronology. Unsurprisingly, the stress on ritual is also repetition in that rituals are repeated actions that invoke the sacred. Such rituals recur repeatedly throughout *Memories*. The little boy who makes a mannikin and hides it in a box with *his* stone is also the older boy who builds a model village, and later still, the troubled psychiatrist who finds comfort in constructing a miniature town (ibid.: 36, 102, 198). Finally, the ritual element of building is materially enacted in the creation of the Bollingen Tower.

Reading and myth remain the literary means by which *Memories* frustrates a causal sequential narrative. The most 'read' text and the source of most of the cited myth is the Bible. Within *Memories*, I would argue, the Bible provides a form of mythological structuring described by Lawrence Coupe as radical typology.

Allegory and radical typology in Memories, Dreams, Reflections

'Personal' myth is the declared core of *Memories*, signifying the mysterious mutation of a life story into a numinous testament and a psychology. One key aspect of the personal myth is the drive to allegory, in which dreams, psychic experiences and events are read for logos, for an abstractable concept or universal meaning. An example of this would be when the dream of Liverpool yields something that sounds like a dictionary definition of Jung's self (ibid.: 224).

Yet allegory is not all. Radical typology is implied in all the narrative methods discussed so far: in repetition and substitution, in the limitlessness of Jungian metaphor, in the intersection of sacred and profane in ritual and monument/building (in which action in time is necessary to evoke a reality beyond time). All these devices deny closure. They open the 'personal' into the mythic by their sense of the other as endlessly unknowable, not ever exhausted by writing. And the most overt way in which radical typology structures *Memories* is in the frequent re-readings of the Bible for mythos, for story.

From the boy nicknamed 'Father Abraham' at school to the likening of the need to renounce his unfathomable No. 2 personality to Adam leaving Eden, to his pre-First World War dream of feeding a crowd with grapes like Christ, the Bible offers a narrative model for the life story (ibid.: 85, 108, 200). Jung's personal myth coalesces around typological readings of the Bible. For example, a vision of a greenish-gold Christ confirms the importance of alchemy, Christ and Buddha are both images of the self in entirely different cultural contexts (ibid.: 237, 309).

It is important to understand the radical extent of this use of the Bible. Jung is not proclaiming himself as a new Christ. Personal myth is *personal* in that it does not claim to be a transcendent revelation fit for all peoples and all times: 'I can only. . . "tell stories",' he says (ibid.: 17). It is also 'personal' because it is a structuring of personal experience of the unconscious in defiance of the most immediate cultural model of his father's Protestant Christianity. The crucial moment comes early. The child Jung is suddenly weighed down with the sense of a forbidden revelation. His way of resolving the tension is to 'read' the Bible story of Adam and Eve as intended to sin by God. Spurred on by the precedent, Jung mentally surrenders to the vision of God letting fall a turd and smashing his Cathedral (ibid.: 53–7). Jung experiences intense psychic relief, but this radical typology mythography severs him from his paternal models both as literal father and the teachings of church 'fathers'. It becomes an early example of radical typology *reading* myth (to relieve acute psychic pressure), that becomes a radical typology *writing* Jung's personal myth.

Radical typology is the chief narrative device delineating the personal myth and is not limited to its most obvious biblical manifestation. People and parents are also subject to its endless reinventions without closure. Both of Jung's parents are treated lightly as figures leading historically circumscribed lives, and repeatedly as types to be mythologically amplified.

To recap, I am arguing that Jung composes his personal myth principally using the narrative method that Coupe defines as radical typology. It is a form that resists closure and makes no claim for universal transcendent significance. Its recapitulation of other mythical stories is potentially limitless: radical typology is *radical* in the notion of rewriting narratives without boundaries, so never producing an 'other' to become a scapegoat. Of course, as I have shown, the tendency to allegory, to abstract a logos or singular 'truth' from the personal myth, does haunt *Memories*. The whole auto/biography is punctuated by interruptions to the personal myth consisting of conceptual statements about the psyche, the nature of dreams and the self. Narratively, the tension between radical typology and allegory (or personal myth and grand theory) rests upon the ambivalence between non-linear and linear elements in the writing.

Consequences of the anti-linear impulse in Memories

Memories is a profoundly anti-linear work in its use of thematic structuring, repetition and substitution, spatiality, ritual and monumentality, reading and myth as radical typological methods of describing the personal myth. Its anti-linear preferences have three major related consequences: *Memories* is against linearity as time, as causality and as conceptual language.

The auto/biography devotes considerable energy to frustrating a notion of linear time as a succession of present moments that determine a life from birth to death. Three ways of presenting time, as family life, as history and as ending in death, are all, through radical typology, shown as participating in time as recurrence or eternity. In fact, the depiction of time as non-linear is one of the main means of representing the unconscious as the mythical land of the dead, including parents, as history reconfigured as spatial.

A consequence of challenging the conventional assumption of time as linear sequence is that causality, in the sense of one action producing another, is similarly questioned. If family life can function as a series of substitutions so that son, Carl, spends much of his textual contact with his father, Paul, acting as the father's mentor – a substitution even more explicit when Freud is said to gaze at Jung as a father figure – then the sense of historical and locatable causes motivating the psyche is diminished. The Oedipus complex gives way to Jung's stress on meaningful non-causal coincidence in the psyche and its interactions with the world. The drive to allegorize this emphasis on meaning produces the concept of synchronicity, enshrining the sense of non-linear time and non-scientific causality within the psychology (see Chapter 7). However, this drive for an abstract logos, or logocentric psychology is explicitly countered by the anti-linear distrust of conceptual language.

Conceptual language is linear because it relies upon words fitting together in a sequence within a sentence. It also implies causality in which one concept infers or produces another. Concepts are the language of science where 'science' signifies notions of a consistent verifiable truth that is abstractable from the context in which it first appeared. For conceptual language is not contextual. It does not depend upon the writing that surrounded it originally to sustain its meaning. Concepts can be abstracted from their first home and applied to another place, another context. So concepts are not the kind of language that is only valid locally, as truths applicable solely to the culture that generated them. They derive from Enlightenment notions of reason as transcendent of cultural variations and split off from the irrational side of the mind.

Memories is suspended between the desire to assert 'concepts' and the realization that such language is itself a barrier to Jung's understanding of the psyche. Despite the urge to allegorize his experience into abstract theory,

Memories offers the overt realization that allegory must defer to radical typology: conceptual language is divorced from psychic authenticity.

> Experience is stripped of its substance, and instead mere names are substituted, which are henceforth put in the place of reality.
>
> (ibid.: 167)

Suggestively, at a crucial period of his life, Jung describes traditional rational science as a rescue *from* the unconscious when he risked being overwhelmed by it between 1912 and 1913 (ibid.: 217).

Memories does not merely prefer radical typology's mythos while being unable to relinquish the temptations of allegorical theory as 'science'. Rather, *Memories* is explicit about the function of personal myth in putting mythos back into logos, or creating a science that is mythological. Not only are myths the earliest forms of science, but today they still *are* science as 'the natural and indispensable stage between unconscious and conscious cognition' (ibid.: 335, 343). For Jung, myth is a mode of science, perhaps a kind of scientific 'mood'. It is both *what happens* in the psyche and also the means of *representing* it. The psyche is mythos in the infinite recreation of stories by which unconscious and conscious mesh. It can only be authentically represented by a radical typology endlessly re-reading the mythical models cast into a life.

What is fascinating here is that *Memories* is both premodern and postmodern on language, science and myth. In wanting to reconnect science and myth, Jung evokes a pre-Enlightenment world before reason and conceptual thinking were split off from mythos, as comprehensively explored by Roger Brooke (2000: 13–24). Jung also wants to reconnect language and psyche in the notion that representation and cognition unite in personal myth. *Memories* shows this principle at work in Jung's most tormented period. Haunted by 'spirits', only *writing* alleviates his suffering (ibid.: 216).

However, Jung develops almost a postmodern scepticism about language and science by stressing the resistances of the unconscious to Enlightenment reason. Language and science have to be invested with myth, not allegorically, but as the renunciation of rational foundations. Mythical emplotment is both representation and reality of the psyche, but it is a reality that forever resists definition, propelling signifiers into myths and story in ways that refuse rational meaning. Such premodern/postmodern articulation is the keystone of *Memories'* portrayal of the self.

Memories, Dreams, Reflections *as writing about the self*

According to Laura Marcus, autobiography enacts the death of the author twice (Marcus 1994: 208–10). First, the genre of autobiography invokes the standpoint of death as necessary for a 'completed' life/work. Second, the death of the author inheres in writing itself through deconstruction's vision that writing undermines self-identity more than it represents it.

Jung's personal myth, the structural form of *Memories* as auto/biography, uniquely plays out a variation of Marcus's dual insight. In the radical typology aspect of the personal myth, death as a perspective for the 'life' becomes one of a series of infinitely extendable substitutions in the drive to defeat linear time, causality and conceptuality. Death as a metaphoric *location* for the unconscious, as the other, therefore becomes a crucial means of resisting closure in the personal myth. *Memories* fuses what Marcus sees as paradoxically distinct: death in genre and death in writing. What Marcus calls the self (that she sees as bounded, *limited* by death), *Memories* portrays as personal myth, writing without origin or closure because any posited origin or closure dwells in an unconscious whose meanings can never be captured in the linear language of rationality. The genre with its standpoint of death is transformed into the personal myth with its endless diffusion of self that is cited/sited far beyond the ego.

So the death of selfhood that deconstruction proclaims is, for Jung, the vital ingredient of ego dissolution that enables the endlessly procreative personal myth to be the Jungian self of (radical typology) myth. The death of the author as the death of the subject of writing (a literal and metaphorical death) and as the death of authority finds a startlingly original form in the personal myth of *Memories*.

Taking the vantage point of death as one of the anti-linear narrative possibilities is a way of writing beyond the ending. Diversions into conceptual language are profoundly inauthentic methods of representing the Jungian self. Such an examination of *Memories* shows what is at stake in defining the self as both centre and totality; as archetype, goal of psychic evolution and as the ever-widening prairies of psychic possibility. For the self is *represented* here through radical typology and *is* radical typology in the personal myth's limitless spinning of tales. *Memories* is autobiography as a mythical reconstruction of psychology.

Perspective is especially important here, as it will be to the comparison with the self in 'Answer to Job'. For *Memories*, personal myth as radical typology is the Jungian self from the perspective of the ego; it is the self as myth-writing-totality. 'Answer to Job' offers another perspective, another *position* altogether. How does a biography of God fare in relation to the 'personal' myth?

'Answer to Job' (Jung 1952/1958, CW11)

Paul Bishop has produced an important commentary on 'Answer to Job' that definitively places the work within its intellectual heritage (Bishop 2002). It is the very different task of this chapter to assess its aesthetic contribution to Jung's use of myth as self-representation.

Common to both *Memories* and 'Job' is an ultimate downplaying of linear sequence in biographical writing in favour of an emphasis on the spatial. Consequently 'ego' and 'unconscious' are conceived as *positions* as much as processes. If *Memories* takes the 'position' of the ego as the threshold for writing (as a way of 'seeing' or speculating), then 'Job' tries to compose the position of the other; the perspective of the unconscious. Paradoxically, 'Job' is also more interested in linear narrative because it is more preoccupied with the interrelationships between culture, history and psyche.

'Job' retells the story of the Judaeo-Christian God as if he were an individuating being. Such a project has an immediate linear narrative drive in two ways. In the first place, 'Job' offers a broadly sequential reading of the Old and New Testaments, in part because the text is interested in individuation as a process in historical time. Second, historical sequence produces evidence for, while being superseded by, a conceptual argument about individuation and modernity. God begins as Yahweh. 'He' is a savage being who torments Job, essentially because he is jealous of the greater consciousness of his creation. The problem is one of individuation; God has a dark side variously incarnated in Satan and in the terrifying possibilities for mass death produced by twentieth-century man. God needs to individuate (for which man has a part to play), and *is* man's unconscious, the site for human striving after the self.

The personal myth is present in 'Job' as the narrative of individuation. It is also to be found in the writing of the strange and passionate story. For Jung openly declares that he is writing out of emotionally charged subjective experience (Jung 1952/1958, CW11: 358). Moreover the 'personal' impetus is assumed deliberately to guarantee a narrative form that resists abstract or transcendent pretensions:

> I deliberately chose this form because I wanted to avoid the impression that I had any idea of announcing an 'eternal truth'.
>
> (ibid.: 358)

The biography of God

'Answer to Job' closely analyses selected biblical verses and draws some startling conclusions. God's jealous doubting of Job's faithfulness is personified as his elder nastier son, Satan (ibid.: 579–86). Fear of betrayal by Job is, of course, an imperfect reflection of the tendency to unfaithfulness in Yahweh himself; a tendency confirmed later when we learn of his two wives. Sophia or wisdom has existed with/in Yahweh for eternity, only to be supplanted by the more legitimate bride, Israel (ibid.: para. 619).

Job is brutally treated by Yahweh. At Satan's suggestion, Job loses everything, family, wealth and health, in a cruel 'test' of his fidelity. His protesting incomprehension of the irrationality of God goes unanswered for millennia. However, his greater insight than his creator 'raises' him in the moral stakes. God's unconsciousness remains a festering sore within divine–human relations (ibid.: para. 606).

The Old Testament prophet Ezekiel provides a second narrative climax. His perceptions of God's nature produce the title 'Son of Man', an indication of greater transformations to come (ibid.: para. 681). For it is Christ who supplies the true 'answer to Job'. Son of God who is at the same time an aspect of God, Christ's incarnation into the sufferings of human beings culminates in his despairing cry upon the cross. An answer to Job rings out across the centuries (ibid.: para. 647).

Unfortunately, such a neatly mirroring recompense does not end the problems of divine unconsciousness. On the one hand, the Bible does not end with Christ. It continues into the apocalyptic horrors of the Book of Revelation, which to Jung suggests that the 'problem' of God for humanity is far from over. What is on one level a theological imperative, is on another a psychological tenet that is also an aesthetic strategy, that narrative closure is anathema to Jung's writing of the self.

The Book of Revelation, Jung concludes characteristically, is likely to have been composed by the Gospel author John, because it sounds so unlike him. Revelation's explosive apocalyptic and overtly pagan fire is the all too predictable compensation for the Gospel's tale of certainty and love (ibid.: para. 698). John's revelation is his 'personal' individuation myth with a cultural dimension in the 'woman clothed with the sun' (ibid.: para. 711). 'She' is the return of the feminine too often excluded from the Christian account of the divine.

'Job' reads Revelation and the whole Bible as a myth-in-history. The personal myth is *vitally* shaped by cultural experiences and exclusions. By exploring a cultural dimension to Revelation, Jung projects John's personal myth forwards into the history of division within Christian churches and the hostility between communism and capitalism in the twentieth century. In an exemplary allegorical reading, religious and political splits are 'both expressions of the unrecognised polarity of the dominant archetype' (ibid.: para. 660). Individuation's personal myth acquires a cultural charge and condenses into the same abstract theory that punctuates the radical typology of *Memories*.

However the myth-in-history does resist complete foreclosure into psychological concepts when it becomes a shaping force in the personal myth of contemporary history. John's warnings of apocalypse are not a distant echo, nor are they even a foreshadowing. The myth-in-history combines chronological time with the perpetual immediacy of everybody's unconscious here and now. Time of prophecy becomes spatial in the structuring of the unconscious for culture past *and* present. John's fears of apocalypse in *his* culture are also of apocalypse now:

The four sinister horsemen. . . are still waiting; already the atom bomb hangs over us. . . and. . . the incomparably more terrible possibilities of chemical warfare.

(ibid.: para. 733)

The myth of individuation, of relationship with the unconscious, cannot end lest it turn into another, far more terribly pervasive myth: the myth of apocalypse. What is now urgently required is a new incarnation: man must explicitly take on the terrible polarities of God within the unconscious (ibid.: 740). The personal myth needs to become a myth of deliverance.

As a linear narrative, God gets a biography as Jung works through biblical episodes in chronological order. The author's penchant for multiple and substitutable father–son relations is reflected in shadowy Satan, the sacrificed Jesus and, most suggestively, in the violent reversals of power versus moral superiority in Job's accusation of Yahweh. The linear sequence is causal: one disastrously unconscious intervention into the human world necessitates another as reparation, and so on. Therefore 'Job' provides a linear argument about the developing psychology of God and the increasing role for human beings in helping Him to greater consciousness. Such linearity is also a myth of history or more precisely, a myth-in-history, as it describes changing human culture as a myth of an evolving religious culture. What I mean by a myth-in-history is that the shaping story is inextricable from the narrative of culture and vice versa. Sacred and profane time both infer and are a means of representing each other.

Despite all this structural linearity, the writing of John's revelation as a myth for the contemporary reader is an indication of non-linear, non-historical drives at work in the narrative. It is a reminder that the 'position' of the other is one in which time and history surrender to spatiality. 'Answer to Job' is a reading of the Bible that is also a myth of history and culture. Simultaneously, the narrative constitutes a personal myth for its author and intended reader.

Personal myth in 'Answer to Job'

As in *Memories*, 'Job' uses non-linearity and repetition. These are less overt, for while *Memories* needed to frustrate linear history to depict individuation, 'Job' is required to maintain it for the same reason. The linear chronological reading of the Bible is the means of representing God's individuation as repeated interventions into human history. Yet individuation cannot solely be portrayed as a straightforward narrative, for that would give too much emphasis to simple causality (and so ultimately conceptuality and rational language). Where on the one hand God's relations with man do suggest in 'Job' a series of causal events, the second half of the work emphasizes non-linear time and structural relations within the godhead.

Indeed, the role of the feminine is the most obvious point of resistance to God's story as sequential. Tempting as it is to argue that it is entirely typical of Jung that the feminine in the divine is forgotten for the whole of the first part of the drama (the agony of Job), it is more symptomatically Yahweh who has forgotten Sophia, his wisdom (ibid.: para. 617). The forgetting of the eternally present feminine becomes a repeated motif impeding divine individuation and therefore blackening the opposites in God. The powerfully threatening 'woman clothed with the sun' is the consequence of the concentration on masculine perfection in the God of the early Christians (ibid.: paras. 710–11).

Moments of tension between God and his creatures are compounded by God's unorthodox family structure. It is unclear whether first wife Sophia is abandoned, forgotten or reincarnated in second bride, Israel. We are told that such divine confusion is reflected in the first man Adam's family problems. He is burdened with a satanic first wife, Lilith, to overshadow his second union with Eve. Such erotic complications are explained as a parallel to God's marital irregularities (ibid.: para. 619).

Parallels and repetitions prepare the way for a narrative device familiar from *Memories*. The story and argument of 'Job' is typological and circular as well as a set of linear consequences. Job, Ezekiel, Christ and modern man are a series of types whose fate is repeated with slight differences across time and cultures. Jung structures his narrative on the model of medieval readings of the Bible as a series of Christ-like types. Yet 'Job' does more than revisit medieval typology. Jung reorients the medieval technique towards modern man and the future. Modern man, not Christ, is the apex of the types and his urgent necessity to individuate the terrible polarities of God/the unconscious locates the consummation of the text, its ultimate meaning, in the future. Where the medieval world looked back to the purity of Christ's teaching from a perspective of decay and the imminence of the AntiChrist, 'Job' is projected forwards as a teleological myth with the potential to turn apocalypse into deliverance.

Furthermore, whereas medieval scholars read the bible as typological for *allegory* so as to extract the true doctrine from Christ's biography, Jung uses radical typology because the myth remains unfinished, open. It is up to modern human beings to continue, to fulfil, the story of God's biography. And it is a story that can never be finished or defined. For future humans will also enter into a relationship with the unconscious in which myth is both the method and the only means of representation.

Both 'Job' and *Memories* offer auto/biography in two senses: these are the historical and the mythical. The historical mode is the events in linear time and culture, while the mythical is the essentially non-linear circum-ambulations of the self. What is not sufficiently recognized is that these two forms of auto/biography are not separable. Heavy editing of *Memories* has de-emphasized Jung's involvement in his own era. So the point is not that Jung is uninterested in history or culture, or finds it of secondary importance to individuation. Rather, history and culture are themselves caught up with unconscious processes and so is the means of representing them. The ego-self in chronological time is inseparable from the Jungian self in which history condenses into spatiality.

God and Christ in 'Answer to Job' are at one level devices for writing from the standpoint of the other. They are ways of writing about the self from the perspective of the unconscious. Both works are auto/biographical writings of the ego-self and the Jungian self. Both versions of self draw Jung into writing myth as radical typology because the ego-self is open to the other, and the Jungian self *is* and is *representable* through endless mythos, without narrative closure.

Allegory remains the technique of abstract concepts and often the narrative means of propelling non-linear items of narrative, such as the record of a dream, into linear events and argument. Interestingly, 'Job' genders allegory and radical typology as the masculine tendency to perfection and the feminine desire for completion, respectively (ibid.: paras. 620–24). In effect, theory and conceptuality are here aligned with masculinity, the mythical writing of the self with femininity. Such a binary falls neatly into the Enlightenment association of the ego with masculinity as rationality, and the irrational (unconscious) other as feminine. Later chapters of this book (in particular Chapters 3 and 7) will look at Jung's lifelong responses to this gendering of modernity.

For Jung, completion, it is important to remember, does not mean closure. Rather, completion is the drive to go on including the other, as failure, darkness, the not known. Since the unconscious is inappropriable territory, completion is a drive, not a fixed state. Completion (to Jung) is never complete; it is the need to go on mythmaking as a way of writing from, with, or for, the position of the other – radical typology. When Jung describes divine incarnation in creaturely man as fulfilment, such a state exists only as 'not yet' as deferral:

> Everything now depends on man: immense power of destruction is given into his hand, and the question is whether he. . . can temper his will with the spirit of love and wisdom.
>
> (ibid.: para. 745)

Memories and 'Job' are both stories of the self from different positions. *Memories* narrates from the position of the ego-self and becomes gradually more and more immersed in the anti-linear spatiality of the Jungian self. 'Job' starts from the position of the 'other' and works towards a projected union with the ego-self in its (personal) myth prophecy of the new incarnation in man. On the one hand, *Memories* and 'Job' are auto/biographies of the inseparable ego-self and Jungian self from different *positions*; the two texts have a spatial relationship. On the other hand, they exist in a linear *consequential* relation since *Memories* functions as a *sequel* to the vast cultural and historical expanses of 'Job'. After all, the best description of the coming incarnation of God in man, the projected *future* of the 'Job' myth, is *Memories* itself.

Conclusion: *Memories, Dreams, Reflections* as a sequel to 'Answer to Job'

> [E]ven the enlightened person. . . is never more than his own limited ego before the One who dwells within him, whose form has no knowable boundaries.
>
> (ibid.: para. 758)

In this chapter I am arguing that the well-known dichotomy in Jung's description of the self, as 'totality' of conscious and unconscious, and as archetype within the unconscious, is directly connected to his two forms of auto/biographical writing. These two forms of writing are not allegory and scientific concepts versus narrative and radical typology because even the ego-self, for Jung, needs to be open to the other. Rather, Jung's two forms of auto/biographical writing are that of the ego-self in historical time and the Jungian self as spatiality: chronology versus positionality. Myth as radical typology allows the ego-self to be perpetually open to unconscious ineffability. Similarly, the sacred time of the unconscious self remains (via linear chronology and sequential argument) rooted in the profane. History and culture are thereby also mythological so long as mythos remains 'radical', open to rewriting and not condensed into allegorical and exclusive abstract principles.

Memories and 'Job' reveal the coincidence of the two modes of the self in Jung's writing as codependence. Without evocation of the Jungian self, the ego-self is inauthentic. Without the linguistic resources of the ego in language and narrative, the Jungian self could not be represented at all. These works are linked spatially and sequentially: spatially by providing the two perspectives on the self, and chronologically by *Memories* being a further stage of the 'Job' myth.

Ultimately, 'Answer to Job' uses mythical radical typology to pivot a myth of deliverance against a myth of apocalypse. 'Everything now depends on man', so it is in the projected and unlimitable future that the possibility of the myth of deliverance may be incarnated in modern man (ibid.: para. 745). In fact, as psychic processes and as means of representation, individuation is presented here as the potential conversion of apocalypse into deliverance and vice versa. A possibility that I can only touch on here is that the *act of reading* 'Job' may be part of that act of transformation and openness to the other in the mind of the reader. Reading is a further body–mind incarnation of the myth (see Chapter 1).

As a sequel, *Memories* takes the apocalypse/deliverance myth of 'Job' and recasts it in a creation myth: the myth of (self) creation. For much cultural theory, the idea of a myth of self creation would signify the formation of a conscious identity in a way that tried to disguise its contingency. Jung offers an alternative to the (post)modern age. For Jung, a myth of self creation is creation by the self; yet it is not the transcendent, potentially knowable core identity of the humanists. One pole of what Jung means by creation by the self is the apparently premodern creation by God, provided that God is regarded as always at home in the human psyche. On the other hand, such an anti-modern notion of the self can also be expressed in more contemporary terms as the active unconscious embracing cultural discourses to shape the ego.

This more postmodern-friendly description of Jung's myth of self creation is, to him, simply other secular words for God's self creation (ibid.: paras. 554–5). The key of this union of the premodern and postmodern is to be found in *myth as both psyche and means of representing* the mysteries of the unconscious. Myth is Jung's writing of self as long as myth is a radical typological openness to endless storytelling. Once allegorical impulses to deduce universal principles from mythos occur, then the writing moves into abstract theory; its language divorced from the unconscious and the self.

Even the two 'conceptual' versions of the self take on narrative form in these two works. For if *Memories'* 'personal myth' is the mode of self as totality, then 'Job' offers the 'other' definition as its *perspective*. 'Job' is its own biographical genre of self as archetype within/from the viewpoint of the unconscious.

Jung's creation myth is myth in the creation of self. Radical typology provides a form of writing that *is* the creation of self as well as representing it. Myth depicts the self as historical and cultural simultaneous with the self of sacred non-linear time for which metaphor and actuality is spatiality. Therefore myth in the creation of self is also self creation in myth. The personal myth of an individual existence is part of the culturally located myth-in-history and inheres within a cosmological religious myth. Reading *Memories, Dreams, Reflections* as a sequel/companion to 'Answer to Job' makes it more explicit that the works are structuring a myth of man's self-fashioning in the cosmos; a myth that does not bypass history and culture.

In this reading of *Memories* and 'Job' as myth and autobiography, I have used studies of these two literary forms in order to look for meaningful echoes between these two works. This is not an argument about 'what Jung really meant', an illegitimate quest given the fragmented state of *Memories'* authorship. Rather, I would like to think that my method has a certain friendly fidelity by seeking out telos and meaning in preference to material causality and origins.

What is finally at stake in this particular reading is the possibility that we should start thinking of Jung's so-called 'concepts' more as overlapping genres of writing. These narrative genres have written into their core a spatial sense of the psyche; they view the psyche from different perspectives. It is not necessary to suggest a priority. For whether concepts result from certain ways that Jung chooses to write (derive from genres), or whether generic writing comes from the need to find expression for the concepts beyond the ego-language of rationality, what is apparent is that the relationship between concept and narrative is a necessary one. Without the link to mythical narrative, concepts exclude too much of the psyche. Without the possibility of thinking in concepts, the ego would lose its being and both 'psychology' as person and 'psychology' as body of ideas would have no direction. For Jung, psychology requires that rationality be set within a myth where there are no borders.

Chapter 3

Gender: The dialectic of anima and animus

Memories, Dreams, Reflections 1963/1983, 'On Spooks' CW18, Jung's Doctoral Thesis CW1, 'Anima and Animus' CW7

> Psychologically the self is a union of conscious (masculine) and unconscious (feminine). It stands for the psychic totality.
>
> (Jung 1951/1959, CW9ii: para. 426)

> The anima has an erotic, emotional character, the animus a rationalising one. Hence most of what men say about feminine eroticism, and particularly about the emotional life of women, is derived from their own anima projections and distorted accordingly. On the other hand, the astonishing assumptions and fantasies that women make about men come from the activity of the animus, who produces an inexhaustible supply of illogical arguments and false explanations.
>
> (Jung 1925/1954, CW17: para. 338)

Introduction

Jung is nowhere more the dualist than in his thinking about gender. His ideas about femininity and masculinity are polarized between an emotional erotic feminine and a rational masculinity. His conventional starting point is made more intriguing if we consider what he is actually describing in the notions of 'animus' and 'anima': the wayward anima is the unconscious femininity of a man; the unworthy animus is the unconscious masculinity of a woman. Although Jung is in one sense an essentialist in believing that female and male bodies bestow an unproblematic gender identity, he also builds in a dynamic of construction to conscious gender. For it arises from a lifelong dialogue with an inner 'opposite' other.

However, rather than pursue the radical implications of psychic bisexuality, the note of hysteria in the reference to 'the astonishing assumptions and fantasies' of women suggests fear in the face of something uncontrollable. Something very interesting is happening here in the writing. At one level Jung is setting out the complementary properties of anima and animus. One is erotic and emotional, the other rational and logical. Anima and animus are 'opposing' or binary manifestations of subjectivity conceived of as dialectical. Jung held that individuation, the constant encounter with the unconscious other, proceeded by a principle of 'opposing' qualities meeting in states of mutual transformation. Since gender (as I shall show) is the chief means by which such an oppositional relationship to the unconscious is structured, so gender is, unsurprisingly, polarized.

On the other hand, there is another level to the second quotation at the head of this chapter; one that threatens to disturb the Jungian dialectic. Just whose fantasies are being presented in the 'astonishing assumptions'? Semantically, they belong to 'women', but the erotic charge of the change of tone in the writing flips them back to the author. Is this account of the animus actually the voice of the other *within* Jung?

Jung's previous sentence warns that men cannot be relied upon to be objective about women. Are the 'astonishing assumptions' Jung the helpful psychologist *deliberately* demonstrating such slippage? A kind of joke? The anima distorts: here is an example! Or does this emotional outbreak indicate something about gender that is *not* under conscious control in the writing?

When Jung allows his anima to speak 'for' him in fantasies about the 'nature' of women, this inner other is immediately implicated in a politics of gender. Moreover, the slippage between 'anima' and 'woman' in the writing complicates the attempt to erect dialectical thinking. For it is not just that descriptions of the anima slide into essentialist and belittling comments about women, it is what Jung calls the anima in himself, masculine erotic fantasy, that seems to be speaking the anima as women. Between the dialectic of 'man' and woman' there is a third that is not stabilizing the dual entities, for it is neither man nor woman, nor synthesis of the two positions. Of course the anima is supposed to be the dialectical other of rational masculine consciousness. Yet the writing betrays, in 'astonishing assumptions', of 'women' *an uncertainty about who is speaking* haunting the dialectical subject.

In this chapter I will examine the role of gender in Jung's presentation of the psyche and its psychology as dialectical. I will show how such a structuring emerges out of something far more complex than can readily be accommodated by a principle of opposition, and also remains haunted by it. Indeed there is something authentically spectral about Jung's encounter with the feminine other. At key moments in his career, 'she' is characterized by an association with ghosts. Spectres by definition refuse the dialectical alternatives of being alive or dead. So the ghost is a trace of something radical and plural attaching itself to the dialectic of anima and animus.

Four significant texts for gender will be considered. Searching for the woman 'within' takes us to two fragments: the 'discovery' of the anima in *Memories, Dreams, Reflections* (Jung 1963/1983), and a ghost story that Jung told as part of a preface to a book on the occult, 'On Spooks:

Forward to Moser' (Jung 1950/1976, CW18: paras. 757–81). To look at Jung's portrayal of gender in relation to other people, I will explore his earliest major work in his doctoral thesis, 'On the Psychology and Pathology of So-Called Occult Phenomena' (Jung 1902/1957, CW1: paras. 1–150). Lastly, I will draw briefly upon 'Anima and Animus' (Jung 1928/1953, CW7: paras. 296–340). First of all, it is worth looking a little closer at the Jungian dialectic.

Jung's dialectical subject

As Joseph F. Rychlak (1984/1991) and Hester Solomon (1994) have shown, Jung considered himself to be participating in a long tradition of dialectical thought. Solomon's introduction to the dialectical vision and its methodology is particularly helpful:

> The dialectical model allows for a twofold view of reality, on the one hand in terms of bipolar opposites in dynamic relation to each other, and on the other hand a unity of opposites towards which each strives. . . The dialectical process begins with a 'thesis' – . . . a starting point from which future developments proceed. In the course of time the thesis is seen to entail an opposite – 'antithesis' – or 'the other'. This opposite is understood in relation to the thesis, such that the thesis is seen to require the presence of the antithesis all along. A third state is achieved called the 'synthesis', which is the result of the dynamic, conflictual, and reciprocal relationship between thesis and antithesis. This resolution has the capacity to hold the two apparent opposites together.
>
> (Solomon 1994: 82–3)

Solomon demonstrates that the German philosopher Hegel's dialectical scheme corresponds to the Jungian procedure of the 'transcendent function' in which opposites in the conscious and unconscious produce a creative synthesis (Solomon 1994: 80–2).

Undeniably, Jung regarded his project as profoundly dialectical, based, as he was fond of reiterating, on a principle of opposites as fundamental to the conscious/unconscious relationship. For example, from connecting to the unconscious via opposition comes the understanding that the creation of meaning is a dialectical process, as is psychotherapy itself with the therapist embodying the voice of the other (Jung 1939/1958, CW1: para. 904).

Additionally, the psyche's propensity to heal itself through being in balance is derived from its intrinsically dialectical procedures (Jung 1943/1953, CW7: para. 92). So there is a kind of innate dialectical impetus in psychic functioning. Dialectical processes are in some sense 'natural', present within the psyche, and therefore must be replicated in the science of the psyche. A dialectical subject entails a dialectical psychology:

> A psychological theory, if it is to be more than a technical makeshift, must base itself on the principle of opposition; for without this it could only re-establish a neurotically unbalanced psyche. There is no balance, no system of self-regulation, without opposition. The psyche is just such a self-regulating system.
>
> (ibid.: para. 92)

We are back in the rational world of binary logic with a vengeance. However, what an examination of Jung's encounters with the other will reveal is the lifelong struggle to *produce* dialectical gender and psychology out of spectral inner figures. These psychic phantoms complicate Jung's dialectical subject on two levels: they are more diverse and plural than simple 'opposition' would indicate, and some of them imply that being which defeats rational categories of life and death: the ghost. Suppose that, instead of dialectical opposition as the fundamental condition of the psyche, what is most innate turns out to be narrative, and a ghost story at that?

Indeed it is particularly resonant that there is a tension between sequential dialectical process in the psyche versus a spectral and spatial narrative of diversity, for it represents another instance of what this book believes to be a perennial Jungian preoccupation: the dialogue between time and space.

Anima: Discovering the soul in *Memories, Dreams, Reflections* (Jung 1963/1983)

One of the features of Jung's feminine other is, I argue, an association with the occult. In this, he anticipates the preoccupation of contemporary cultural theory with ghosts and haunting. To deconstruction (see Chapter 2) it is the idea of ghosts, or more properly their representation as beings that defy the binary logic of being present or absent, alive or properly dead, that disturbs the rational and dialectical systems of modernity (Wolfreys 2002: 2).

In *Memories, Dreams, Reflections* it is suggestive that gender as the inner other arrives in the company of ghosts. Such a spectral genesis both sustains and undermines Jung's ability to generate a new psychology out of his haunted psyche.

Here is his representation of the anima:

> I once asked myself, 'What am I really doing?. . .' Whereupon a voice within me said, 'It is art.'. . . I knew for a certainty that the voice had come from a woman. . . Later I came to see that this inner feminine

figure plays a typical, or archetypical, role in the unconsciousness of a man, and I called her the 'anima'. I was like a patient in analysis with a ghost and a woman!

(Jung 1963/1983: 210–11)

In the context of this passage the ghost probably refers to Philemon, a masculine imaginal figure. What is indicative here is the association of 'ghost' and 'woman' as markers of the other. That the 'other' when feminine is touched with inferiority is reinforced by the slippage in professional status. Jung identifies the voice as that of a patient, thereby suggesting a reassuring notion of authority and control (ibid.: 210). He later finds *himself* in the subordinate patient role. At the inception of the anima, ideas of gender alterity are caught up with professional barriers.

Symptomatically, Jung takes on another position associated in his career with that of a patient: he becomes a medium. When he reflects that the anima lacks physical embodiment, he allows her temporarily to usurp his conscious control of speech – he enables her to speak in his voice just as a medium invites a spirit to use her vocal organs (ibid.: 210). Not only is this highly suggestive of the anima's talent for 'taking over' Jung's voice in other writings, but also the exchange of roles between the patient and the medium binds this fragment (very late in Jung's life) to the extraordinarily creative early work, the doctoral thesis (Jung 1902/1957, CW1: paras. 1–150).

Building upon the invaluable research of F. X. Charet (1993), I have shown elsewhere that Jung's writing about women is focused through a slippage from medium to anima (Rowland 1999). Charet shows that the nature of the anima is modelled upon his portrayal of the medium. Jung then becomes the medium in the depiction of masculine subjectivity in *Memories*. This work reveals Jung's inner gender alterity prompting him to adopt the (feminized) patient–medium position, thus displacing the feminine to the (occult) inner other.

My argument is that in order to engage with the inner feminine, Jung has to take what for him is a feminized role. The struggle to maintain any semblance of secure identity is played out in writing. By 'writing letters' to the anima, Jung stages his battle for inner authority through authorship (ibid.: 211). How far is the construction of the anima as a dialectical concept actually a desperate strategy to assert conscious command of this unruly inner voice? Certainly the struggle to define the descent into fantasy as art, science or nature seems to be the battleground for Jung's sanity:

Thus the insinuations of the anima, the mouthpiece of the unconscious, can utterly destroy a man.

(ibid.: 212)

Here the anima is that familiar gender stereotype, the nagging, destructive woman. I propose that she be regarded as having this aspect; one mask of the anima is that of the culturally conditioned fears of the other gender invading Jung's writing, just as he so obviously fears this invader in his head.

Yet there is another way of understanding the persistent irrationality of the anima. As well as an abject portrait of the feminine as destructive woman, she is far more in embodying that which denies to consciousness control of meaning. In effect she resists rationality, theory and science. 'As mouthpiece of the unconscious', she refuses to be consistent, defined, corralled into concepts and stable truths. She is a textual anarchist. She is the unconscious as something radical, sublime, that forever eludes incarceration in conscious definitions.

This anima represents the founding presence of Jungian psychology (as mouthpiece of the unconscious) as a founding absence. That which is most fundamental, the unconscious, is also the most undermining of any fixed conceptual scheme. Unlike Freudian psychoanalysis, the unconscious is not only that which is produced by the splitting of the subject, it is additionally the pre-existent given. Jung's unconscious as collective, the inheritance of all humanity, is the originating concept *that by its very definition* undoes, makes provisional, puts under erasure, all other Jungian concepts.

In the language of deconstruction, the unconscious is the 'supplement' necessary to produce Jungian psychology. The concept of the anima, from this point of view, is merely a feminizing of this radical other. How far is the notion of the anima a culturally inflected tactic? One that serves to repress the unconscious other just enough to generate a dialectical theoretical schema that will be professionally viable?

By portraying the anima as a nagging woman, Jung is able to cloak himself with an intellectual authority over her transgressions based upon a moralized gender authority. Or to be more sympathetic, moral self-control of inner unruliness is linked to rational command of theoretical argument. What Jung never considers is the suspicious resemblance between controlling a gender other within and the conventions of masculine authority in exterior social relationships. Such an omission leaves his work open to the speculation that conventional social relationships are a spectre haunting Jungian psychology. Cultural misogyny can be detected in the interiority of dialectical gender that aligns masculinity with rationality and femininity with its opposite.

In *Memories* the figure given the definition of anima becomes an emblem for unconscious contents that require 'a technique for stripping them of their power' (ibid.: 211). Such a reconquering of interiority requires that unconscious forces be personified so that they can be brought into a dialectical relationship with consciousness. Curiously, 'relationship' here seems to be equated with disempowering of the other. What seems to be at stake is the ability to define, name, or acquire a social context to the inner other; one that enables an ego understanding with the properties of ego governance.

Jung's whole project in engaging with his inner spectres (those voices he came to treat as a medium treats her ghosts) is to convert the spectral into the dialectical. The spectre that disrupts identity is repositioned as a figure in a relationship. Together the ego and the figure of the unconscious will perform identity as an ongoing dialogue. The concept of 'anima' (and animus, shadow, self, individuation, etc.), is both a means and a consequence of adopting a dialectical model of subjectivity. To personify entails naming; a dialogue means that a duality is brought into being.

Memories' depiction of the anima demonstrates the Jungian techniques of explication, active imagination and amplification. She, the inner voice, is explained through personification. Then active imagination brings forth a ghostly and fantasized drama. Finally amplification builds this personal activity into a concept: Jung decides to call her the 'anima' after the soul in Christian myth (ibid.: 210). The reader is informed that such inner pioneering results in the 'personal myth' (ibid.: 224), that pivotal term signifying both Jung's intensely individual striving for meaning and the scheme of his 'theory', his psychology as given to the world (see Chapter 2).

What the negotiation of the anima in *Memories* demonstrates is Jung *making* knowledge out of the irrational, in an attempt to undo and revise Enlightenment rational categories. However, it also shows him falling into the Enlightenment tendency to erect binaries by setting up a self seemingly founded upon gender trouble. In both challenging and repeating the Enlightenment feminizing of the other, Jung proves himself its enemy and its heir.

Telling ghost stories: 'On Spooks: Forward to Moser' (Jung 1950/1976, CW10)

Since part of my argument is that Jung anticipated deconstruction's turn to the spectral, it is worth looking at the nature of postmodern haunting. Jacques Derrida suggests that the spectre is that which is neither alive nor dead (1997: 12). It inhabits a gap between two ontological categories of being. The spectral is not a logical or a dialectical constituent. For Derrida and the deconstructionists, ghosts are nothing in themselves. What is truly uncanny is what their representation does to the logical or dialectical structures of modernity:

> A third term, the spectral, speaks of the limits of determination, while arriving beyond the terminal both in and of identification in either case (alive/dead) and not as an oppositional or dialectical term itself defined as part of some logical economy.
>
> (Wolfreys 2002: x)

'On Spooks' is a short piece in which Jung discusses the nature of the occult in culture and psychology before offering his own contribution to a collection of ghostly tales. In an uncanny anticipation of deconstruction he begins by unsettling rational categories: he disputes the binary alternatives false/true when applied to the existence of spirits. Ghost stories may be a means to a truth that is not what they purport to describe. Jung asserts that such tales cannot prove anything about survival after death. So they are neither 'true' in the sense of being actually proven emissaries of the dead, nor 'false' in the sense of having no 'reality' at all.

Deconstructionists speak of a 'gap' in rational categories of alive and dead and which is not subject to dialectical reasoning (Wolfreys 2002: x). To Jung, the gap between 'true' and 'false' expands into a conceptual space, the landscape that he is seizing for his psychology, into 'territory. . . this vast and shadowy region, where everything seems possible and nothing believable' (Jung 1950/1976, CW18: para. 757). Part of the architecture of this space is narrative or, more particularly, biography. For Jung identifies psychological precursors in the biographical works about occult practitioners such as mediums and somnambulists (sleepwalkers) (ibid.: para. 757). Crucially, Jung identifies the *narrative* telling as the antecedent rather than the occult-inclined persons themselves.

Jung makes another fundamental claim in keeping with deconstruction by arguing that the occult is *produced* by the exalted structuring of rationality in the Enlightenment. The very production of binary logic results in a residue of disorder haunting the structure: 'the more rationalistic we are in our conscious minds, the more alive becomes the spectral world of the unconscious' (ibid.: para. 759). Like the anima voice in *Memories*, occult phenomena exists as a challenge to traditional empirical science. Modernity's response is to define this unruliness as non-science, non-knowledge, 'other', hence 'occult'. Jung's contrasting tactic, as I have indicated earlier, is to literally establish a dialogue with the exiled other in order to pursue a dialectical model of science, fed by the unknown. One form he gave to this revision of modern science is that of myth (see Chapter 2).

After establishing the spectral as phenomena that transcends true or false logical categories, Jung recounts his own ghost story, purporting to describe his experiences of 30 years ago. He describes his occult encounters and then follows it with an analysis.

In the summer of 1920 Jung made an extended visit to London to give lectures on his new psychology. It became customary for him to spend weekends at an old farmhouse in Buckinghamshire accompanied by an English colleague named only here as Dr X. The two men were waited upon by local women, who made a point of leaving the premises well before dark. On the first weekend Jung had a bad night, afflicted in bed by a strange exhaustion that seemed to inhibit sleep. There was also an unpleasant smell in the room that he could not trace to any physical origin. Indeed, driven to search for a parallel to the smell in his memory, he recalls an elderly woman patient with a noxious wound.

The next occurrence was that the horrible smell was joined by the sound of a dripping tap. Again, a search of the room and good weather outside revealed no rational origin. So much for the first weekend. On the second, things became worse. By the third night the unnatural 'torpor', the smell and the dripping tap was added to by a loud knocking and noises like a dog-like animal rushing around the room (ibid.: para. 770). It was on the fourth weekend that Jung tentatively broached with his host the notion that the house was haunted. Proving a proper scientific sceptic, Dr X laughed. However the female servants confirmed the house's spooky reputation and their own nervousness. Jung's sufferings became even more acute. A narrative climax was at hand. Waking from drowsiness, Jung, at last, has a vision of the spectre:

> There, beside me on the pillow, I saw the head of an old woman. . . The left half of the face was missing below the eye. . . I leapt out of bed with one bound.
>
> (ibid.: para. 774)

Fortunately, Jung's troubles were nearly over. After spending the rest of the night on a chair, he changed bedrooms and endured no more nocturnal disturbance. Yet the narrative cannot cease until the erosion of rational categories is complete. In other words, the complacent scepticism of Dr X must be defeated. Challenged to spend a night alone in the house, Dr X is actually driven out of the building by occult tumult. The house is given up and eventually has to be demolished because no one will buy it.

Given Jung's trope of space, of new 'territory' for psychology at the start of this short text, it is worth noting that this account is, in essence, a story of Jung *in the wrong room*. He has to shift literally and bodily from the passive position, lying in bed, to active self-possession. He leaps out of bed, he changes bedroom, as a kind of physical prelude to challenging Dr X. Jung then *moves on* into 'explanation', a final section analysing the experience.

Here it may be significant that Jung starts by announcing that he cannot account for the dripping noise. He refuses even to consider that it was a 'delusion' (ibid.: para. 778). This occult fragment remains outside definitions of true/false, and even outside Jung's revision of his psychology as a dialogue with an unfathomable psyche. It remains truly (and doubly) spectral. For most of the rest of the disturbances he first of all provides a bodily cause. Rustling and creaking perhaps are noises inside the ear. The knocking could be heartbeats somehow projected onto the exterior walls of the room. The bodily lassitude may be a somatic registering of fear. Unconscious of his terror, Jung's unease is manifest in the body until the vision of the old woman causes it to break through into consciousness. As for the apparition herself, she was probably a hallucination of the former patient (ibid.: para. 778).

The animal, now named a dog, is said to represent Jung's intuition. In a complex bodily-verbal creative episode, intuition becomes conflated with the physical sense of smell in sniffing out something strange about the room. Those critics who argue that Jung is uninterested in the body should look very carefully at this text. For Jung seems to be portraying the somatic depths of the psyche by mapping bodily responses through the narrative medium of the ghost story. A classic Gothic literary form becomes a means of speaking the body.

What is even more fascinating (and Gothic) is that Jung refuses to ascribe a secure origin to these events in either the body or the psyche. While arguing at one point that the room may have possessed an ancient and barely detectable smell that the body is registering, the contrary may equally be valid. The psyche's anxieties could be transmitted physically and bodily as the smell of fear that gradually assumes even more monstrous shapes in the dripping, the knocking, the dog and the spectral crone (ibid.: para. 780).

The search for origins here occupies a doubly spectral landscape. It is both openly ghostly and theoretically so in defeating any attempt to maintain another two distinct categories of body and psyche. Is Jung's bodily sense of smell picking up a physical trace, or is his psyche's agitation provoking a bodily performance? Separation of body and mind is intrinsic to the construction of positivist rational science. Instead of a rational scientific sequence of causal origins, Jung provides narrative.

The emphasis on 'telling a tale' occurs multiply: once in the reference to biography as the precursor of psychology, second in the structuring of this experience through the genre of a typical haunted house story, and third as that which enables the formation of a body–psyche dialectic where one operates far more in partnership with its 'other' than for Jung's treatment of the anima in *Memories*. It is time to look more closely at the gender dynamics of this ghost story.

Significantly, Jung again takes a feminized position in this occult encounter. And again the feminized position is marked by inferior social status. Until his final overthrow, Dr X is not a picture of a human being nor even a literary character. Rather he is a narrative device consisting of two features: he is sceptical of ghosts and he is a doctor, a male colleague with professional status. He is therefore a metonym of the rational scientific establishment in its scoffing rejection of the occult as phenomena that might contribute valuable, if contentious, new forms of knowledge.

By contrast, Jung is being made positively ill by events; in body by sleeplessness and in mind by not being able to categorize his experience and hence assert his sanity. His fears and sufferings ally him with the frightened female servants and his sickness forces him dangerously close to the role of a patient. That, indeed, is literally the climax of his tale: when he sees the ghost in close proximity on his pillow, it is an image of his own position at that moment. Jung *has to move* because he is lying down next to a feminine incomplete 'other', in a narrative that structures him into the role of inferiority: occult (not scientific), feminine, and socially subordinate.

Here on foreign ground, in England, where he is trying to convince a sceptical masculine medical fraternity of his strange new ideas, Jung's gender trouble is theory trouble and vice versa. Just as Jung's physical leap away from the ghost is simultaneously a move into conceptual understanding, so again his brief occupation of a feminine position is a disturbing, yet productive loss of inner identity. For it allows him to rebuild an internal coherence that is also a shaping of his professional psychology.

The bodily leap is also a leap into Jungian psychology. It is a movement from a space that is not limited by a binary logic of gender (Jung is neither masculine rationality or wholly abandoned to the feminine occult), nor of the ontological categories of alive and dead. *Jung's gender trouble is spectral because it is where he is with those who are neither alive nor dead.* This ghost story is a demonstration of the way that Jung's theorizing both defeats and seeks to re-establish Enlightenment binary logic, only in new dialectical terms. Yet, in converting a binary opposition into a dialectical process with the other, Jung imports the space of the spectral into his writing. Jung's entire psychology is a negotiation with the spectre of the unconscious as that which defies rational meaning. At the same time the persistent association of the feminine with the occult is a poignant demonstration of its haunting power in his imagination.

In fact, 'On Spooks' is structured around three narrative positions that together interact to form what might be called a 'Gothic economy'. The text opens with a firm rejection of Enlightenment rationality as neither natural nor sustainable. Rather, the creation of rationality by the splitting off of irrationality, or the unconscious, produces and magnifies occult phenomena. Second, Jung enters his own argument through the medium of narrative: the ghost story. In the haunted bedroom Jung experiences the trauma of the territory of the spectral where neither gender, nor theory, nor the category of alive or dead offer certain knowledge. His psychology becomes spectral because his inner being is spectral. The story culminates in a third narrative position where Jung steps out of the realm of the spectral without losing touch with it all together. By moving into a different bedroom (in the same house – distance from the spectre still maintains a spatial relationship), and by involving Dr X as a second bodily agent in the story, Jung *performs* physically his conversion of the spectral into the dialectical.

In effect the ghost story is a bodily and scriptural performance of the roots of Jung's responses to the Enlightenment and the structuring of his ideas. Such a minor text is, paradoxically, a powerful demonstration of

Jung's notion of the psyche as embodied, and of gender as an agent of alterity. It is narrative, and specifically here the genre of ghost stories, that permits this performance of physical, psychic and conceptual positions to be staged. Hence I would argue that 'On Spooks' reveals a Gothic economy at work in which narrative is the founding act from which theoretical positions can be derived.

Both the fragment about the anima from *Memories* and 'On Spooks' are late works in the Jungian corpus. They could both be read as referring back to his very early doctoral thesis, 'On the Psychology and Pathology of So-Called Occult Phenomena', which appears as the opening text of *The Collected Works*. The thesis focuses upon the activities of a female spiritualist medium known here as Miss S.W. Later research, notably by F. X. Charet, has identified her as Jung's teenage cousin, Hélène Preiswerk (Charet 1993).

The doctoral thesis contain citations of Freud's *The Interpretation of Dreams*, yet was written and published before Jung had corresponded with the great man (Freud 1899/1976). As a work before the encounter with Freud, it is also a work before Jung. Jung built his psychology upon a productive dialectics with the unconscious *after* the break from Freud and *out of* the subsequent breakdown in his mental equilibrium. On the other hand, the thesis is revealing of Jung's inner conflicts and, in particular, demonstrates the way gender, authorship and authority become mutually implicated throughout his work.

Writing anima in 'On the Psychology and Pathology of So-Called Occult Phenomena' (Jung 1902/1957, CW1)

An extensive text of some 150 paragraphs, the doctoral thesis contains three movements with numerous subdivisions. The first section offers brief details of a number of patients, mostly women, with abnormal states of consciousness. Symptoms range from hysterical fits, amnesia, sleepwalking and descriptions suggesting epilepsy. Several patients have problems in distinguishing the living from the dead. They hallucinate corpses or hear weeping from graves (Jung 1902/1957, CW1: 9–13).

After establishing the wide variation in the pathology of abnormal states of consciousness, the second section gives information on the spiritualistic medium, Miss S.W., followed by Jung's extensive analysis of the phenomena. In this chapter I am going to concentrate on the doctoral thesis as a piece of writing and not refer overtly to the later research on Hélène Preiswerk, much of which challenges or modifies Jung's conclusions. Specifically, I am not trying to trace 'what really happened' in these late nineteenth-century séances, although the hints of intimacy between the investigator and the medium are important. Rather, I am going to look at

Jung's writing methods at this formative stage of his career. In particular, the portrayal of gender in the thesis betrays a seminal struggle over origins and authorship.

Jung opens his account of S.W. by describing her as a Protestant teenager from a family with a history of mental disturbances. Of average intelligence and inadequate education, she is discovered to be 'an excellent medium' after trying out table turning as a joke (ibid.: para. 39). The first spirit claims to be the medium's grandfather and soon the medium tells of visions of white veiled figures. During spiritualist episodes, S.W. enters a partial hypnotic state where she assumes a far more mature personality. She begins to let the spirits take over her own voice in séances and she becomes greatly influenced by a book about a famous woman medium (ibid.: para. 49). Now she produces a frivolous and gossipy spirit called Ulrich von Gerbenstein, followed by a much more impressive spectre, Ivenes. This latter figure is known as S.W.'s own spiritual self, a superior being whose physical appearance is said to be 'of a markedly Jewish type' (ibid.: para. 59).

As S.W.'s education in the Beyond continues, she starts to pass on cosmic instruction about star dwellers and the inhabitants of Mars. Alongside the cosmological stories go the multiplying adventures of Ivenes. Although as a very special being, Ivenes does not need to incarnate herself as often as most, she still manages a wide variety of sensational and sexual exploits, often involved with earlier incarnations of Jung himself. For example, when burnt as a witch, she had then been Jung's mother and he was, naturally, much affected (ibid.: para. 63). Jung characterizes S.W.'s proliferating narratives as either 'family romances' (Ivenes) or 'Mystic Science' (cosmos) (ibid.: para. 64).

Eventually the exuberance of these psychic productions falters and S.W. is finally caught out faking. Here Jung moves to take control of his writing by inaugurating the third movement entitled: 'Discussion of the Case' (ibid.: para. 72). The investigator puts much of the phenomena down to S.W.'s reading as inspiration of her desire to 'act out' the role of a great lady. The grandfather could perhaps be like an image from a dream as described by Sigmund Freud, yet precise identification with Freud's theory is impossible because 'we have no means of judging how far the emotion in question may be considered "repressed"' (ibid.: para. 97). I will consider the implications of this provisional use of Freud later.

Jung is fascinated by Ivenes and suggests that she represents a fantasy expansion of S.W.'s everyday ego. His second reference to Freud differs significantly from the first in its wholehearted endorsement of the other thinker's position of dreams as sexual wish fulfilment. S.W.'s 'romances', her potentially endless weaving of stories of Ivenes's sexual adventures, are directly equated to dreams in a Freudian theoretical framework, acknowledged in a footnote:

> [T]he whole essence of Ivenes and her enormous family is nothing but a dream of sexual wish fulfillment, which differs from a dream of a night only that it is spread over months and years.
>
> (ibid.: para. 120)

From re-examining the other spirit personalities, Jung finds himself able to group them under two headings: 'the *serio-religious* and the *gay-hilarious*' (ibid.: para. 126) – as essentially two different subconscious personalities. Ivenes herself signifies a way of the psyche trying to mediate between two extremes. 'She' is an orientation towards a possible future self (ibid.: para. 116).

There is so much rich material in the profound encounter between nascent psychologist and unruly feminine subject that I am only able to begin the analysis of the significant struggles over meaning and gender. For example, in the originary work for Jung as a professional practitioner (his *doctorate*), S.W. herself produces several theories of origins. Particularly startling is her answer to one of the greatest spiritual and intellectual traumas of the nineteenth century in her narrative of reconciliation between Darwin's theory of evolution and the Bible story of the creation of Adam and Eve. Religion and science are blended in a web of storytelling that includes the 'family romances' of S.W.'s spirit world. Europe's population, we are told, is descended from materialized spirits and evolved monkeys (ibid.: para. 64).

Also in a fantastically resonant passage, Jung suggests that S.W. confounds the logical sequence of origins in reading. While arguing that much of S.W.'s occult performance can be traced to her reading, that act itself is not the origin. Rather it is the means for the medium to become her own origin. Ivenes is not a copy of the medium in the book; 'she' is the true original (ibid.: para. 116).

Such a description of a performance of gender as its own origin shows it as a mask that constructs a truth rather than concealing it, a mask that is not a veil of some originary identity. This portrayal anticipates the work of Judith Butler on gender as performance (Butler 1990). That this performance may be energized and psychically shaped through reading infers its spectral nature. Reading is that which is neither alive nor dead, real nor unreal, but a gap or space where reality or identity can be performed.

However, S.W. is not yet done with origins. She produces for Jung what he calls 'Mystic Science' and orders him to draw a diagram of cosmic forces (ibid.: para. 65). The mystic system is distinguished by the way it combines spiritual and material powers (ibid.: para. 66). Its completion marks the end of the most significant séances and allows Jung to move on to his analysis.

Probably not a moment too soon, for the creativity of S.W. represents a serious challenge to Jung for control of the text. Despite not formally being Jung's patient, S.W. nevertheless provides the earliest example of the unconscious psyche in *The Collected Works*. Yet she is also the first, the *origin* for Jung in another sense. In staging her narrative web of theories of origin, the first (not quite) patient displays an expansive territory of ideas that later find habitation as the stuff of Jung's distinctive psychology. S.W.'s tales could claim to be the occult origin of Jung's theories and therefore the origin of his masculine professional identity. The 'patient', whose pseudonym conceals her familial intimacy to Jung as a cousin, is too proximate in a textual sense as well.

On one level the doctoral thesis is a text about authorship. Is S.W. the author of her extraordinary fertile fantasies? Her occult narratives, we are told, are not produced out of her conscious mind. Only at the end does she consciously and deliberately fake, and this material is not given in the thesis. Does S.W.'s inner 'other' create originals from her reading, her spiritual inspirations, her overheard conversations? This appears to be Jung's belief by his comment on her reading. So if S.W. is some kind of divided author – her inner creative other mediated by her ability to represent it bodily and linguistically – the question remains how far Jung tailors her productions in order to become the author of his own thesis? Certainly, as I shall show, the position Jung adopts in the thesis *vis-à-vis* the theoretical control and explication of S.W.'s narratives is woefully narrow in the face of her expanses of creativity. (In fact it is the very position that Jung later spends years condemning in Freud.)

The question of authority in authorship becomes ever more acute if we consider the way that S.W. could be said to anticipate or 'originate' key elements of *The Collected Works*. Does S.W.'s performance of gender, which includes occulted philosophy, theology, science, romance writing, constitute her as the 'anima' of Jung's *Collected Works*? I would like to suggest that the structural resemblance between the struggle over art, science and nature with the anima in *Memories* and the drive to occupy these fields in the thesis (through controlling the definition of S.W.'s creativity), represents a crucial dialectic in Jung's thinking. It is a dialectic explicitly created out of, and as a way of limiting the play of, the spectral feminine.

Prompted by a (mis)represented real person, S.W.'s fate is to function as anima to over 20 volumes: 'she' is the spectre of gender in the writing. Let me try to substantiate S.W. as textual anima. In her obsession with origins she performs a mediating narrative (that Jung was later to call the 'transcendent function'), which seeks to heal the split between science, religion and philosophy. She also links body to mind in mending the Enlightenment severing of rational discourse (science, philosophy) from sexuality. Since her narrative mode is erotic and domestic, S.W. enacts a femininity that challenges the gendered division of masculine intellectual affairs in 'the world' versus the romance that exiles women to the home. Instead of romance as both narrative genre and signifier of the erotic being exorcised from those determinedly masculine spheres of science, religion and philosophy, for S.W. romance is their chief means of expression. In this occult process, art, religion and science are connected in a web of narrative with S.W. as a truly Gothic author.

S.W.'s Gothic romance overturns Enlightenment presuppositions and categories. Jung, the male medical author-ity may wish to dismiss the material as phenomena to be subordinated through his professional tools, but S.W. would appear to be suggesting much of his later preoccupations. Yet, where Jung will eventually produce 'concepts' as his tokens of scientific discourse, S.W. presents ideas wholly in the realm of narrative, and in one of its least rationalizable modes: romance. No wonder S.W. is finally dismissed as a fraud as her 'scientific methods' prove intolerable, too feminine, too occult, too abject.

An example of S.W.'s occult gifts to Jung is her asserting the supreme reality of the psyche through the medium of the séances. Early in the proceedings she valiantly defends the genuine nature of the spiritual experiences against charges of illness or fraudulence (ibid.: para. 43). Then again, the journey of S.W. through the séances is recognizably one of individuation. Ivenes stands for the model and goal of her ideal self. When Jung concludes that S.W.'s multitudinous spirits actually consist of her torn between two psychic extremes, Ivenes is said to be a means of mediating between opposites. Therefore in the performance of the exciting story of Ivenes can be found individuation, the transcendent function, the future-oriented teleological psyche, the role of dreams and the self:

> The patient. . . anticipates her own future and embodies in Ivenes what she wishes to be in twenty years time. . . she dreams herself into it.
>
> (ibid.: para. 116)

Of course, in the notion of 'mystic science' we have Jung's interest in religion as a dimension of psychology through providing a record of psychic activity. That the mystic science of S.W. is devoted to reconciling spiritualism and materialism suggests a prototype of Jung's development of synchronicity or meaningful acausal coincidences of events that may point to the relativity of time and space (see Chapters 6 and 7).

In addition to Jungian concepts, the mode of narrative itself may have proved formative, since it returns creatively in the later writing. Here in the thesis, Jung needs to assert textual organization of meaning by starting the conversion of spectrality into dialectics, occult romance into 'opposing' movements and concepts in S.W.'s psyche. He has to draw back from absorption in S.W.'s fantastical world (and does not acknowledge that he may have a role in stimulating her erotic fantasies). Jung will claim distance from his feminine subject into order to corral her fertile psychic spaces into a construction of knowledge based on an *encounter* with the other. It is not yet the full dialectic, a creative dialogue with the other.

The doctoral thesis is Jung before the full establishment of his dialectical psychology, before he is able to trust in a fully dialectical science, for which myth will become an authentic mode of expression. Therefore at this point in Jung's career the confrontation with the spectre is very interesting in the methods used to shore up his scientific credentials. In the first place he adopts the tactic that he also retains later of converting multiplicity into duality. Second, he uses the tool that he emphatically later rejects: that of 'nothing but' language characteristic of the Enlightenment split between rationality and irrationality.

Duality is imposed by firmly grouping the spirits into two types: gossipy and frivolous, versus serious and religious (ibid.: para. 126). These then become the two extremes through which Ivenes wends a mediating path. The 'nothing but' language, is, on the face of it, a more startling development. For it is the explicit means, and only place in the thesis, where Jung wholeheartedly adopts the theories of Sigmund Freud.

> It is the woman's premonition of sexual feeling. . . that has created these monstrous ideas in the patient. . . From this point of view the whole essence of Ivenes and her enormous family is nothing but a dream of sexual wish fulfillment.
>
> (ibid.: para. 120)

As Renos Papadopoulos (1991) has shown in his seminal essay on Jung's 'Other', this linguistic device, 'nothing but', 'nothing but sexuality can account for', 'nothing but childhood neuroses', Jung later criticizes as peculiarly Freudian (Jung 1939/1966, CW15: para. 68). To the later Jung, 'nothing but' argument is far too constricting to contain the fields of fantasy that are his creative psyche. Yet here in the early thesis, 'Freud' becomes a masculine textual position as a cited 'authority' and a literary means of carving out distance from a dangerously proximate feminine (patient).

Such language enables meaning to be controlled in a way that is simultaneously a construction of knowledge. As in 'On Spooks', Jung is in danger of being suspended between a rational identity (that he genders masculine and which casts out the occult other as 'nothing but'), and feminine occult narrative. Yet, unlike in 'On Spooks' and the anima in *Memories*, Jung embraces the masculine position that *he* identifies as Freudian. If Jung's gender trouble is theory trouble and vice versa, is it also the fatal narrative of his trouble with a powerful male theoretician? Certainly 'Freudian' Jung in the thesis is not yet ready to learn from his anima, despite his provision of a peculiarly potent one for his *Collected Works*.

S.W. is a redoubtable proto-author. She is also a portrait of gender identity as performance. Her staged self is magnificently literary and multilayered because it is a narrative uniting reading, speech and bodily performance. Her story weaves together intellect and body, science and spirituality, and a spectral deconstructive space where gender can never be binary. Her spectral performance turns the gap the deconstructionists speak of as the liminality between two ontological categories into a Gothic romance.

Derrida refers to the ghostliness of modern technologies as accelerating the spectrality of modernity:

> Contrary to what we might believe, the experience of ghosts. . . is accentuated, accelerated by modern technologies like film, television, the telephone. These technologies inhabit, as it were, a phantom structure.
>
> (Derrida 1989: 61)

What this depiction of modernity leaves out is the spectral technology that preceded film, television, telephones in a thoroughly non-causal genealogy. Jung's writings demonstrate spiritualism as a technology producing stories of the other that undo the supposed unity of the rational subject. Rather than simply portraying the spectral pollution of the (post)modern subject, Jung provides a methodology for living with a ghostly interior: the conversion of spectrality into a dialectical subject. The doctoral thesis shows this methodology in its infancy and incomplete.

What can be detected here is the eroticization of the inner other conducted via the psyche of another, in S.W. Ivenes, in particular, becomes a magnetically sexual heroine whose multiple roles as siren, seer and adventurer across time, space and cultures answers all the perceived inadequacies of the historical, poorly educated Swiss teenager. The question of who might perceive inadequacies, S.W. or Jung, is unanswerable since the desires of both are caught up in the imaginative potency of Ivenes.

Similarly, for the later dialectics, Jung produces, a little crudely, the tactic of reducing multiplicity to duality in insisting upon a basic structure of opposing forces in S.W.'s spirits. He does the same job on the personality of S.W. as his language polarizes her portrayal between silly schoolgirl and magnificent Ivenes. What is incomplete with regard to the later Jung is the sense of a knowledge necessarily in dialogue with a creative unknown. Perhaps only the reader brings this quality to this fascinating text. For who could feel satisfied with the 'nothing but' device of reducing S.W.'s spectral proliferation to one definitive answer: puberty?

This lack of reader satisfaction is the trace of the absence of narrative completion. Later Jung was to perceive this lack as important to his dialectical subject. It is a version comparable to the Lacanian model of 'lack' yet remains distinctively Jungian in its core dialectical role in his psychology. This lack of *satisfaction* as the desire to know fully, to complete the story, is the misfit between a neat conceptual idea and the imaginative outpourings of the unconscious. In the guise of his struggle to comprehend the textual space of Miss S.W., it was to haunt Jung all his life.

Conclusion: Writing concepts of gender in 'Anima and Animus' (Jung 1928/1953, CW7)

[T]he dissociation required for our dialectics with the anima is not so terribly difficult.

(Jung 1928/1953, CW7: para. 323)

At the end of 'Anima and Animus' Jung justifies his style of writing about gender as experiential. He insists that he is describing psychic 'empirical facts' that could be expressed abstractly, yet are only truly communicable in a more intuitive manner (ibid.: para. 340). Here is stated again, more obliquely, the notion that rational language is wanting when it comes to representing the psyche. Without experiential imaginative writing, factual psychology is 'an empty web of words' (ibid.: para. 340). Jung's use of the term 'empirical facts' is a reference to psychic material. So how far is this essay of Jung's 'about' gender, which purports to stake out his concepts of anima and animus, marked by tensions 'within' the author?

For example, it is hard to reconcile the potentially exciting idea that when a woman embodies a man's anima she has the ability to extend a man's vision with the later pronouncement that, for a woman, anything outside her husband is in a sort of fog (ibid.: para. 338). Clearly, where the woman incarnates the anima she has unconscious powers denied to her independent self. It may be possible to justify this psychologically, but the sense remains of the woman *getting lost* in the writing of the anima.

However, this stress on vision recalls the importance in Jung's work of perspective. Just as 'Answer to Job' was an attempt to write from the point of view of the other, 'Anima and Animus' uses the vantage of the male ego and the male other, the anima (see Chapter 2). Hence the slippage from anima to women in the description of gender properties. Jung performs his psychology (experiential language), for to write without immersion in the energies of his own psyche, his own perspective is, to him, to be divorced from 'psychic facts'.

Also, in gazing upon gender in his own society through the lens of his personal biases, Jung is consciously offering of such a practice a *methodology* through the concepts of the anima and animus, rather than an absolute truth about the nature of gender identity for all time. Had he acknowledged his own *animated* writing then his descriptions of independent women would be less likely to be taken as either pure prejudice (to be unthinkingly dismissed) or as deep insights into the true path of contented women.

What is also interesting here is his demonstration of the methodology as amounting to a critique of the relativity of the western psyche. For it is the 'extraverted attitude of the western mind' that fetishizes material reality, so provoking a compensating inner spiritual figure (ibid.: para. 303). The anima's aura of immortality is a consequence of the spiritual poverty of western modernity. Indeed, Jung goes further to suggest that European denigration of the cultural 'other' is a projection of their own inferiority (ibid.: para. 326).

In giving the anima a cultural genealogy and geography, Jung comes closest to admitting the socially situated nature of his own conversion of spectrality into gender dialectics. The material obsessed, worldly western male generates an anima of unmappable dimensions. Yet Jung does not refer in 'Anima and Animus' to 'her' connections to his own history. (Such candour has to wait for *Memories, Dreams, Reflections* and the 'personal myth'.) This is not just the argument that the model for the description of the western anima can be traced back to S.W. Rather, there is also the aspect of S.W. in which she presents in occult guise (and Jung represents) the *future history* of his writing. S.W. was certainly the anima-woman who 'saw further' into Jung's future endeavours than the 'nothing but' writer of the doctoral thesis. And not only the anima can be traced back to the enigmatic work. By insisting upon the animus as a plural figure, 'like an assembly of fathers or dignitaries', 'he' recalls S.W.'s ghostly multitudes (ibid.: para. 332).

S.W.'s combination of overblown gravity and facetiousness in her masculine spirits survives in Jung's typical description of an animus (ibid.: para. 332). Jung is adamant that the anima is an historically resonant unity while the animus remains a plurality of conventionally minded patriarchs. He does not develop this highly suggestive polarity between diachronic and synchronic time. 'Anima' implies a feminine linear history and future, whereas 'animus' is a masculine command of the present. So the dialectical anima/animus can be unpacked as three separate polarities: as feminine versus masculine, singular versus plural, and linear versus synchronic time. Together it forms feminine singularity in linear time versus masculine multiplicity across present cultures.

It seems to me very suggestive that this complicated dialectics resembles the *literary form* of the doctoral thesis. For there a singular S.W., a figure from Jung's own history, faced a multitude of spirits including masculine dignitaries. There too was born the tactic of converting multiplicity into duality as Jung declares that S.W.'s spirits can be *understood* as two opposing character traits: the silly and the pseudo-profound. As Ivenes, S.W. also has the quality of immortality, existing through endless incarnations where her 'masculine dignitaries' appear more circumscribed by their culture. Chapter 7 will explore this gendering of time and space in two further works.

Perhaps the position on 'nothing but' language has not changed quite so much as Jung claims in 'Anima and Animus' (ibid.: para. 319). He misses the opportunity to consider a more complex dialectics of time and culture, or oneness versus multiplicity, in favour of the conversion of gender into straightforward 'opposition'. Against such simplification into polarized concepts, the spectral traces of Jung's past remain. They are the ghostly forms of a narrative process behind the emergence of a dialectical subject; one inflected by means of gender.

Two conclusions are implied in this account of Jung's efforts to produce gender and psychology as something comprehensible, identifiable and stable. First of all, that for Jung, gender, identity and theory are mutually constructed. Second, narrative remains the irreducible ground of his science. Close reading of Jung's gender reveals a dialectical ideal whose fundamental pairings are not actually solvable through dialectical synthesis – *and such tension produces as much as it fails to account for* a ghost story. Much of the energy of Jung's writing on gender is devoted to configuring dialectical concepts from spectral narrative. Yet glimpses of something more radical and plural are retained in the works as necessary to the psyche's endlessly generative mythmaking. Later chapters of this book will explore these less charted territories. Invoked or not invoked, gender is the spectre haunting the dialectical inception of Jung's psychology.

Chapter 4

Argument: Writing beyond tragic science in 'On the Nature of the Psyche'

CW8

> A novel is a medicine bundle, holding things in a particular, powerful relation to one another and to us.
>
> (LeGuin 1996: 153)

> The psyche is the world's pivot: not only is it the one great condition for the existence of a world at all, it is also an intervention in the existing natural order, and no one can say with certainty where this intervention will finally end.
>
> (Jung 1947/1954/1960, CW8: para. 423)

Introduction

The psyche brings the world into being for human understanding. We cannot know the extent and consequences of this intervention in the natural order. The above quotation from the essay 'On the Nature of the Psyche' is taken from late in the work and suggests that the argument is essentially open ended: that which is posited is not wholly susceptible to traditional means of validating knowledge (Jung 1947/1954/1960, CW8: paras. 343–442). In this chapter I will examine the ways in which Jung creates an argument about that which we cannot ever completely know.

'On the Nature of the Psyche' is a difficult text to read and an important one. It is quite possible that its difficulty and its importance are allied for it is here that Jung looks at the premises of his work. What quickly becomes apparent is the variety of forms of argument Jung finds necessary in order to move from established intellectual positions to his revolutionary notions of psyche. Indeed, I shall suggest that the text's daring use of creative methods amounts to the formation of a new hybrid genre between scientific essay and science fiction. Jung is a pioneer in writing that could be properly called science aesthetics.

On argument

Argument is conventionally divided into two types: either conceptual or empirical. Conceptual argument, as the name indicates, teases out the implications of concepts. It debates the nature of ideas or figures and, if resolvable, needs no recourse to extra-linguistic information. Conceptual argument is focused upon the densely packed meanings within a pre-existing term.

Empirical argument, on the other hand, requires the results of observation, experience or data. Most scientific papers are a blend of these two categories: empirical data serves to modify concepts, or concepts are used as the basis for further observation. Both these kinds of argument can be found in 'On the Nature of the Psyche'.

In terms of methodology, argument exists in a spectrum. At one end, argument is weighted with rational logical proceedings, at the other extreme are the rhetorical arts of persuasion. No argument can be either wholly logical or wholly rhetorical. For logical thinking cannot entirely do without the metaphorical qualities of language and the purest rhetoric has some recourse to reason for its powers of persuasion.

A useful analysis of the logical strategy is that by Stephen Toulmin, Richard Rieke and Allan Janik (1984). They divide 'sound' argument into four component parts: claims, grounds, warrants and backing. Here the 'claim' is the assertion put forward for public acceptance and the 'grounds' are the specific facts supporting it. 'Warrants' constitute the basis for connecting the grounds to the claims. An example is provided by scientific formulae. When applied as warrant these convert grounds to claims. Lastly the backing validates the warrant. 'Backing' refers to broad statements that explore or make explicit the experience establishing the reliable nature of the arguing in any particular instance. These four functions are knitted together in a sound argument. The additional presence of two other modes, those of 'qualifiers' and 'rebuttals', turn a sound argument into a strong one. Qualifiers such as 'probably', 'possibly', 'presumably', show the degree of trust to be placed on the conclusion of the argument. In turn rebuttals and exceptions explore the special circumstances that might undermine the logical process.

Perhaps surprisingly, Jung can be found in all of these rational positions in 'On the Nature of the Psyche'. However, particularly in the latter stages, there is a tendency to deploy claims and backing in isolation. Such a practice omits the connecting features of grounds and warrants. There is also a highly suggestive frustration of logical order, in that he frequently advances claims at some textual remove from the grounds that would support them. I shall look at the consequences of these devices later.

Toulmin *et al.* also make a distinction between those kinds of argumentation (the activity of 'doing' argument), that follow existing procedures, in effect using established warrants and backing for new grounds and claims, as opposed to those other arguments making a radical break with conventions. 'Regular, rule-applying' arguments are the application of theories that are not themselves being challenged. The contrary 'critical, rule-justifying' arguments are essentially subversive of current thinking. These latter challenge the basis of existing theories and ideas. Of course, a rule-applying argument in one area may become a rule-justifying one in another. Jung makes extensive use of this technique in his analogies from particle physics. 'On the Nature of the Psyche' is, naturally, primarily critically rule justifying. It therefore provides, in a useful division proposed by the educationalist Sally Mitchell, a voyage of discovery rather than a traveller's tale (Mitchell 1996: 12).

The logical model of argument is a significant constituent of 'On the Nature of the Psyche', and is combined with the conceptual in looking at the borders of consciousness. What rapidly becomes apparent is that the combination of logic and conceptual thinking cannot serve Jung's greater purposes, for it leads to the repeated resting point that 'psyche' must simply equal consciousness. In fact logical methods become identified with the regular rule-applying notion that psychic selfhood is ego thinking only. The problem here is itself one of logic: how is it possible to argue, to construct *knowledge* of that which lies beyond the comprehending role of the ego? If Jung is going to argue for the existence of the unknown (and to a certain extent unknowable) psyche, then argumentation will have to seek resources beyond that of logic. Wholly rational strategies need to give way, at times, to the rhetorical in order to set up rule-justifying new premises.

Rhetorical argument moves away from intrinsically rational criteria and towards the arts of persuasion. One frequent strategy is to introduce an academic persona to suggest credibility for ideas. Often the persona is used to set up a dialogical type of argument in which interaction with the assumed position of the audience is a key ingredient. Rhetoric is also more likely to set up an argument as an open-ended process, as an activity carried on between two or more positions that may never reach a final agreement. In addition to logic and reason, rhetoric invites validation from the affective and experiential.

In terms of judging a rhetorical argument, the emphasis shifts to whether it works in a given context. A crucial factor about different styles of argument is their role in the mechanisms of power. Politically, argumentation oriented towards the logical end of the spectrum is inherently monological, closing down opposing positions or the voice of the 'other'. A rhetorical argument with an emphasis on the dialogic makes less of a claim to power through knowledge. Rather it provides a network to connect different social and epistemological standpoints.

One device particularly germane to rhetoric is the pivot, which I have already suggested is familiar to Jung. A pivot turns ideas around and gives them a new direction. It is to be found in all types of argument, but is an intensive feature of 'On the Nature of the Psyche', with consequences that I shall explore.

A pivot, for Jung and elsewhere, often introduces or frames the use of 'evidentials'; a functional category in English of words denoting attitudes to knowledge (Barton 1993). Evidentials indicate the degree of validity or strength of the knowledge claim. They are broadly used by Jung here in the following five ways: in problematization to show the inadequacies of traditional approaches to the psyche; in establishing a credible academic persona; in the citation of 'authorities' (frequently to undermine them); in the process of constructing his argument both logically and rhetorically, and, in setting up a general epistemological stance (a starting point for building knowledge).

I will suggest that the need to incorporate the unknown psychic into the argument demands the expansion of evidentials, usually confined to such overlooked phrases such as 'I believe that' or 'reports', 'demonstrates', 'thus', 'as a result'. By contrast the imaginative resources required by Jung's argument extend evidentials into aesthetic qualities of language. Suggesting attitudes to knowledge using metaphor and figurative writing is always possible in arguments leaning towards rhetoric. What remains distinctive about 'On the Nature of the Psyche' is that aesthetic evidentials are a defining feature. With these techniques the argument pivots by means of intertextuality, cross-disciplinarity (as rule-applying argument in one discipline becomes rule-justifying in another), metaphor (particularly of light and space), analogy and the model.

Indeed Jung's argumentation is methodologically diverse. From the conceptual he moves into the empirical, and on to suggesting a 'model' as an 'as if' structure that would provide a way of figuring his ideas. His argumentation then uses textual analysis, in particular for works on alchemy. At this point the argument becomes explicitly hermeneutical, and draws from the texts themselves the principles by which they, and the psyche, may be understood. After textual analysis, Jung's essay offers 'the net' as the final figure for its rhetorical writing of an inherently dialogical psyche. So the argument runs from concept to empiricism, to model, to text, to net. I will conclude by looking at the implications of figure of the net with the help of the writer Ursula K. Le Guin. One advantage in the net is that it helps the wary reader come to terms with the circling wheel-like style of presentation.

'On the Nature of the Psyche' (Jung 1947/1954/1960, CW8)

Jung's essay consists of eight numbered sections with a final unnumbered 'supplementary' addition, which I will treat in order. They are named:

1 'The Unconscious in Historical Perspective' (ibid.: paras. 343–55)
2 'The Significance of the Unconscious in Psychology' (ibid.: paras. 356–64)
3 'The Dissociability of the Psyche' (ibid.: paras. 365–70)
4 'Instinct and Will' (ibid.: paras. 371–80)
5 'Conscious and Unconscious' (ibid.: paras. 381–7)
6 'The Unconscious as a Multiple Consciousness' (ibid.: paras. 388–96)
7 'Patterns of Behaviour and Archetypes' (ibid.: paras. 397–420)
8 'General Considerations and Prospects' (ibid.: paras. 421–33)
'Supplement' (ibid.: paras. 434–42).

Broadly the text begins with the position that the psyche has not hitherto been a recognizable object of study, and ends with the overwhelmingly urgent appeal that only psychic understanding can avert the catastrophe implicit in the development of weapons of mass destruction. Ultimately, for Jung, the psyche is a moral, social, cultural and political entity of the greatest importance. The essay therefore moves from outside of Jung's psychology to its rhetorical heart in the apocalyptic myth (see Chapter 2).

'On the Nature of the Psyche' begins by establishing the need for a separate discipline of psychology and concludes by manifesting itself as a textual net cast over all ways of knowing. Its argumentation is not linear. The claim of the truly *revolutionary* nature of the psyche occurs early and late. Jung's methodology *enacts* his revolution by proceeding wheel-like and by building rhetorical and logical validation through repetition. Key Jungian terms such as 'archetypes' and 'complexes' are seeded early in the essay, so discreetly as not even to amount to claims for future validation. Their repeated citation gradually expands into argument with a strong emphasis on operating rhetorically by accretion. This is how Jung presents his case.

1 'The Unconscious in Historical Perspective'

'On the Nature of the Psyche' opens by problematization and by setting up an epistemological stance. Prior to the development of psychology as a discipline, the soul or psyche was not regarded as an object meriting study. This stems from the attitude that the psyche was a known common property, and also that the exercise of reason could exalt the human condition without recourse to the irrational. However the greater differentiation of consciousness in modern times revealed something unexplored in beliefs about the psyche. Unable to claim the human mind as a wholly transparent organ, philosophy gave way to empirical psychology.

The basis of Jung's recourse to problematization throughout 'On the Nature of the Psyche' is his resistance to the idea that the psyche only extends to the knowable part of the mind. In the very first paragraph he produces an evidential of his scepticism by saying that there is an unconscious acceptance of 'subjective opinions' as universal (Jung 1947/1954/1960, CW8: para. 343). There are several clever layers to this building of problematization, which is constructed via setting up an epistemological stance, or fundamental way of regarding knowledge.

For calling general opinions 'subjective' in the first place is a rhetorical blow to the argument that the psyche is a transparent window onto the world. A refusal to consider opinions as subjective is a logical consequence of the proposition of a largely rational mind. Such a prejudice is portrayed as the survival of the outmoded non-psychological attitude now disproved by the emerging empiricism. And finally, this opening remark slips in the word 'unconsciously' in a way that anticipates much of Jung's later arguments. Indeed, the second paragraph repeats three times Jung's position that all ideas and doctrines are at least partly 'a subjectively conditioned confession' (ibid.: para. 344).

Since there is as yet no observation or data, Jung is making a conceptual argument and he does so rhetorically by repeating the contrast he has set up between the erring non-psychological past and today. Part of Jung's rhetoric in the early paragraphs is temporal. He institutes a mistaken past and then seeds *his* ideas as the common position of the enlightened present. He is, therefore, setting up a powerful persona as the embodiment of widely accepted intellectual knowledge.

The repetition in this paragraph is also a tiny example of his 'wheel' and 'seeding' structure employed throughout 'On the Nature of the Psyche'. Crucial ideas are slipped in early as unproblematic ingredients of modern attitudes to the psyche. Only later will the argument wheel round to explore those items. In fact, the repeated notion here of the subjective, *psychological* nature of all human systems is returned to again and again. It anticipates its much later expanded restatement that psychology *is* psyche (ibid.: para. 429).

As well as the wheel-like shaping, another major device is that of analogy, and in particular an analogy where the two components threaten to fuse together. He compares psychology to a psychic function that is only allowed to register in consciousness insofar as it agrees with conventional attitudes (ibid.: para. 347). This analogy is extremely subtle because again it is an insertion of a significant Jungian idea that will be explored later. Part of the rhetorical force of 'the wheel' is that when notions are returned to, the reader cannot help being half-familiar with them. In particular, the early structuring of Jung's far from conventional epistemological stance and core concepts as 'common knowledge' bestows credibility upon the Jung persona in the essay when these 'general premises' are revealed in fact to be his.

The analogy above teaches the reader an argument as a *figure* of writing before it is introduced as a *claim*. Psychology in a hostile society is analogous to the function of repression of inconvenient truths.

If we return to the Toulmin *et al.* model of logical argument, then Jung is shifting around claims, backing and warrants to occupy several different positions. Analogy is a very useful figure for this strategy. Instead of the hierarchical logical model with the claims resting on warrants, which are in turn rooted in the backing, etc., analogy is more of a web or network. In comparing psychology to an inhibited psychic function, the text is offering a horizontal argumentative structure that rhetorically implants key elements of the Jungian frame.

The second half of 'The Unconscious in Historical Perspective' proceeds by evidentials of citation. Jung gives us late nineteenth-century psychologist Wilhelm Wundt as 'representative' (ibid.: para. 348). He is said to regard the unconscious as of very minor interest. Embarkation on extensive citation marks a shift of methods designed to expand the argument. Having suggested a few core Jungian principles as common knowledge, the text only then reveals the presence of contrary views, so moving the persona into the realms of heroic struggle. Wundt does not stand alone. He possesses a 'school' of followers who assert that the psyche must signify only consciousness.

To defeat these enemies, several methods are brought into play. For example, Wundt is given the evidential of a 'drastic' situation in medical psychiatry (ibid.: para. 348). The position of Wundt and school is that which counts as truly psychic is only that which can be known; in other words, consciousness. This is a conceptual argument and Jung devotes much energy into breaking it down. Wundt himself grants 'more dimly conscious' psychic elements rather than considering the term 'unconscious' of value (ibid.: para. 351). Within this citation of Wundt is the first glimmer of the light metaphor so prominent later in 'On the Nature of the Psyche'. The fact that the metaphor is first glimpsed in the words of another is suggestive of the way the whole essay both sets up differences and ultimately seeks to absorb them. The light metaphor, in a very submerged fashion, could be said to continue a dialogue with Wundt.

Eventually, Wundt's stance is presented with an overtly belittling evidential as one that 'boggles' before the notion of unconscious representation (ibid.: para. 352). This gives Jung an opportunity for a fantastic double pivot: first, if 'contents' is substituted for 'representations' then the unconscious can possess properties. Second, he claims that he will later trump Wundt with an account of unconscious representations. This use of the double pivot suggests something of the multidirectional nature of Jung's argumentation.

Jung is here displaying his ideas by playing off a repeatedly cited 'authority'. Knowledge is explicitly competitive. Jung 'wins' by twisting the terms and then by projecting a future complete overturn of Wundt's language. Indeed, repeating the language of this opponent allows the insertion of the concept of archetypes – unadvertised as such – partly clothed in the language of the other: the 'inborn pattern' (ibid.: para. 352).

Repetition with a difference leading to argument by persuasive accretion was earlier Jung's method of secreting his principles as everyday truths. Now it has become a technique for argument via citation. Competitive citation is certainly dialogic in bringing in multiple voices, but here there is a powerful monological drive to pivot the language onto Jung's own ground.

The essay is careful not to overplay the persona's lone heroic stance in this competitive arena. Some citations can be pivoted to Jung's position, some are simply assimilated such as the mention of 'Adolf Bastian' whose 'elementary ideas', are today's 'archetypes' (ibid.: para. 353). Here the citation operates as backing for Jung's claim by pointing to a general body of knowledge supporting it. It also enables the insertion of the key word 'archetype' into the text. Citations such as these act like analogies in setting up comparable propositions.

'The Unconscious in Historical Perspective' draws to a close by final undermining evidentials of Wundt (ibid.: para. 353), followed by a pivot to the revelation of several counter-authorities who unequivocally back the notion of a significant unconscious (ibid.: paras. 353–5). After heroic struggle, the persona sights allies coming over the hill.

2 'The Significance of the Unconscious in Psychology'

The convoluted argumentation of part one of 'On the Nature of the Psyche' may perhaps be attributable to the way that its fundamental proposition eats away at its drive for legitimation. The fundamental proposition is that notions of fact are subjective or psychically conditioned by unknown factors. Having established, rhetorically and dialogically, that the psyche is more than known consciousness, part two explores the nature of the unconscious as a concept. To do this, the essay first examines the role of concepts in themselves. After all, the conventional definition of a concept leaves scarce room for unknown psychological elements.

First, the effects of the hypothesis of the unconscious are to extend the area of the psyche as both 'known and unknown' (ibid.: para. 356). 'Old psychology' is thereby radically transformed in a way comparable to the turn in physics on the discovery of radioactivity (ibid.: para. 356). Immediately, argumentation becomes even more dialogic because it is open ended: it now concerns the known, the unknown and the unknowable.

Second, this moment sees the introduction of the crucial analogy of psychology and particle physics that will become a structural feature of the whole essay. Indeed, the fate of this analogy is symptomatic, in that the gap between the two entities bridged by 'likeness' becomes so intensely charged as to evaporate. Jung will finally posit a complete meeting of psychology and particle physics in the union of the psyche with atomic matter. Fascinatingly, the analogy is introduced here embryonically as a figure for the changing of the discipline. Like other seeded devices (such as the light metaphor) and inserted terms (such as archetypes), this first mention is the apex of a triangle as repetition expands the domain of the figure or Jungian term. In this opening of the second section, Jung stresses the unpredictability of the psyche and that this is connected to the way it is examined:

> The moment one forms an idea of a thing and successfully captures one of its aspects, one invariably succumbs to the illusion of having caught the whole. . . One has taken possession of it, and it has become an inalienable piece of property, like a slain creature of the wild that can no longer run away. It is a magical procedure such as the primitive practises upon objects and the psychologist upon the psyche. . . he never suspects that the very fact of grasping the object conceptually gives it a golden opportunity to display all those qualities which would never have made their appearance had it not been imprisoned in a concept.
>
> (ibid.: para. 356)

The language here is instructive. Conceptual argument is limited to the ego's way of understanding and when applied to the greater psyche it amounts to a distortion. No concept is wholly adequate to grasp all aspects of the psyche because it has roots in the unknown. Inevitably, this conclusion also extends to such concepts as 'psyche' and 'unconscious' themselves. There is a logical argument here but it is built upon the grounds that an active psyche affects the functioning of consciousness and its ability to rely completely on rational processes. It is worth remembering that these logical 'grounds' emerged rhetorically and competitively from the essay's first section.

Particularly interesting is the assertion that conceptual thinking itself acts dynamically upon psychic manifestations and that the process resembles 'primitive' magic. Again, we have the secretion, by analogy, of a significant direction in the argument: the dialogue with the colonial other. Although the term 'primitive' denotes a degree of racial condescension, the tenor of the analogy here, as later, is more horizontal. In fact, Jung's web-like dialogical arguing (in preference to a hierarchical logical methodology) starts to come into its own with the citing of voices from other cultures.

Also the simile of the wild creature is suggestive. Concepts imprison; they are an act of possession, such as that of killing an animal as a trophy. These metaphors are powerful evidentials of attitudes to knowledge. There is an intriguing ecological and postcolonial structuring here with the concept-maker as the great white hunter. 'He' assumes that his mastery is the rightful order, when it is rather an intervention that corrupts the true state of the wilderness.

Here the argumentation is particularly open ended and generative, constructing positions from analogy and metaphor. It is also, of course, a justification for its own methods. If concepts are distorting and imprisoning, then a logical analysis of their work is an unsuitable methodology. Much better to push rhetoric into the aesthetic dimension of language and seek the flickering images of an untamable realm.

Language is an intervention into psychology, not a neutral medium for it. Such a position amounts to a qualifier of the argumentation on the nature of the psyche, but also, paradoxically, a backing. It is an epistemological stance that simultaneously undermines and augments the subjective, psychically provisional substance of all doctrines and ideas (as propounded in section one). Consequently, this challenge to conceptuality is a challenge to the nature of logical argument itself. It does not mean that logic, deduction and linear thinking are invalid. Rather, it has been decentred as the dominant mode for this essay. The body of the argument comes to justify the rhetorical mode of its presentation. Rhetoric moves more centrally away from being just a tool of argument to being more authentically the way the psyche works.

The physics analogy is also a conversion of a rule-applying argument in physics to become a rule-justifying one in psychology as it supports the radical effect of the unconscious hypothesis. This leads to an expansion of the epistemological stance to encompass vast regions. By mentioning the unimaginably small and the incomprehensibly large in electron microscopes and light years, Jung draws all human knowledge within his psyche. He asserts that every science and all knowledge stems from the psyche (ibid.: para. 357):

> Nobody drew the conclusion that if the subject of knowledge, the psyche, were in fact a veiled form of existence not immediately accessible to consciousness, then all our knowledge must be incomplete, and moreover to a degree that we cannot determine.
>
> (ibid.: para. 358)

Again we have a developed epistemological stance as backing without the logical hierarchy of grounds or warrants for what is now an expansion of the hypothesis of the unconscious. In a way, the rejection of concepts as providing complete arguments works rhetorically very cleverly here. The unconscious as a concept has its boundaries removed, which facilitates its hyper-inflation to cover all human understanding.

Also, the word 'nobody' reconnects this second section with the epistemological stance (disguised as an historical narrative) of the opening paragraphs. 'Nobody' realized that the logical consequences of the unconscious revolutionize epistemology. This negative evidential cleverly positions this notion (of epistemological revolution) as now wholly accepted and unquestionable. It is a momentary sinking of the Jung persona into what he will later tell us is the collective consciousness: the voice of generally agreed truth.

Having recalled the powerful rhetorical technique of situating his argument as the commonly held position, Jung briefly returns to philosophy. There is no attempt to delve into the writings of Hegel, Schelling, Schopenhauer, Carus or Nietzsche here. Instead Jung uses the citation of these potent figures to refine the historical narrative as a structure that can now take inserts or seeds of some of his more sophisticated and cultural ideas. Whereas previously the historical narrative was based on a crude binary of past error versus present (Jungian) enlightenment, now the philosophers are given specific roles in Jung's argument as he begins to embed his historical account. What started as a rhetorical device is becoming a cultural analysis.

For example, Hegel is more properly a psychologist whose excesses of idealism ultimately lead to the explosion of daemonic energy prophesized by Nietzsche and so to the 'catastrophe' of modern Germany (ibid.: paras. 358–9). Two crucial moments stand out here. Via this historical analysis, Jung introduces 'compensation' as a defining property not only of the individual unconscious, but also of the epoch. Second, this is the first mention of modern Germany. The brief excursion into cultural criticism again widens the scope of the essay by its wheel-like movement from basic structures to expansion of territory and accretion of specific details.

As well as setting up a space for cultural criticism, Jung's deployment of philosophers is also an argument about epistemology. It is a drive to substantiate his claim of the radical effect of the unconscious on knowledge by dragging the epistemological terrain away from the philosophers and onto his own ground. If the psyche really does denote mere consciousness then total knowledge is possible, depending upon the parameters of any particular epistemology. Or, put another way, the philosophers (in Jung's description of their work) have it. Yet, if the unconscious exists, then the margins of what can be known become permeable. The question of the border arises. For it is then no longer a question of general epistemological limits, but of a 'flimsy threshold' between ego and unconscious contents (ibid.: para. 362).

A pivot back to conceptual argument allows a logical reinforcement of Jung's epistemological stance that underpins all of the essay: the concept of the unconscious is, in effect, warrants and backing for the position that knowledge is psychically relative to an unknown degree. Jung repeats the metaphor of the threshold, derived from citation in section one, three times in paragraph 362. The threshold metaphor is then converted into grounds for the following argument about unconscious contents. For if the border of consciousness is really like a threshold, then it suggests that some unconscious contents may possess the higher energy needed to cross it.

This second section, 'The Significance of the Unconscious in Psychology', ends with a wheel-like recapitulation of the mode of part one. Wundt's objection that unconscious processes make no sense because there is no 'representation' without ego, without subjecthood, is 'nullified' (a nice draconian evidential!) by a counter-citation that the unconscious can be effective without representation (ibid.: para. 364). Then the section finishes off with an engaging fusion of rhetoric and logic. Wundt (or more properly what he is made to stand for in Jung's argument – a discounting of the unconscious) is decisively trumped by the analogy of the dog. For this friend to man seems to enjoy a psyche without consciousness (ibid.: para. 364).

So psyche can and does exist without conscious subjecthood. Such a final flourish rhetorically returns the persona to the firm ground of common sense. The analogy is partly so effective because it is a logical argument; that dogs exhibit psyche without self-consciousness. It thus provides the grounds to support the claim that psyche can exist disconnected from the ego, *if* you then infer a backing that dog psyche and human psyche are members of the same order.

Jung is supplying a kind of ecology to his rhetorical environment in addition to clothing it in historical analysis and cultural criticism. Distantly, the dog echoes the tragic 'slain creature' at the start of the second section. Just as the killed animal is the consequence of the misguided psychologist as great white hunter, so the dog (and later analogies of ant and weaver bird) metonymically stand for the psyche as natural habitat.

3 'The Dissociability of the Psyche'

The end of part two marks the point where 'On the Nature of the Psyche' considers the existence of an active unconscious as established. Part three starts to unpick the presumed unity of consciousness. 'The Dissociability of the Psyche' shifts the largely conceptual argument onto more empirical grounds by discussing pathology. It seeks, literally, to break up the concept of consciousness as unproblematic unity. This is the real start of considering the psyche as intrinsically dialogic.

In paragraph 365, the notion that the psyche can become dissociated, split or fragmented, is justified in three ways: by tradition, by appeal to the 'primitive', and by psychiatry. The tradition of more than one soul is a seeding of an appeal to the past as a source of useful unorthodox knowledge. This 'seed' will flower in a forthcoming section upon alchemy. It marks a dramatic modification of the rhetorical historical narrative, in that now the past has an obscured layering of knowledge. So, mistaken 'old' philosophy and psychology rest upon an underlying 'tradition' of true intuitions.

Reference to the primitive level here is so brief as to be unclear whether it refers to contemporary other cultures or to the distant past. The pivoting possibility connects the modern western psyche to earlier citations of 'primitives' and later to Jung's accounts of his travels. Tradition and 'primitives' provide backing for a claim about a dissociated psyche while psychiatric experience could be regarded as a warrant if substantiated. Grounds such as psychiatric evidence from case histories are not supplied here. Rather Jung moves on to his 'threshold' description for the margins of consciousness (ibid.: para. 366).

Logically, some kind of hinterland between conscious and unconscious can indeed be inferred. Here, however, the threshold metaphor becomes concrete as it serves as the basis for an argument about psychic energy. For unconscious processes to be manifest in any way at all to the observing ego they must be charged with sufficient energy to cross the threshold. Why do they not simply do so? Jung claims that dissociation from the ego is not accidental. Rather, the gap between unconscious contents with energy, and consciousness, is caused either by repression (because the elements are incompatible with the ego), or because the ego lacks the capacity to perceive something new and strange.

Both repressed or 'foreign' unconscious contents first appear to the ego as symptoms. They may either prove semiotic in referring to something known, or symbolic in pointing to the unknown. In most cases, contents never before conscious are at issue, 'like the demons and gods of the primitives or the "isms" of modern man' (ibid.: para. 366). Such a simile repositions 'primitives' and modern man in a net-like horizontal relation (rather than colonial hierarchy) and further substantiates the historical-cultural narrative by seeding future cultural criticism.

'The Dissociability of the Psyche' then embarks upon one of Jung's famous near-collapsing analogies. Consciousness can be compared to the senses in having upper and lower thresholds as we do for sound and light (ibid.: para. 367). Here we have the insertion by analogy of a spatial notion of the psyche that will be greatly developed in the next section on instinct and will. A discourse on the term 'psychoid' follows with Jung offering his own reservations about the term: he will use it as an adjective not a noun. 'Psychoid' denotes only the quasi-psychic such as reflexes, to distinguish a category that is neither wholly of the body nor completely psychic.

Now the argument moves both back and forwards. It goes back to the matter of the epistemological stance and forwards in a considerable expansion of it. If the unconscious is regarded as a system, maybe with some sort of subject or ego, it would entirely change our worldview (ibid.: para. 369). What can verify this radical shift? Perhaps surprisingly for Jung, the avowed empiricist, he says that matter in the unconscious with which one can have a dialogue can be verified *only* by the 'interpretative method' (ibid.: para. 370).

A revolution in the worldview is achieved by a kind of psychic hermeneutics. As the arts of interpretation and the principles underlying those arts, hermeneutics will take an active role from now on in the argumentation of 'On the Nature of the Psyche', especially in the alchemy section. Here, of course, it is the psyche that is being treated like a text: psychic hermeneutics will validate itself, will bring into being the dialectical 'other'. An appeal to 'interpretation' here seeds both its development into the practice of Jungian therapy, and into the Jungian analysis of alchemy as the drawing of 'tradition' into Jung's argumentation. The interpretative method as key to verification is also a stance on the side of rhetoric because it is the kind of argument that 'makes' its own evidence by the act of interpretation. Jung's psyche is itself rhetorical: it is about what works in a given context. It is about the arts of constructing meaning.

4 'Instinct and Will'

Empirical methods are not wholly given up, however, with the citation of the evidence produced by Pierre Janet and Sigmund Freud in this section. Instinct and will are shown to be an unsatisfactory dualism to accommodate Jung's now explicitly multiple dialogic psyche. Logically the duality of instinct and will comes unstuck because Jung refuses to derive the psyche from an instinctual base, although he asserts that it is connected to it. Rhetorically, this simple division will not do because of Jung's seductive web of language of revolution and limitless horizons.

'Instinct and Will' not only functions by its internal dynamics but also by its position within the whole of 'On the Nature of the Psyche'. By ending with the overtly circular pseudo-conclusion that psyche must equal consciousness (ibid.: para. 380), Jung not only expresses the inadequacy of conceptual argument when dealing with the unknown, he also leaves a rhetorical deficit, a need for more, beyond logic and reason.

This section also contains an exercise in marginalizing the core notions of Freud. Described fairly with Janet as one of the 'pioneers' (ibid.. para. 371), his theory of repression is introduced by the qualifying evidential of an 'initial discovery' (ibid.: para. 373). None of the colourful details of the Oedipal theory are included. Indeed, the rhetorical deficit on the splendid potentials of the unconscious here is a good example of the essay dialogically positioning the reader *within* the argumentative matrix. Jung starts to tantalize the reader by refusing to tell all he 'knows' here about the transformation of unconscious contents (ibid.: para. 372).

On the other hand, in this section Jung makes his views on instincts, the body and the psyche exceptionally clear and in unusual detail (ibid.: paras. 375–80). The psyche has an instinctual base bound to the body and a part under the control of the will operating in consciousness. All psychic processes therefore have a real connection to the body. Yet it is incorrect to say that the psyche *derives* from the body and instincts, because it is capable of greater complexity than can be accounted for by the known laws of organic systems. Indeed, the psyche can cease to be oriented to instinct and can attain an existence Jung calls spiritual; although complete disengagement from instinct and body is impossible.

Since psyche is not a derivative of the body and body is not subordinated to psyche, both the domains of spirit and instinct are autonomous and limit the ego's will (ibid.: para. 379). The psyche has imprecise borders with both body and spirit; it is in a state of tension or conflict between compulsive instinct and will.

A result of the straightforward exposition is both a spatial and a conflict notion of the psyche. Intriguingly, the *matter* of these ideas bears a strong resemblance to his *methods* of arguing for them throughout the whole essay. 'On the Nature of the Psyche' moves between the competitive and the truly dialogic (other voices are in part dismissed, in part contribute), and develops spatial methods of inserting ideas, figures, terms, analogies as 'seeds' that expand into fields of argument.

However, the description of instinct and will does use a rhetoric of emancipation in breaking free from instinctual bonds (ibid.: paras. 377, 379). At last, instinct is exhausted and the definition of the psyche as the realm of the will ends at the conceptual impasse: psyche is logically identical to consciousness if restricted to acts of the will. 'On the Nature of the Psyche' needs to rediscover its argument of the last section, that dissociation and potential multiplicity problematizes the simple division between conscious and unconscious. Again the logic of concepts is shown to be not enough. And this repetition of the conceptual impasse should be seen as a potent rhetorical device. For Jung is about to propose a different kind of argument altogether.

5 'Conscious and Unconscious'

Jung needs a critical rule-justifying argument in order to develop his ideas about the unconscious. Here the physics analogy starts to become a vital ingredient because it offers more than one way of observing events. Physics discovered the requirement for different methods of recording light either as waves or as particles: light behaves differently according to the method of observation. Recalling Jung's discussion of psychological language as an intervention into the psyche rather than a neutral reading of it (ibid.: para. 356), we are now offered a new figure for scientific argument in the 'model':

> It is not a question of. . . asserting anything, but of constructing a *model* which opens up a promising and useful field of enquiry. A model does not assert that something is so, it simply illustrates a particular mode of observation.
>
> (ibid.: para. 381)

Again a seed is expanded into argumentation as the physics analogy becomes the backing for the model method. The 'model' is the claim, given backing from physics without the intervening logical stages of grounds and warrants. This, of course, is precisely the point of the model: it is a map of an unknown territory, a perceptual scheme that does not derive from actual exploration of that unknown land. The model suggests ways of proceeding, but is not, and can never be, a guidebook. Jung's argumentation about the unconscious becomes an avowed voyage of discovery.

The model Jung actually adopts is his dialectical psyche; that the relationship between unconscious and consciousness is one of self-regulating 'oppositions' (see Chapter 3). In this chapter I am going to start using 'dialogical' for 'dialectical' for three reasons. First, as I tried to show in Chapter 3, the classical beauty of dialectics struggles to give home to something more complex and narrative in Jung's psyche. The most fundamental relationships that Jung encounters are not *resolvable* through dialectical synthesis, mainly because they consist of polarities within a multiplicitous field. So second, 'dialogical' is a more appropriate term because it suggests something more flexible, adaptable and plural for Jung's psyche, where a number of 'others' might speak. My third reason for promoting 'dialogical' is the subject of the following chapter when I look at Jung's treatment of the psyche, nature and texts. Jung's 'dialogical' model might constitute the concrete embodiment of the pivot, a multidirectional perspective to cast a net of language over a glittering psyche.

Now in the essay Jung is free to describe the margins of consciousness as 'alternating shades of light and darkness' so picking up of the light metaphor as it starts to become the leitmotif of this and the succeeding section (ibid.: para. 382). After noting a numinous mythological quality to unconscious contents, the light metaphor is amplified in the direction of the physics analogy by bringing in the colour spectrum. Just as light has a red end to the spectrum so there is an instinctual bodily pole to the unconscious: red evokes blood and instinct (ibid.: para. 384). On the other hand unconscious complexes can be drawn into consciousness where, as Jung puts it, 'dialectical' procedures can be used (ibid.: para. 384). The conflict model of the psyche is more properly one for dialogue.

The remainder of this section is dominated by two main argumentative pivots that make rhetorical use of the light metaphor. First, in the no man's land of alternating light and shadow of the psyche's conscious margins, the unconscious too has areas close to consciousness. Here unconsciousness is relative. Although it can never be known or proven, it is possible that all conscious contents have unconscious counterparts and vice versa (ibid.: para. 385).

A second major pivot returns to the issue of consciousness as identified with acts of the will. Given that the unconscious produces contents *as if* there was a subject present, then it is possible to consider them as quasi-conscious. Non-ego consciousness is 'virtually unthinkable' yet may, in fact, exist (ibid.: para. 387). So there is no need to be so 'absolute' about the ego.

Echoing the helpful dog of part two, Jung offers the analogy of animals who may be said to possess consciousness without ego, so ego-consciousness could be imagined as being 'surrounded by a multitude of little luminosities' (ibid.: para. 387). Here the light metaphor is enlarged to justify a major modification to the internal dynamics of the psyche. It also serves as a pictorial anticipation of the next section on alchemy. At this point metaphor is more than an evidential: it is the plastic material by which argument is constructed. Section five, 'Conscious and Unconscious' is a rhetoric of metaphor and analogy.

Also the intensive use of the pivot device to suggest multiple directions in the argument heralds a notion that Jung will later make explicit: that the psyche itself is subject to reversals, to enantiodromia. As the whole essay progresses, the methods of argumentation become ever more fused with the subject of the work. Method is inseparable from matter. Surely the wheel-like motion of 'On the Nature of the Psyche', the seeding, repeating and expansion of motifs into claims, arguments and dialectical figures, mimics the repeating action of archetypes? Or as Jung could himself deduce, the notion of archetypes might stem from just this sort of argumentation?

As a portrait of the decentred ego, the developing spatial metaphor is amplified into a landscape. If infantile unconscious is 'like a chain of islands' then even an adult has a capacity for 'indefinite expansion' (ibid.: para. 387):

> Gleaming islands, indeed whole continents, can still add themselves to our modern consciousness.
>
> (ibid.: para. 387)

There is a complexity in the rhetorical power of this visual evocation. Its persuasiveness rests in showing both psyche and argument as open ended. Again the reader is drawn into a world of limitless horizons; such expanses can be glimpsed while never being wholly known. Consequently the 'model' is firmly embedded as something of a net in which the reader is caught as much as the author.

Of course the language of undiscovered continents does recall a colonial dynamic, so it is salutary to note both the warning about approaching the psyche as a big game hunter, and the care with which the essay has already renounced claims to intellectual mastery of this new world. The introduction of the model as a method of argumentation is an example.

Conquest by the ego, in the sense of converting it all to the domain of the will, is not an option as a later section will detail. For now, the light metaphor has been united with space in a landscape of psyche. Alchemy will expand the inner world further into an internal cosmos. Space, vast and minute, cosmos and atomic particles, is a seed that has become a topos. It is also about to become a key ingredient in Jungian hermeneutics or the 'interpretative method' (ibid.: para. 370).

6 'The Unconscious as a Multiple Consciousness'

In the previous section, the light metaphor is used to enact an unspoken analogy between psychology and alchemy in the notion of multiple luminosities. Section six opens by offering a more logical, yet general backing for the link in the co-location of symbolic images in alchemy works and in the psyche. The argument becomes even more orientated towards the logical when grounds for the analogy are supplied by describing the psychological language used in this esoteric tradition.

Yet the attentive reader would be hard put to pick out the logical ingredients of claims (that alchemy is an important precursor to psychology), grounds (alchemy's psychological terms), warrants (the common practice of developing symbols by amplification – not even stated – although implied dialogically in the argument of sections six and seven), and backing (the co-presence of similar material in alchemy and in modern dreams and fantasies). In fact this functioning logical argument is barely discernible. It is partly obscured because it is not presented in a rational order.

Instead what is foregrounded is the powerful imagery of alchemy substantiating the 'multiple luminosities' by poetic and rhetorical effect. Logic seems sunken here by the desire for hermeneutics, the *arts* of interpretation. It is by textual analysis that the critical, rule-justifying argument is demonstrated that alchemy was a technique for relating to the unconscious.

What is especially significant about this is the whole essay's preference for *showing* the practice, over and above logically arguing for it. 'Showing' here constitutes a rhetorical argument that engages with logical justification while remaining paramount. In particular, the stress on alchemy's images in section six is deliberately multidirectional in pointing forwards and backwards in the text. Through the images Jung seeds his own conceptual language of collective unconscious, self, anima and synchronicity, to be developed into argument in later sections. Again, this is a distinctively rhetorical device of familiarizing the reader with the terms before introducing the ideas formally. However, it is also a device about to be elevated from 'mere' rhetoric to epistemological stance by the claim in section seven that psychic images form the empirical matter of his psychology. Yet again the psyche proves to be rhetorical as the arts of argument are naturalized as the principles of Jungian psychology.

The section on alchemy highlights hermeneutics, which, Petteri Pietikanen states, 'can be viewed as a reciprocal process of understanding between the interpreter and the text or other symbolic referent (such as the unconscious. . .), which calls for deciphering' (Pietikanen 1999: 29). It is from the contemplative analysis of images that psychological argument is sought.

There is another very strong link between the method of constructing argument here and what Jung goes on to suggest about the psyche as perspective and time. First of all, through hermeneutical treatment, Jung stresses the theme of many eyes in alchemy: as fish eyes glowing in the dark, the many-eyed god, the dragon that is all surveying. Such images include the uroboros or tail-eating snake that connects the all-seeing with time (ibid.: para. 394). Hence unconscious archetypes, those multiple luminosities, like many eyes with multiple perspectives, have a relation with time, which 'points to the synchronicity' of events influenced by archetypes to be described later (ibid.: para. 394).

So in one respect of argumentation, as the *matter* of the writing, the tail-eating serpent is another appropriate figure for the wheel-like shape of 'On the Nature of the Psyche' itself. Indeed, the reader here enters the nature of the uroboros in the peculiar argumentative shape where the necessarily linear time of reading is staged also as a circular accretion of meaning.

However, the most prominent aspect of the link between psyche as perspective, as time, *and as method of argumentation* proves to be cultural location. Let me put it this way: it could be considered as rhetorically excessive for 'On the Nature of the Psyche' to focus so extensively on symbolic alchemy. After all, the essay has not yet explored psychic imagery in more orthodox medical conditions such as Jung's consulting room. If, on the other hand, we take a look at the progress of the expanding argument on time and multiple perspective, then the apparent diversion into alchemy and astrology makes some kind of sense. Why look for evidence of the collective unconscious in the images of a distant, half-forgotten tradition? The answer is to *enact* not just describe the notion that the unconscious has a different relation to time, so that ancient and modern images possess a real organic connection. The structure of the work performs the argument.

Additionally, alchemy and astrology are important because they are not wholly 'open' conventionally held beliefs, then or now. As esoteric, partly hidden traditions practised by few and given to secret arts, they embody a certain diversity, 'otherness' in the culture. Alchemy and astrology are by nature inclined to subverting of dominant attitudes and so represent the multiple nature of the 'luminosities'. Cultural as well as temporal plurality reflects the dialogical psyche.

It is worth remembering this rhetorical stress on the cultural nature of collective symbolic images as characteristic of Jung's committed, if unorthodox, immersion in history. Chapter 6 will explore the topic of Jung and history further. Here, the rhetorical stress on the value of alchemy has amounted to a transformation of the simple historical narrative introduced in part one of the essay. Now history is a many-eyed multidirectional figure (as the psyche faces forwards and back), of dominant and submerged cultures constituting a layered psyche. Such a portrayal provides backing for Jung's argument from the past as well as present. History has become an *aspect* of the web-like argumentation of 'On the Nature of the Psyche'.

7 'Patterns of Behaviour and Archetypes'

Section seven, by far the longest in the work, looks back to the epistemological stance concerning the effects of the hypothesis of the unconscious upon knowledge. It contains what some might say is a much delayed account of Jung's therapeutic practice in the context of further discussion of the value of concepts. Extensive use is made of the pivot to encompass reference to other cultures, to mythological material, and to orient the light metaphor back to the sphere of physics. All in all, section seven represents an expansion of Jung's deeply held ideas in which rhetorical power is gained from their prior seeding in the essay.

Returning to the notion of biologically rooted instinct, we are told that instinct is fulfilled psychologically in an image (ibid.: 398). In a delightful return of eco-logic, the leaf cutting ant's behaviour is one example of inborn possibilities lived out in the right conditions (ibid.: 398). What is suggestive in this analogy is the way that fulfilling an image is, in fact, a form of integration with the environment.

Nevertheless this happy coincidence of empirical science and Jungian psychology cannot last. Instinctual patterns in man are not subject to empirical proof since there is an inherent logical problem that the organ requiring proof of its aspects is, of course, also the only means of perceiving the proof. Because there is no position outside the psyche from which to observe the psyche, 'direct' proof is not possible. Analogies from animals are not classed here as direct empirical proof; an admission of the missing warrants that would link animal and human minds to the same order. Instead we move back to the territory of images as an indirect proof via active imagination.

By allowing psychic images to develop spontaneously, archetypes can be seen at work producing instinctual patterns of behaviour. Such an argument is conducted by the persona's transformation into a therapist. Very cleverly, this so-called 'indirect proof' gains credence by the professional context that shows Jung learning from observation. Argumentation shifts into empirical mode (developing by observation and experience) and discovers grounds in psychic images for the claim of the theory of archetypes. Here we witness the interpretative method (earlier deployed as a mode of *verification*), succeeding therapeutically in reducing 'pressure' from the unconscious (ibid.: para. 400). What was a method of argument is now a method of therapy. Jung explicitly fuses both therapy and argument in presenting activity in the consulting room as research (ibid.: para. 400).

From this overtly experiential learning, Jung states that his 'views' are derived from such observations, so privileging the empirical mode of argument, which has hardly been the most dominant characteristic of 'On the Nature of the Psyche'. However a claim to empirical argument rests upon his evolving epistemological stance that knowledge is provisional to unknown factors. An unknowable 'dark impulse' is at work guiding the painter and the dancer as well as the psychologist (ibid.: para. 402).

Significantly, the persona is here ranged with the *artist* not the empirical scientist or the philosopher. In the same paragraph we are told that science needs to draw generally valid concepts from such experiential learning; an experience of the effect of the unknowable. Science writing is therefore a form of translation from the timeless domain of the archetypes to the 'scientific language' of his time (ibid.: para. 402).

Jung's epistemological stance is with the artist: his work as defined as traditional science is one step removed from the true nature of the psyche. So it is unsurprising to hear that an archetype may behave 'like a ghost' and act like magic on the modern psyche saturated by 'isms' (ibid.: para. 405). Indeed the next few paragraphs betray the limitations of scientific language before calling for a poetic rhetoric of psyche to realize its darker side.

Therapy itself must be rhetorical for it is far truer to the characterization of the psyche as a tension of oppositions (Jung's dialectics), as motion in e-motion. In order to come to terms with the pain of the inferior part of the personality or shadow, poetic language is indispensable. To heal the inner damage of the shadow it is necessary to conduct a kind of dialogical argument with an inner opponent *using some of its own emotional register* (ibid.: para. 409). Awareness of a dark interior other 'should not be twisted into an intellectual activity' (ibid.: para. 409).

Earlier, the argumentation stressed the limitations of rational logic in the inability to find a perspective outside of the psyche from which to examine it. The multiple perspectives and dialogical qualities of the argumentation, and its object, the psyche, have unknown borders, yet psyche remains a constant human quality. 'Confrontation' with unconscious contents is an ethical necessity lest the modern citizen be no more than a cipher 'mass man' (ibid.: para. 410).

Indeed, the need to recognize the feeling value of archetypal configurations is reinforced by Jung's depiction of his encounter with the spiritual Elgonyi in East Africa (ibid.: para. 411). The 'primitive' tribes people are compared to Europeans whose Christmas trees are a custom honoured without rational explanation. Again, the use of the cultural other is more comparative and horizontal than colonial and hierarchical. Just as for Jung, alchemy is not a naive attempt at psychology in unenlightened times, but rather a sophisticated symbolic system appropriate for another age, so any lingering sense of 'primitives' as a culture 'behind' the west should also bear in mind the whole essay's frustration with the Enlightenment myth of linear progress.

In fact, it has become evident that history, time and culture are major leitmotifs in this work. In the movement of the argumentation from concept, to empiricism, to model, to text (alchemical hermeneutics), to net, notions of culture, history and time have followed a similar route. Where part one set up a simple rhetorical linear history of mistaken past versus correct Jungian present, the whole strategy of 'On the Nature of the Psyche' is to show linear thinking (conceptual, logical, causal) as one-sided. From the viewpoint of the dialogic psyche, culture and history are multidirectional and have many perspectives.

Section seven continues by wheeling back to debates upon the existence of archetypes and on to pivot the light metaphor back to the more scientific sounding ground of the spectrum. Of course, the usefulness of the light spectrum is in showing the integrity of the dynamic poles of the psyche: the blood-red instincts are realized in the mystically coloured violet archetypal images. In such an area the dialogical psyche can also be regarded as an intrinsically narrative one.

For consciousness is perpetually engaged in the hero myth (ibid.: para. 415). On the one hand the ego-hero fights the instinctual depths for the light of consciousness (ibid.: para. 412). On the other hand, the unconscious is also the 'spiritual goal', 'the sea' and 'the prize' (ibid.: para. 415). The pivot in the argument represents the pivot in the psyche, as the unconscious is that realm the ego must separate from, while also needing continually to reimmerse itself in, in order to be renewed. In Chapter 7, I consider Jung's intuitive sense that the hero myth of consciousness is in need of radical *treatment* for the modern age, not least because of its gender implications.

The final part of section seven, 'patterns of behaviour and archetypes', turns to the relationship between psyche and matter. Throughout the whole essay, the physics analogy plays a number of significant roles in the argumentation. Its main rhetorical function is to prepare for the suggestion made now: that 'psyche and matter are two different aspects of one and the same thing' (ibid.: para. 418). In the mode of logical argument, the claim is introduced with three statements of backing: that psyche and matter exist in the same world; that they are in continuous contact, and that they derive from irrepresentable factors (ibid.: para. 418). Synchronicity, in which the non-psyche and psychic can behave like each other without a causal relation, 'point. . . in this direction', in a qualifying evidential (ibid.: para. 418). (See Chapters 6 and 7 for more on synchronicity.)

There is a final pivoting analogy to draw in spirit to the dance of psyche and matter. Instincts are rooted in the body and form a bridge from psyche to matter (ibid.: para. 420). Archetypes, as is all reality, are mediated through the psyche. Since it would be facile to describe everything as merely psyche, this argument should be applied also to the true status of archetypes (ibid.: para. 420). The nature of archetypes is more properly described as 'spirit' and situated beyond the realm of the psyche (ibid.: para. 420).

On the one hand metaphysical daring (presented as speculative *argument*), on the other hand, this move is in keeping with the web-like development of 'On the Nature of the Psyche', and, of course, with the epistemological stance of the revolutionary effect of the unconscious hypothesis. Looked at from the latter point of view, this expansion of argumentation into matter and spirit is coherent, developmental and even necessary to sustain the web-like structure posited for knowledge.

8 'General Considerations and Prospects'

> I fancied I was working along the best scientific lines. . . only to discover in the end that I had involved myself in a net of reflections which extend far beyond natural science and ramify into the fields of philosophy, theology, comparative religion, and the human sciences in general.
>
> (ibid.: para. 421)

This rhetorical use of the persona brings to textual consciousness the figure of the net to embody the argument of the whole essay. The net, I contend, is the enactment of the model referred to earlier in 'On the Nature of the Psyche'. Intriguingly, the persona as 'orthodox' scientist provides a voyage of discovery resulting in the evocation of the net or, put another way, a multidirectional opening of pathways.

A net of reflections is profoundly resonant. A matrix of twine that can be pulled in different directions, knowledge is connected while not pinned to orthodox positions: it can change in ways that will ripple out to the rest of the network. And the net of reflections also suggests what is now often referred to as 'intertextuality', that all links on the net are made out of combinations of other texts, other forms of knowledge and disciplines.

The psyche is a web engineered by discourse: we cannot escape the parameters of our languages of psychology, philosophy, religion. However, to realize that these languages are conjoined in a network is to envision a seeing *through* of discourse as each may – in fluid and temporary form – take the place of the unconscious 'other'. What is offered here is a dynamic intertextuality in which movement and growth is possible, but not in the linear triumphant mode of demolishing 'inferior' past positions. Rather the net of reflected discourses offers many directional paths, multiple cultural positions, a uroboros of discourse.

Jung's net is both the form of his argument in 'On the Nature of the Psyche' and its resulting vision of knowledge. That Jung has a sense of cultural imperative about his net of argumentation is evident from the connection made in this section between traditional logical (heroic) science and the mindset of war. After collapsing the physics-psychology analogy wholly to identify them in the union of psyche and matter, Jung follows this *conjunctio* with the proper rites of separation. Psychology lacks the mathematical qualities of physics. It is also without the crucial exterior position from which to offer objective examination. Psychology can only portray itself and so is an experiential procedure in which human errors of both doctor and patient unite (ibid.: para. 421). By contrast, physics can provide material proof of its atomic theories:

> Physics, on the other hand, is in a position to detonate mathematical formulae – the product of pure psychic activity – and kill seventy-eight thousand persons at one blow.
>
> (ibid.: para. 421)

Such a typically double-edged argument sinuously reunites psychology and physics at the very climax of their separation. Physics's intervention in matter kills; psychology is not so directly lethal. Yet physics is a psyche-logos: the psyche is also the architect of physics, as much as it is of any human endeavour. Perhaps the mode of argument here rhetorically borrows the cultural power of physics while creating a distance from its most devastating application. For of course, the crucial pivot in this argument is the statement of the psyche itself as pivot:

> The psyche is the world's pivot: not only is it the one great condition for the existence of the world at all, it is also an intervention in the existing natural order, and no one can say with certainty where this intervention will finally end.
>
> (ibid.: para. 423)

The epistemological stance (radical effect of the unconscious upon knowledge) is here pivoted to encompass the contemporary social malaise that is the theme of section eight. It indicts modern consciousness as frailly 'suspended' over a chasm between collective consciousness and collective unconsciousness (ibid.: para. 423). To Jung, the loyal Swiss citizen, the 'sovereignty' of the ego is a problem (ibid.: para. 423). To avoid a repetition of the *psychic* disaster of the Second World War, the ego must be strengthened through progressive integration with the collective unconscious. Lest the cultural narrative become too narrow in its location, modernity requires an-other, balanced and integrated with the insights of modern science. What this signifies is an internalization of science (as Jungian psychology), that needs to wake up to its own limitations as rationality. Hence this science of the inner being to be fully itself needs to be conjoined with an attitude of 'medieval' mysticism because it is the closest cultural form to the 'correct' attitude to the unconscious (ibid.: para. 426).

So Jungian psychology needs an intertextual relation with an internal and external other in order to function as itself. 'Medieval' thinking is an example of what is necessary to keep Jung's 'science' from becoming concrete; to preserve the 'gaps' that are an essential aspect of the net. Such an 'other' marks and enacts the vital space for the unknowable to live as a dynamic part of the psyche. It creates an inner and outer 'border' for Jung's conceptual language. Therefore, medieval thinking is an other in the *discourse* that performs simultaneously to structure the other in the *psyche*, as the languages we accord knowledge shape the psyche's action in the world.

Jung, in effect, recommends the splicing of diverse discourses to break up the dangerous monoliths of contemporary ideologies, his dreaded 'isms'. The modern psyche needs to live by the net and not by singular, western imperialist ideologies. This need is urgent because psychic mass destruction is an equivalent danger to physical mass destruction. Indeed, one infers the other. The collapsed analogy physics-psychology when the atom bomb is acknowledged to be also psychic, is here reinstated, temporarily. The terrors of history have a mythical dimension that expresses the non-linear aspect of time as humankind faces the possibility of another biblical flood (ibid.: para. 428). (How prescient of Jung in an era of global warming!) Pessimistically, Jung fears that only a few are capable of developing the necessary inner resources.

Reflections upon psychology as a discipline lead again to the pivot. Before the psyche was the world's pivot, now psyche loses its distinction from psychology. Psychology is, of course, a matter of (rational) accounting for psychic processes. It is therefore in itself an inner process, a 'coming to consciousness' of the psyche (ibid.: para. 429). It is not and never can be a 'pure' unmediated perception of all psychic functions because to 'explain' is to make conscious, is to intervene in the 'nature' (psychic nature) you purport to describe. The psyche can only demonstrate itself. Psychology is a discourse abutting onto the unspeakable. Psychology speaks of the unspeakable in a process of active transformation of it. It needs to concede that much of the 'unspeakable' remains outside its grasp:

> Psychology is doomed to cancel itself out as a science and therein precisely it reaches its scientific goal. Every other science has, so to speak, an outside; not so psychology, whose object is the inside subject of all science.
>
> (ibid.: para. 429)

Psychology is the web of all discourses. There is no outside text. Hence it is entirely appropriate that the methods of argumentation in 'On the Nature of the Psyche' have tended to coincide with its subject. The pivot from psyche to psychology is the realization of the epistemological stance that psychology is *all* the conscious aspect of the psyche. So psychology is theology, philosophy, art, all the disciplines, all human culture in all times and in all places. 'Psychology' is the name of the net of reflections: it is the discursive web connecting the gaps, holes of unknowing. The unknown, unknowable, non-linguistic is that 'other' necessary quality that makes the net a net.

Without holes, gaps, the multilocational, multidirectional nature of the web would be lost along with its potential ethical properties in a post-colonial, post-human twenty-first century. As Jung states in this contemporary oriented section, his web, his psychology is designedly ethical. In a web there is no centre and no margin. There is no secure position of dominance and nowhere to relegate the 'other' to the margins.

Just as 'On the Nature of the Psyche' itself has no centre and no margin, concern in the final paragraphs of section eight wheels back to fears of misunderstanding the clean and proper role for the ego, given recent European horrors. Repetition is a key component of the argumentation here and its dimensions become more apparent as the web-like structure surfaces in the work.

Repetition also *enacts* the net, in that *reading* 'On the Nature of the Psyche' is to partake in a dialogical process of rhetorical and logical construction of meaning in a reciprocal exchange between text and reader. The rhetorical use of the pivot implicates the reader; structures a subject position for the reader in meaning making. Consequently, to read 'On the Nature of the Psyche' is to participate in a dynamic process (with the reader's conscious and unconscious creativity invoked) over time. Therefore one effect of the wheeling repetition-accretion mode of argumentation is to embroil the reader in time itself as both linear and circular. The reader enters the uroboros.

It is significant that the final paragraphs of section eight, originally the end of the whole essay, repeat and repeat again the immense dangers besetting the European psyche. A late pivot stresses the concern of this section with cultural healing as integral to individual well-being:

> Individuation does not shut one out from the world, but gathers the world to oneself.
>
> (ibid.: para. 432)

In this peculiarly graceful expression, 'gathers the world to oneself' evokes the net-like qualities of the psyche that extend infinitely into the world as the multiple pathways of individuation. With the imperious ego decentred, there is no centre-margin figuring of the psyche. The psyche-in-individuation is a net that extends into the web of culture, history and through time.

With a flourish, the persona concludes this section by testifying to the heroic endeavour of the reader in such a demanding essay (ibid.: para. 433). Such an address acknowledges the dialogical structure of 'On the Nature of the Psyche', while the citing of it as a 'sketch' strengthens the open-ended nature of the argumentation (ibid.: para. 433). The text as net is more truly a net when author and reader have subject positions in a reciprocal exchange that is not closed down.

Supplement

The very existence of this supplement is suggestive of a certain net-like basis to Jung's writing. A text for him is something that can be added to (rather like the periodic additions to the Bollingen Tower), rather than being a discrete intellectual monument. Unsurprisingly, these additional paragraphs are concerned with the web-like notion of matter and a corresponding net-like matter in the argument. Revisiting the animal and physics comparisons leads to the discussion of the accretion of ideas in the whole essay by roping in ever more analogies.

First of all, the persona opens in vigorous dialogical mode by proposing to dispose of 'prejudices' in a succinctly dismissive evidential that admits contrary arguments into the text by means of summarily rejecting them (ibid.: para. 434). Prejudice one, that archetypes signify inborn *ideas* (and hence are false is to be dialogically inferred) is rhetorically exploded by the analogy of the weaver bird's instinctive nest building (ibid.: para. 435).

Prejudice two is that Jung is providing a philosophy of myth. This is indignantly denied upon the grounds that what is actually being offered is a psychology of images based on a therapeutic practice. Argument moves deftly into empirical mode to justify claims based upon observation and experience. Other dialogical contraries are quite brusquely dismissed as 'stumbling-blocks' (ibid.: para. 436). Jung is quite capable of apparently closing off argument, but here does so in such an overtly partisan manner that the rhetoric, somewhat paradoxically, has an equalizing tendency with the reader. Consequently, the *rhetorical* rather than logical use of rebuttal actually opens up the argument by the very act of closing it in a blatantly incomplete response to critics.

Jung returns to the consideration of light. Both psyche and light mediate reality as conscious perception depends on the psyche and light is the perceiving medium (ibid.: para. 437). Light and matter behave like particles and like waves (ibid.: para. 438). Causality gives way to a matrix or a web of 'invisible fields of probability in multidimensional spaces' (ibid.: para. 438). Unconsciousness also seems to be dual faceted in behaving subjectively (as if it had subjecthood, Jung means), and yet also objectively as an exterior 'other' to consciousness (ibid.: para. 439). It is therefore impossible to imagine the underlying reality of archetypes so they cannot certainly be identified as psychic (ibid.: para. 439).

The argument now explicitly wheels back to the rhetorical climax of the physics-psychology analogy in its collapse into the union of psyche and matter. Physics can resolve the contraries of particle/waves only by factoring in an observing consciousness (ibid.: para. 440). Archetypes 'must' have a non-psychic aspect on the 'grounds' of synchronicity (ibid.: para. 440). Synchronicity is the cord connecting the net of psyche to the phenomenal world: the psyche's mysterious powers of affinity ceases when the unconscious element becomes conscious.

At this point the argumentation produces evidentials of citation from C. A. Meier and more from the physicist Wolfgang Pauli. These enable Jung to suggest a relation of complementarity between physics and psychology in understanding synchronicity as possible point of interchange between conscious, unconscious and matter (ibid.: para. 440). Physics aims to measure quantities while psychology focuses upon qualities. Both forms of valuation and evaluation abut onto each other at the point where consciousness loses itself.

The argumentation also promotes synchronicity rhetorically by calling it a 'highly unscientific pretence' to ignore it as mere coincidence (ibid.: para. 441). It is a borderline concept because it is inferred rather than known, and itself marks a borderline as the net of Jungian psychology is knotted by it onto the particle web of physics. Of course, the argumentation manages a highly complex pivot to this wheeling restitution of the *analogy* of physics and psychology. If the different concepts of energy in the two disciplines reinstate the separation built into analogy, then it is to be remembered that the physics' notion of energy derives from an ancient psychic one (ibid.: para. 441).

Psychology is both the *ground* of physics and also an-other. It is a net abutting onto physics and its interior unconsciousness of itself as a form of knowledge, like any form of knowledge, dependent upon the activity of the psyche.

The last paragraph pivots about the very notion of analogy. While 'On the Nature of the Psyche' has striven to establish certain analogies, these do not constitute absolute proof. The claims have insufficient grounds, warrants and backing for indisputable evidence. In a pivoting around of the sequence of logical argument, the claims are warranted by the analogies:

> The existing analogies, however, are significant enough in themselves to warrant the prominence we have given them.
>
> (ibid.: para. 442)

Open-ended argument (not proven so not closed to further dialogue) is justified by its net-like structure of analogies; those analogies are made principally by rhetoric, yet also by logic and reason. And the use of rhetoric comes to signify the dialogical rhetorical nature of the psyche itself.

The final flattening of the persona into the multiplicity of 'we' leaves the reader as one of many within the web of argumentation of multiple relationships. The prominent, rhetorical conscious device of the pivot is a marvellous evocation of a centreless structure *representing* by *enacting* a dialogic psyche.

I am going to close this chapter by taking another look at what is hinted at several times in 'On the Nature of the Psyche': that its net of reflections spans the culturally divisive ground of science and of art.

Conclusion: 'On the Nature of the Psyche' and the Tragic Myth of Science

The poet and science fiction writer, Ursula K. Le Guin, is also a critic of aesthetic form. She offers a fascinating perspective on the figure of the net, which she sees as an important alternative to more orthodox linear models of heroic enterprise in art or science (Le Guin 1996: 149–54).

In the first place linear structures suggest origins in very early human modes of behaviour. The earliest discovered cultural artifacts tend to be stone tools for cutting or spear points for hunting. These appear to offer a thematic continuity to those later cultures that so venerate the arts of war that weapons are found in their graves. Warrior cultures bequeath the hero myth and 'his' epic literature to succeeding generations. Hero myths remain potent in western culture and are to be found, for example, shaping Shakespearean tragedy, the Hollywood western and early science fiction.

So seductive is the masculine-identified myth of the rise of Man the Hero, that it also informs complex cultural productions such as the hard sciences and technology. Science is conceived as Promethean, Herculean, a linear arch of triumphant progress that contains within its myth a dark 'other' of tragedy. For 'heroic' modern science wrestling ever more energy out of cleaving matter risks invoking tragic apocalypse. 'On the Nature of the Psyche' reveals Jung to be only too well aware of this.

Fortunately, linear narrative is not the only western literary structure just as the hunting spear is actually probably *not* the first cultural object. It is merely the most durable. It is likely that the *real* first creative products were not the phallic spear, but rather a carrying device for that most basic essential, food:

> A leaf a gourd a shell a net a bag a sling a sack a bottle a pot a box a container. A holder, A recipient.
>
> (Le Guin 1996: 150)

If hard science, such as physics, follows the myth of the hero in a triumphant smashing of matter casting a tragic shadow in potential holocaust, then its literary equivalent is heroic tales of conquest. Its psychological equivalent, as Jung knew well, is the hero myth as the triumph of the ego at the expense of the unconscious 'other' (see Chapter 7 for more consideration of this in Jung's work). On the other hand, the marginalized feminine culture of the carrier object could be said to find realization in the novel, and, I would suggest, in the net that is 'On the Nature of the Psyche'.

The novel, significantly favoured by women writers, is the literary counterpart to the carrier bag or bundle because it dethrones the hero as sole object of interest, and forces him into a network of relationships. As in the quotation at the head of this chapter, it is a dialogical form that suspends ideas, feeling and characterization in multiple pathways that include the reader as an active participant. Although novels can try to adopt the linear heroic model, they work best as a different kind of literature.

As Le Guin is keen to suggest, the novel as carrier object can reimagine science and technology in an attempt to move it away from its tragic-apocalyptic myth. Le Guin calls the science fiction she writes under this imperative, 'realism':

> It is a strange realism, but it is a strange reality.
>
> (Le Guin 1996: 154)

The mood of this comment matches some of Jung's own reflections on the strange outcome that is 'On the Nature of the Psyche'. I would like to suggest that Jung anticipates Le Guin's call to expose the tragic myth of hard science and technology by some 30 years. In particular, 'On the Nature of the Psyche' betrays a cultural anxiety to implicate psychology in physics. The looming potential for physical mass destruction made possible by hard sciences is shown to be a psychological disaster that has both happened (in science's part in the western divorce from sacred uncon-sciousness), and has not yet been materially enacted to its full extent.

In taking 'argument' away from relying mainly upon linear models of conceptuality and empiricism, and into the matrix possible with the model, the hermeneutical text and the net, Jung addresses his culture's past horrors and immediate terrors. It would be facile to call 'On the Nature of the Psyche' a conventional novel or science fiction because that would belie the way it deconstructs the deep cultural division between science and art. I would rather call it science-aesthetics, or perhaps, more pedantically: speculative science-aesthetics.

'On the Nature of the Psyche' is argument that both describes and enacts the rhetorical psyche. It posits a web of culture in which meaning is a product of a complex negotiation of multiple positions. It is also a myth of healing deep cultural divisions, and its open-ended emphasis on the 'personal equation' prevents it from ossifying into a grid-like prescription. 'On the Nature of the Psyche' is argument as a net of reflections of cultural discourses. To the alienated modern psyche, it offers the world for its soul.

Chapter 5

Nature: Alchemy and ecocriticism
Psychology and Alchemy, CW12

> [G]iving up on language betrays our own human nature. I think that the
> human form of display, in the ethologist's sense of 'display,' is rhetoric.
>
> (James Hillman 1989: 295)

> Language is basically biological; it becomes semi cultural as it is learned
> and practiced.
>
> (Gary Snyder 2000: 130)

Introduction: The dialogical archetype

During the 1930s, two very different thinkers each developed a sense of a
fundamental dichotomy in culture. The dichotomy was between a unifying
force that tended to homogenize meaning, structured in perpetual tension
with a decentralizing, dispersing energy that produced plurality and difference. The two thinkers were C. G. Jung and Mikhail Mikhailovich Bakhtin.
The latter's seminal work, *The Dialogic Imagination*, only appeared in
English in 1981, yet was written as lectures, in Russian, in the 1930s
(Bakhtin 1981: xxiv).

For Jung, the powerful dichotomy found a home in the theory of archetypes. His volume, *Psychology and Alchemy*, first published in English in
1953, is based on two lectures given in the 1930s. A hypothesized unifying
energy, unknowable in itself, is the impetus towards similar forms of cultural expression and meaning. Yet this centralizing dynamic of the archetype can only be represented by the archetypal image. These images are
signs of difference in that each one, although born of the archetype, takes
on the colouring of its particular historical moment. In dreams, archetypal
images mediate the unknown domain of sublime archetypes to an encultured subject; they are a speck of embodied time.

Dreaming an archetypal image expresses the continuum of body–
psyche–culture in the constant structuring and destructuring of the human
subject, which Jung called 'individuation'. Archetypes therefore are at one

extreme sublime creative energies, at the other the lived moment polluted by personal, cultural and historical context. Archetypal images are part of the dialogue of social exchange. The image pole of the archetype is the dimension of plurality and difference as the centralizing sublime dynamism is incarnated via the multiple discourses of any particular society.

So archetypal images are not restricted to dreams. In the Jungian scheme all cultural activity, by extension all human activity, has an innate archetypal core that can only ever be manifest in the diversity of archetypal expressions. If dream archetypal images are part of the dialogue between known and unknown parts of the mind, then more public images in art extend the dialogue to the social. Ultimately all cultural products and myths partake of exchanges between conscious and unconscious – all express the dichotomy inherent in the production of meaning, between a drive to homogeneity that is simultaneously only realizable in heterogeneity. In a sense, archetypal theory enacts the realization that meaning is an attribute of the other; such meaning structures subjectivity as the individual's participation in social representation.

Bakhtin gave the term 'the dialogical imagination' to the formation of culture through the creative meshing of centralizing and decentralizing forces in language as socially active. It is the contention of this chapter that Bakhtin's dialogics clarifies tensions within Jung's writing between his dialectical ideal and narrative complexity, as indicated in Chapters 3 and 4. Chapter 6 will extend the comparison with Bakhtin further, into the domain of history, space and time.

Raya A. Jones has posited a connection between Bakhtin's dialogical approach and Jung's archetypal theory (Jones 2002, 2003). I want to take this link in a different direction by considering a Jungian *text* (Bakhtin is a critic of literary texts) in the light of dialogical criticism, as a prelude to developing an argument about Jung and nature. Reading Jung with Bakhtin, moreover, does more than offer new perspectives on Jung. It also, as I shall show, provides fascinating opportunities for literary theory. In particular, I will use Jung's textuality to augment and extend Bakhtin's dialogism for discursive constructions of nature, and for the development of ecocriticism.

Bakhtin and Jung

To begin, I am not going to argue that Bakhtin and Jung had hit on exactly the same ideas. Jung deals in a dialogic psyche while Bakhtin locates most of his dialogics in language. This enables Bakhtin to elaborate a far more materialist conception of social interaction. Jung regards materialism as an unnecessary metaphysical choice, while Bakhtin's paradigm of language and social representation is of a constant battle between centralizing energies that aim to standardize meaning and linguistic form, versus centrifugal forces of dispersion and difference as language is embodied in actual social situations.

I have referred to Bakhtin as 'more' materialist than Jung, because as Caryl Emerson and Michael Holquist, his editors and translators, point out, his proposition of the dialogic imagination relies upon a priori categories. It rests upon an underlying metaphysics:

> This conception has as its enabling a priori and almost Manichean sense of opposition and struggle at the heart of existence, a ceaseless battle between centrifugal forces that seek to keep things apart, that centripetal forces that strive to make things cohere. This Zoroastrian clash is present in culture as well as nature, and in the specificity of individual consciousness; it is at work in the even greater particularity of individual utterances.
>
> (Bakhtin 1981: xviii)

Like Jung, Bakhtin's centralizing energies, those that he calls 'centripetal', are an enabling hypothesis or 'model', not a metaphysical principle that is provable from the linguistic evidence before him (see Chapter 4 for Jung's 'model'). The key Bakhtinian terms for his scheme are the centripetal forces of language that are inevitably manifest in 'centrifugal' expressions, and the resulting complexity and diversity, which he called 'heteroglossia'. Essentially Bakhtin sees language and culture as layers of heteroglossia in which centrifugal social diversity is limited by centripetal drives. If centripetal forces could exist in pure form in culture, then they would constitute a 'unitary language', a cultural structure of absolute meaning that is identical with power.

Fortunately, unitary language can never be purely present. Dialects and cultures of the powerful come closest to embodying unitary language, yet its purity is an impossible ideal in the face of concrete social experience. Power dreams of unitary language, but its reality is always contaminated by heteroglossia to a lesser or greater degree:

> A unitary language is not something given. . . but is always in essence posited. . . and at every moment of its linguistic life it is opposed to the realities of the heteroglossia. But at the same time it makes its real presence felt as a force for overcoming this heteroglossia, imposing specific limits to it, guaranteeing a certain maximum of mutual understanding and crystallizing into a real, although still relative, unity – the unity of the reigning conversational (everyday) and literary language, 'correct language'.
>
> (Bakhtin 1981: 270)

So centralizing forces in language and culture are necessary lest social polarization causes the heteroglossia (linguistic and cultural diversity) to fragment into mutual incomprehension. The drives that seek a unitary language limit heteroglossia into intelligibility, while the drive producing heteroglossia fragment the awe-ful purity of power. Bakhtin regards any language or culture as irretrievably diverse: diversity in language is the articulation of diversity in society through class, race, gender, occupation, etc., and diversity within the individual through multiple social roles and the unconscious. What makes communication or dialogue possible within all this fragmentation is what *must* somehow exist, a unifying centralizing energy, always operating in tension – dialogically – with the realities of social and psychic dispersal. Any form of social expression, any utterance, is a dialogue between the absolute specificity of that moment in that person, place, society, etc., and the forces of centralization that limit singularity. This is the dialogic imagination.

It is possible to say something very similar about archetypal theory. The polarity in the archetype between its irrepresentable essence and the particularity of its every representation in archetypal images is equally a condition for language and culture to be regarded as dialogic. Of course, there is an apparent difference between Jung and Bakhtin in that the latter assimilates diversity in representation to the mechanics of social power. The ideal of a unifying language is, to him, an engine of social hierarchy. Elites aim for a monopoly of meaning production. The most banal example of an unitary language is the notion of a 'standard' form in everyday use by government, to which all regional dialects, idiolects and individual idiosyncrasies must defer in order to speak to power.

Bakhtin himself gave an intriguing list of social languages that aspired to centripetal functions. Religion, art and philosophy are prime sources of the mobilizing of power via the centralization of meaning. Examples included Aristotle's poetics, and the medieval Church's one language of truth (Bakhtin 1981: 271). In the realm of literature, Bakhtin finds that poetry is particularly redolent of centripetal drives. Hence the explicit part played by lyric and epic verse in sustaining aristocratic values. By contrast, the novel is the true child of centrifugal pluralism. It is against the nature of the novel to be confined to one form of social language; it therefore embraces the dialogic imagination rather than is polluted by it. Where heteroglossia is most evident, there is to be found the greatest challenge to the centralizing tendencies of power. To Bakhtin, the novel's articulation of diversity was cause for celebration (Bakhtin 1981: 259–422).

For Jung, on the other hand, it is easy to allege that he was more on the side of the politically conservative centripetal pole of the dialogical archetype. Certainly he produces his own attempt at unitary language (that impossible ideal) in the concepts and practices of analytical psychology. Also, as is evident in *Psychology and Alchemy* (see below), he emphasizes the centralizing tendency in individuation as a positive healing process. This emphasis is replicated in cultural terms in a frequently expressed desire for renewal in religious symbolism that could culturally reinvigorate the centripetal dynamics of the archetypal imagination (see Chapter 7 on culture).

However, as I have shown in earlier chapters, what is most basic to Jung's position, as opposed to its conservative social colouring, is his sense of the psyche's dimension of the unknown, and its crucial role in all knowledge making. This is what I am calling here, the *dialogical* aspect of the psyche. For both Bakhtin and Jung, pure unitary language/archetype is the impossible, irrepresentable, engine of representation. The only material existence it can have is a mutation of its sublime energies as it mediates difference.

Jung's overt desire for centralizing is a way of underlying the dialogical nature of the archetype because it is explicitly a centre of unknowing to which the ego becomes subordinate. Consequently the centre can never be wholly manifest: it can only be posited by images dialogically engaged with its un-image-able being. His treatment of alchemy is a fascinating instance of his belief in a dialogical psyche finding expression in a dialogical notion of psychological doctrine. For what is at stake is both Jung's dialogical structuring of archetypes and the founding of his psychology with its centripetal claims to be a 'unitary language'.

Ecocriticism: A dialogue with alchemy and nature?

Alchemy is part of the heteroglossia of medieval and early modern theology, philosophy and science. Necessarily diverging from the orthodoxy of the Christian Church, the question remains as to how far its emphasis on finding the spirit in matter (as opposed to the divine as separated from the material world), represented a subversion of Christian teaching. In particular, alchemy as the ancestor of modern chemistry could be said to have a dialogical relationship to one of the most powerfully centripetal languages of modernity: empirical experimental science. In turn, this places alchemy in an interesting position *vis-à-vis* recent attempts to fracture the centralizing tendency of western monotheism and western science, in the cause of that despised subordinate partner, nature.

Ecocriticism has two roles. It is, on the one hand, the desire to understand how centripetal languages have got us to the position where the biosphere is configured merely as an inert 'tool' or 'resource'. Equally, ecocriticism wishes to create a new dimension of the heteroglossia; a dialogue with the 'other' that is nature. So ecocriticism is both a *criticism* of western modernity, and a creative rethinking of its premises. Such an aim inevitably means that ecocriticism has to examine the 'othering' of nature by centuries of patriarchal Christian theology. So far there has been little ecocritical analysis of alchemy as a signifying system, as aspect of heteroglossia, where centripetal energies were weakened because of its divergence from attempts at a unitary language in Christian orthodoxy.

Alchemy represents a cultural practice before the Cartesian split between subject and object, mind and body, god above and inert matter, was generally accepted. It contains representation of nature, plants, animals and landscapes, as essential aspects of becoming human. The rest of this chapter will suggest that Jung's writings on alchemy may prove fruitful for ecocriticism in unpicking the *absence* of a dialogical relation of the other that is nature. I will suggest that the heteroglossia that makes up *Psychology and Alchemy* (both within the work and as the work stands for a repressed dimension to the centripetal languages of orthodox science and religion) offers a way to heteroglossia more open to the voices of nature.

It is not enough to want simply to talk to animals. Ecocriticism knows that it needs to unravel the discursive strategies by which they are made mute. Jung's alchemy offers a way through layers of cultural representation through his own sense of being in dialogue with, not imposing meaning upon, other cultures. The cultural dimension of the dialogical archetype is a sense of the possibility of a creative transformation of historical conditions. First of all, it is important to look at the intellectual argument of ecocriticism, a critical practice sorely lacking a Jungian perspective.

Ecocriticism and the necessity of remaking 'man'

Introduction

Like the critical orientations of feminism, postcolonialism and queer theory, ecocriticism seeks to reposition an entity long marginalized in western patriarchal and monotheistic thinking. Unlike these recent innovations in theory, ecocriticism has to look beyond human culture in order to do so. Indeed, ecocriticism's radicalism challenges the very structures of meaning by which 'human' as opposed to 'non-human' nature is defined. Twentieth-century literary theory emphasized language as an enclosed system with only a conventional connection to the non-human 'referent'; this connection became ever more attenuated with the advent of new technology. Laurence Coupe (2000) describes theory's preoccupation with language to the exclusion of 'the world' as a semiotic fallacy with ethical implications:

> But it should be pointed out that, in failing to move beyond the linguistic turn, theory. . . has committed what might be called the 'semiotic fallacy'. In other words, it is assumed that because mountains and waters are human at the point of delivery, they exist only as signified within human culture. Thus they have no intrinsic merit, no value and no rights.
>
> (Coupe 2000: 2)

The natural world cannot be thought of apart from the symbolic systems of human culture. However, this inevitable human or discursive dimension should not obscure its existence beyond human language and interests. Nature has a being apart from human culture (although it abuts it). In this it is truly an-'other', moreover one upon which humans remain dependent for survival. The habitual ways of regarding nature merely as an exploitable resource should be challenged, if only in our own interest. Yet ecocriticism does not suggest that the situation is just one of human culture as a whole failing to comprehend that treating nature as a resource is self-annihilating. Rather, environmental degradation is also a politics *within* the human sphere. Culture, understood dialogically, is a history of powerful elites that construct their privilege by 'othering' marginal persons and setting them with/against nature, the ultimate mute. It is not a coincidence that women have been 'othered' by being associated with nature in opposition to 'masculine' culture. The reverse is also true as nature is feminized to dissociate it from patriarchal culture or religion.

Of course, a necessary part of analysing the way that 'nature' has been constructed as the inferior term of the nature/culture binary is to look at the complex uses of that very word. Kate Soper highlights at least three ways of articulating the term 'nature' (Soper 2000: 125). Used as one half of a binary with culture, 'nature' is essentially a metaphysical concept through which difference and definition are inferred.

Second, 'nature' occurs in the phrase 'the laws of nature', as a realist notion of the powers functioning in the physical world that include human beings. Such processes including generation, gravity, molecular structures, are the objects of natural science. Third, there is the largely visible nature that western culture has separated itself from and despoiled. For this 'nature', an aesthetic response is intrinsic to the demands it makes upon the human psyche. It is this 'inbuilt' aesthetics that is of particular interest to ecocritics (Soper 2000: 125).

Soper also discusses the effects of the gendering of nature as feminine from the ecocritical perspective. Today the feminization of nature has two faces. 'She' is both the nature of 'natural laws', the true object of scientific enquiry, and also, the feminized spatial ground, territory to be conquered and encultured through agriculture (Soper 2000: 141). Nature is therefore the generative source, the womb of all human endeavour, and site of seduction; she is both mother and spouse.

Evidently, this complex apparition is a remnant of a goddess of nature, a myth that might once have served to guarantee respect for her sphere. However, the triumph of patriarchal religion has weakened the goddess into becoming a sign of nature's inferiority, rather than of her superior position over human beings (see Chapter 7 for Jung's treatment of the goddess). It is time to turn to the drastic effects of Christianity on the figuring of nature.

Father-god and silent nature

In the discourse bequeathed by western Christianity, nature is silent. It is a symbolic presence only, an 'object' mediated by language and symbolic systems designated as purely human. Nature does not speak; culture speaks *of* and *for* nature.

There is an alternative position to nature as mute and it is characteristic of some pre-Christian societies and some contemporary non-western ones. To believe nature to have voices, to be capable of dialogue, is the attitude of animism. A perspective that holds all the phenomenal world to be animated, not just the biological, animism regards rocks and trees, rivers and animals as possessing articulate spirits. Such spirits are capable of entering into communication with humans under certain conditions.

Historically, the Christian Church was implacably opposed to 'pagan' animism. Not only was God a 'sky-father', his proclaimed transcendence of nature was shared, to a large degree, by the resulting definition of 'man'. Lynn White Jr argues that the eradication of animism allowed Christian culture to treat nature as a despised resource (White Jr 1996):

> The spirits *in* natural objects, which formerly had protected nature from man, evaporated. Man's effective monopoly on spirit in this world was confirmed, and the old inhibitions to the exploitation of nature crumbled.
>
> (White Jr 1996: 10)

By moulding 'man' in the image of a sky-father god absolutely divorced from natural processes, western Christianity created a new human subject. 'Man' requires himself to be defined against those elided inferior terms 'woman' and 'nature'. In particular, the construction of man silenced nature, replacing the pluralism of *animated* nature's many voices with a mute realm for 'his' indefinite expansion.

In response to such thinking, Christopher Manes calls for the lethal fiction of 'man' to be swept away and replaced by a different conception of the human subject: '*Homo Sapiens*: one species among many millions of other beautiful, terrible, fascinating – and signifying – forms' (Manes 1996: 26).

However, the overthrow of the western subject needs to be accompanied by a radical overhaul of one of 'his' most centripetal languages: science. Lynn White Jr traces the evolution of modern science as a direct descendant of Christian theology (White Jr 1996: 111–12). To early Christian culture, God may be transcendent of nature, but he also made it and so its study was legitimate. So-called 'natural theology' took two forms. In the early Church and the Orthodox east, nature was constructed as a symbolic communication from God to Man. For example, the behaviour of animals was regarded as embodied sermons. So nature was viewed aesthetically as a source of meaning and revelation.

A contrary movement began in the Latin west by the thirteenth century, which shifted natural theology into the attempt to understand the mind of God through experimental investigation of his creation. The mind of God, or the logos, became identified more and more with the knowledge of science. In a sceptical age, the identification of logos/truth with the divine is discarded. Just as modern science is a continuation of natural theology in pursuit of logos, so its creation, technology, is a consummation of the Christian practice of dominating nature as an object. Logos, as rational knowledge transcendent of nature, has mutated conceptually from the mind of God, to the knowledge of science, to the principles and codes of modern technology. Yet it is still arguably a Christian patriarchal tradition in which present day (so-called secular) attitudes to science, technology and nature, are mired (White Jr 1996: 12).

Unsurprisingly, part of the process of alienation from nature can be understood by examining textual practices. The Christian Church *produced* the notion of logos, of reason transcendent of matter and nature by its form of reading, explains Christopher Manes (1996: 20). In doing so, of course, it created the outlines of rational 'man' as the powerfully pervasive fiction of the human subject:

> Exegesis established God as a transcendental subject speaking through natural entities, which, like words on a page, had a symbolic meaning, but no autonomous voice. It distilled the veneration of the word and reason into a discourse that we still speak today.
>
> (ibid.: 20)

In Bakhtinian terms, the textual practice of the Church was a major engine of its centripetal drive to create a unitary language of power. Of course, the Church never achieved a purely unitary language as that is not possible in the face of social complexity. Yet exegesis, the mode of reading for the one truth, for the transcendent mind of God, became a potent construction of the notion of authorship as authority that still informs reading practices today (see Chapter 2).

Nevertheless, reading for logos or singular truths is now challenged by literary theories such as poststructuralism that regard texts as inherently plural, so containing many voices. In fact, it could be argued that post-structuralist reading is a return of animism – with the many voices of nature shifted to texts: '[a]t one time nature spoke; now texts do' (ibid.: 19).

So poststructuralist reading can be regarded as a form of animism. It seeks dialogue with many textual voices and treats meaning as something to be negotiated rather than extractable as a whole, and inherently tran-scendent of textual *matter*. On the one hand, the return of animism is a welcome development for the ecocritic. On the other hand, its restriction to Coupe's 'semiotic fallacy' remains a problem. The question stubbornly lingers: how to get from texts to nature, to hear the authentic voices of the 'other' from beyond human technological culture.

Poststructuralism as a project and ecocriticism overlap. Together they share the critique of objectivity, of the assumption that thinking can stand outside the 'object' to be studied. For if the critic is always part of a larger system (such as language or 'nature'), then rather than powerful centres of meaning such as God, reason, logos, we need to think in terms of networks of interrelated systems. Consequently, the traditional human subject or 'man' is no longer the centre of meaning and value: 'man' and his logos are decentred and meaning is dependent upon a relation with the 'other'. Bakhtin's dialogics is one model of meaning constructed mutually, although his is, in part, a description of the effect of unequal distribution of power, and only in part hints at more plural possibilities.

Unfortunately, establishing a dialogical relationship with texts is not enough. Ecocritics want to go further and reconstruct the animism of nature. It is necessary to extend dialogics into the natural world as a way of articulating difference in a relationship. Something like an optimistic version of Bakhtinian dialogics is called for in order to do away with the annihilating binary of nature versus culture. The notion of centrifugal plurality replaces the fiction of a single inert 'other', and enhances the chances of bringing the non-human into the production of meaning. Patrick D. Murphy sees Bakhtin's theory as fruitful for ecology's vision of the planetary ecosystem as a field of inter-animating relationships, including the human (Murphy 2000).

But Bakhtin did not extend dialogics to the non-human, limiting his analysis to a description of the operation of human language and power. So ecocriticism is left with an immense challenge. If the animation of nature through the dialogical imagination is to be conceivable at all, then language (in the broadest sense) has got to be rethought as no longer exclusively human. And logos, the rational language of knowledge constructed as transcendent of its object, will need to be reconfigured as *one* mode of knowing among a network of others, rather than lauded as the supreme form of cognition.

For example, aesthetic engagement with nature may turn out to be more potent in reordering human subject relationships with the non-human than the traditions of modern science. One crucial tactic for ecocriticism is to undo modernity's hierarchy of knowledge perspectives, in which rational science reigns, and replace it with a spectrum, network or web of dialogical relationships.

In such an eco-logic environment, it becomes apparent that language is not a symbolic system existing as separate from other symbolic systems by which we interact with the world. Indeed, language can be shown to trouble the nature/culture binary rather than be a means of reinforcing it. Gary Snyder sees languages as inherently nature *and* culture (Snyder 2000). In the quotation at the head of this chapter he asserts that language begins as part of the child's natural being, while becoming ever more cultural as the child is socialized. He suggests that language never stops being intrinsic to the human body as it is conscious experience that remains, in some sense, wild:

> Consciousness, mind, imagination and language are fundamentally wild. 'Wild' as in wild ecosystems – richly interconnected, interdependent, and incredibly complex. Diverse, ancient, and full of information.
>
> (Snyder 2000: 29)

James Hillman is suggesting something similar in the other quotation at the start of this chapter. He declares rhetoric to be part of the 'nature' of being human (Hillman 1989: 295). Of course the core importance of rhetoric to the human psyche was one of the themes of Chapter 4. When Jung posits a continuum between psyche and matter in that essay, he is implying that psyche is part of the ecosystem. An intrinsically rhetorical psyche cannot therefore be seen as distinct from the phenomenal world.

Certainly, it is axiomatic that ecocritics are paying careful attention to the extent that humans, as biological beings, demonstrate a continuity (rather than transcendent separation) with nature and the environment. Neil Evernden explains that interrelatedness of the ecosystem, including the human animal, is actually more deeply involved than hitherto believed (Evernden 1996: 93). Humans do more than walk upon the earth; they contain within themselves other life that they cannot do without.

In this analysis, the biosphere does not consist of discrete beings. Even the western conception of interrelatedness as causal connections turns out to be too modest or too predicated upon an ethos of individualism. Rather living beings dwell in a state of interpenetration just as a forest soil is a delicate margin instead of a firm boundary. Humans, for example, could not survive without countless inner bacteria, let alone the animals that we breathe in and out. It is possible, Evernden says, to see animism return via this acute ecological insight:

> For once we engage in the extension of the boundary of the self into the 'environment,' then of course we imbue it with life and can quite properly regard it as animate – it is animate because we are part of it.
>
> (ibid.: 101)

Another shift in perspective away from the human subject as rational 'man' comes from the refreshing proposition that human culture is banal and simple compared to the complexity of the ecosystem. Joseph W. Meeker alleges that the closest 'ecological' aesthetic form that humans have developed is comedy (Meeker 1996). Eco-logic is discernible in comedy's acceptance of life as cyclical, including birth and death, as well as the acceptance of necessity (ibid.: 163). Yet compared to the immense web of complexity that is nature, human culture is arid. Meeker comes close to Bakhtin's diagnosis of centripetal simplification as the expression of power. For he argues against the 'civilized' habit of suppressing (bio)diversity in order to convert landscape into 'pure' production, a banal factory. When it comes to the dialogics of 'man' and nature in western farming, 'man' is a centripetal creature seeking to squash the centrifugal complexity of the biosphere. Replacing 'man' by 'homo sapiens' is an important early step in transforming that particular dialogics of power.

So if we can take seriously ecology's premise that human beings do not exist separately from the natural world, 'man' is a dying fiction. It is to be hoped that he dies conceptually before his presence in western culture proves more literally lethal.

The ecological human subject is one regarded as continuous with the environment. It follows that aesthetics is both contributor to the change of 'man' into homo sapiens and itself subject to radical revision. Arnold Berleant, for instance, proposes a new environmental aesthetics stemming from the realization of human continuity with nature (Berleant 1992). After all aesthetic engagement becomes material participation if human beings can no longer separate themselves off. 'Experience' proves to have an inherently aesthetic dimension. From such a position, so-called scientific 'objective' methods of enquiry into the natural world appear to be a false fictional construct; a deliberate stripping away of 'natural' aesthetic and affective bonds.

Such ideas are very close to the position of the Romantic poets, in particular William Blake, as noted by ecocritics such as Betty and Theodor Roszak (Roszak and Roszak 2000). Romantics and new romantic ecocritics want to correct the bias of rational science by augmentation with imaginative, aesthetic and affective modes of human understanding. The aim is a new animism that would enfold all living beings, the phenomenal world and the cosmos, in its embrace.

In the rest of this chapter, I am going to argue that what may prove particularly interesting in Jung from the point of view of ecocriticism is his *difference* from the attempted unitary language that is Christianity, and indeed, how that very difference reveals heteroglossia within the most powerful western myth. Additionally, I will suggest that a significant factor of his writings on alchemy is his explicit embrace of heteroglossia (obviously without using that term) at the level of cultural representation. Despite Jung's own centripetal desires (to write his own unitary language as analytical psychology), and conservative longings for centralizing forms of cultural discourse, his adherence to the centrifugal and plural is an enduring legacy.

It remains to be seen whether he is centrifugal or 'other' enough to let nature into the dialogue. I want to suggest that Jung's acute, though often neglected, sense of historical and cultural *location* offers possibilities as a starting point for a culturally sophisticated rethinking of human relations to nature. After all, if alchemy has a *place* both within Jung's work and in his sense of it as a social practice, then the spatiality that I have already described as innate to his writing (see Chapters 2 and 6) begins to look like eco-logic.

Jung and alchemy

Introduction to Jung's alchemy

Jung's writing about alchemy is writing about texts. Although he alludes to its mythological origins in ancient Egypt, he never strays far from analysing an astonishing variety of works composed in Europe in the early modern era. In focusing upon a specific period in the complex legacy of alchemy, Jung is stressing certain key features as innate to his conception of the art.

For Jung, alchemists worked on matter and mind simultaneously with no sense of division between the two activities. The popular view that they were straightforwardly aiming to convert lead into gold for purely mercenary purposes was never a sufficient explanation for him. Rather alchemists worked to produce a base substance known as the *prima materia*, and operated upon it to achieve a higher 'golden' form known by such names as 'spirit', 'elixir of life', 'philosopher's stone'. There was general agreement that the transformation would proceed by stages. Originally four stages are mentioned: blackening, whitening, yellowing, reddening (Jung 1944/1953, CW12: para. 333). These are reduced to three around the fifteenth century by omitting the yellowing. Jung attaches importance to the fundamental oscillation between four, the number of the elements of that period, and three, with its echoes of the Christian trinity. More on the link to Christianity later.

Native to alchemy is a centrifugal drive into heteroglossia. Although there are common laboratory procedures and general consensus on the stages, alchemy texts work by multiplying images for its powerful substances. There is a proliferation of terms for the potent initial prima materia, and for the final object of desire, the *lapis* or stone. Even these two items themselves are not always separable, in a crucial clue to alchemy's frustration of modernity's belief in the logic of so-called 'inert' matter. It possesses a 'poetic' bias, as I shall show:

> For one alchemist the *prima materia* was quicksilver, for others it was ore, iron, gold, lead, salt, sulphur, vinegar, water, air, fire, earth, blood, water of life, *lapis*, poison, spirit, cloud, sky, dew, shadow, sea, mother, moon, dragon, Venus, chaos, Microcosm.
>
> (ibid.: para. 425)

This heteroglossia is, for Jung, the clearest evidence of the centrifugal pole of the archetype. Alchemists, all unknowing, had projected their unconscious psyche into matter. Therefore they needed their own individual symbols for the unknown substance before them. The framing argument of *Psychology and Alchemy* is that these early modern texts bear witness to archetypal symbolism by way of alchemy's investigation of the then relatively unexplored domain of matter.

> As is shown by the texts and their symbolism, the alchemist projected what I have called the process of individuation into the phenomena of chemical change.
>
> (ibid.: para. 564)

Jung is acutely aware of the historical specificity of this 'psychic' evidence. He carefully traces alchemy's transmutation into chemistry in the eighteenth century as the study of matter parted company with the excitation of the psyche (ibid.: para. 332). Alchemists regarded themselves as 'philosophers' working with texts and ideas; study was obligatory. Yet it was crucial that alchemical philosophy has a material dimension of working in a laboratory. When that link was broken modern chemistry was born and the psychic work, according to Jung, had to wait for its re-emergence in analytical psychology.

Jung's alchemy and analytical psychology

Alchemists did not regard themselves as in a state of projection. They believed that there was a divine spirit imprisoned in matter. It was their task to release or produce the spirit/lapis etc., through successive transformations of the matter of the prima materia. Through study and physical chemistry *together* alchemists sought to evoke a third realm between mind and matter, between philosophy and chemistry. This space, in which the prima materia and the lapis may be manifested, is known as, 'the intermediate realm of subtle bodies' (ibid.: para. 394).

   The medium of the subtle body or 'subtle reality' is the place of the Jungian symbol. As part of their work, alchemists believed in an imaginative power in the human mind that had the capacity to transform matter. In describing this potency at work through symbols, Jung allows himself to reach beyond alchemy as projection to conceive of it instead as a psychic continuum between inner self and outer world:

> The imaginatio, as the alchemists understand it, is in truth a key that opens the door to the secret of the *opus*. . . The place or the medium of realization is neither mind nor matter, but that intermediate realm of subtle reality which can be adequately expressed only by the symbol.

The symbol is neither abstract nor concrete, neither rational nor irrational, neither real nor unreal. It is always both.

(ibid.: para. 400)

Despite this sympathy with the alchemist's pre-Cartesian holism, most of *Psychology and Alchemy* stays firmly within the frame of projection. Indeed, the governing trope of projection serves to emphasize the intrinsic hetero-glossia of alchemy. For if alchemists are projecting the unknown contents of their own psyches, it is unsurprising that they do not understand each other, since each projection/archetypal image must be uniquely nuanced for that individual (ibid.: para. 401). Moreover, there are times when alchem-ists do not even comprehend their own symbolism, so greatly is it saturated with the unknown within.

In this, Jung's alchemists are artists rather than scientists. They do not produce a public code to be deciphered. Alchemy is not primarily oriented towards exercising wide cultural influence as a centripetal social language. Rather, its centripetal dimension inheres in the broad agreement in three alchemical stages, the philosophical outlook, and the concrete desire for money or transcendence. These aspects are almost obscured by centrifugal symbolic images in their texts. Alchemists make works of art, or at least individual texts built with their own analogies (ibid.: para. 403). A centri-petal set of conventions serves to license and limit centrifugal analogies producing heteroglossia as a kaleidoscope of images.

If the alchemists work by analogy, then it is this method that embodies the active transforming principle of the imagination. Jung explains that just as multiple sense impressions distil an idea, so the primal substance finally condenses an ethereal spirit: the analogy is a material cause; a process of the mind working upon matter (ibid.: para. 377). In effect, alchemists employ what Jung calls 'active imagination'. For the alchemists, the active power of the imagination transforms matter. For Jung, active imagination trans-forms the matter of the psyche (ibid.: para. 394).

Amplification is a particular species of analogy that Jung considered important both for himself and the alchemists. An organ of spatiality in Jung's thinking, amplification enlarges a phenomenon until it reaches intelligibility (ibid.: para. 403). It is a process of assimilation of psychic experience such as a dream into textual and cultural experience by using myth or a discourse. So amplification is an interesting link between the notion of territorial expansion and the production of meaning. But what can it do for nature?

Jung's alchemy and nature

Forging a connection to matter is not the same as forging a connection to the natural world as something to be respected in its own right. A great deal of exploitation and environmental degradation has occurred in the name of exploring the matter of the biosphere. It is not for nothing that Jung identifies alchemy as the begetter of natural science that treats nature as a mute object of study. Alchemy's relation to chemistry can be construed as legitimating the torture of nature to force her to give up her secrets. Boiling organic extracts in test tubes would appear to be an unpromising basis for a new ecocriticsm.

And yet the story of alchemy, as Jung tells it, crucially complicates the descent of the Christian logos from transcendent God, to scientific abstraction, to cybernetic codes. Although medieval alchemists claimed to be loyal members of the Church, their trade carries a counter-cultural charge. While apparently adhering to the transcendent redeemer in the ether, above material earth, they nevertheless also located a divine source in the phenomenal world (ibid.: para. 356).

Additionally, alchemy dramatically alters the Christian construction of divine–human relations. Christianity offers the saviour God of every human soul. By contrast the alchemists saw themselves in the divine role; they are called to be redeemers of the god trapped in matter (ibid.: 420). On the one hand Jung discovers or recreates his own favourite myth of the necessary human redemption of divine unconsciousness from the matter of the psyche (see Chapters 2 and 6). On the other hand, what Jung does not overtly say here is that alchemy challenges orthodox religious hierarchies.

For alchemy deconstructs Christian transcendence. No longer is God only to be found 'above' man, and therefore licensing a version of his creature as similarly transcendent of nature. No longer is the human, 'man', in the sense of imitating the logos (as transcendent reason) alone, thereby denying his eros (as connectivity to earth, matter, body, soul). A god *in* nature as well places human beings in nature too. Ecocriticism's 'homo sapiens' live in Jung's alchemy.

Consequently, the nature symbolism in *Psychology and Alchemy* is indicative of, if not fully embracing, eco-logic. For example, Mercurius is the transforming substance in humanoid form, sharing attributes with 'serpent, dragon, raven, lion, basilisk, and eagle' (ibid.: para. 173). Although Mercurius can take Christian form as Virgin clasping dying son, 'he' is also a green lion, a tree, and birds whose flight signifies fantasies (ibid.: paras. 305, 498–9).

It goes without saying that Christian priorities make significant inroads into alchemical symbolism. Mercurius is also associated with the devil and Jung mentions animal symbolism in a series of dreams as showing a 'lower' aspect of the psyche. It is not only the Christian colouring of the alchemical writing that weights Jung's commentary towards the traditional hierarchy of man above nature. However, the exposition of animal symbolisms as intertwined with Christian, and Mercurius's dual devil–saviour aspects, means that Jung is fully aware of the way that alchemy breaks up the linear, distinct, and transcendent, in favour of a network of interanimating symbols that refuses to fix a hierarchy of divine, human and nature.

The important point here is that Mercurius is not reliably or inevitably the *higher form* over the animals in incarnating the stuff of alchemy. Rather the innate *substitutability* of images where any can stand for each 'other' deconstructs simple 'man' based hierarchy. The emphasis on minerals and the philosopher's stone extends the network to the phenomenal world: all are animate.

Bakhtin had a name for this kind of deconstruction of centripetal categories: carnival. And although, the heavy presence of Christian culture within alchemy texts constellates a bias towards the human as *the* source of meaning, alchemy nevertheless represents a vital fracturing of Christianity's drive to become monolithic, or a unitary language. A particular focus of *Psychology and Alchemy* is an exploration of the attempt to fuse alchemy and Christianity in the extensive analogy between the *lapis* and Christ. Jung is aware that the alchemical–Christian combination is both contradictory and potentially explosive.

He admits that if the alchemist had any sense of his unconscious then he would have had to recognize Christ as a symbol of the self, and his own role in redeeming the God (ibid.: para. 452). Even Jung's extensive analysis of alchemy's parallel between the object of the quest and Christ cannot force alchemy to unite with orthodox Christianity. Indeed, Jung does not want it to. A dialogical relationship between alchemy and the official Church will serve his purposes of first generating his analytical psychology, and second, for his larger project of redeeming modern culture.

The result is a portrayal of Christianity, for all its centripetal drives to power, as saturated with heteroglossia. Here alchemy takes its dialogical position. As part of the heteroglossia of Christianity, the legacy of alchemy can be read two ways. One inheritance is its descent into chemical science and its transmission of Christian logos into becoming, in turn, the dominant language over its religious relation. A second, more obscure inheritance remains a counter-discourse that Jung's text allows to surface: a destabilizing of Christian dominance that preserves the possibility of hearing the voices of nature.

Significantly, the lack of realism in alchemy's natural symbolism is an indication of the psyche's participation. True, animals, stones and birds are not imaged in alchemy for themselves and invited to a genuinely dialogical relationship. Rather, they feature as a 'way' to the sacred *for* man. Yet it remains a path that acknowledges the participation of nature in the phenomenon, in the *being* of humanity. Alchemy is an expression of the continuum of human identity into the phenomenal world: human animation reaches out to an animate nature. Alchemy was a material/psychic practice of aesthetic engagement that knew no bounds to the self in both the conventional and Jungian sense. Jung's alchemy makes it impossible to deny the importance of the non-human in the very roots of our being.

Therefore alchemy as Jung portrays it is not a simple source of ecocriticism. In the first place, the kind of dialogics it exhibits is overtly in the interest of the human over the non-human. The repeated insistence of alchemy as psychic projection is a theoretical expression of alchemy as self-interest, from the point of view of a Cartesian self (subject severed from world as object), as opposed to alchemy's attempt to regard subjectivity in continuum.

Second, alchemy veers away from ecocriticism by bearing the marks of the Christian drive to remove the divine from immanence to transcendence, despite its intrinsic embrace of the phenomenal. Locating the sacred in matter does give alchemy a stake in the non-human. Unfortunately, the alchemist's understandable tendency to make analogies and amplifications to Christianity *as a narrative* pushes alchemy in the direction of exploiting matter and nature in order to restore the sleeping god to his true transcendence.

Yet, in the cause of ecocriticism, alchemy powerfully demonstrates a native heteroglossia to Christianity as culturally embedded. Alchemy is liminal to Christianity in that it represents heteroglossia within Christian culture and functions as a marginalized 'other' to its norms. So it even preserves a trace of animism within the Christian ambience.

More significantly still, Jung provides the animism of texts. He liberates alchemy's many voices in multiple readings and quotations. His textual animism is then explicitly linked to the tongues of the other in the phenomenal world. This crucial matrix occurs because alchemists worked in the laboratory as well as the scriptorium, but most importantly because they believed (like some ecocritics) that imagination possesses material properties. The symbol brought into being subtle reality between consciousness and the world. Rather than language and texts seen as pre-structuring reality in a way that renders its non-human qualities as 'outside' signifying, Jung's alchemy suggests an *animated* matrix in which textual voices form part of a dialogic web of interanimating presences: human, textual and non-human.

It is now worth looking at the structure of *Psychology and Alchemy* to see how it works as textual *matter* rather than just as the argument I have abstracted from it (in a thoroughly non-ecological manner!). How does this volume fare as an entity with its own unique shape, offering psychotherapy for the voices of another age; a *treatment* of texts?

Psychology and Alchemy (Jung 1944/1953, CW12)

Basic structure of the opus

The structure of the volume of the *Collected Works*, *Psychology and Alchemy*, consists of three parts. The first section is a relatively brief introduction followed by the much longer Part II on dream symbolism in relation to alchemy. Part III on religious ideas in alchemy is even more extensive. It has chapters on the making of symbols, the role of myth, the work of redemption, parallels with Christian iconography and ends with a study of unicorn symbols, which extends into non-Christian religions.

From the evidence of the part and chapter arrangements, *Psychology and Alchemy* is an expanding structure. Its inner spine of three parts widens in scope and detail as the book progresses. In essence the book spirals, beginning at the centre with great circular sweeps on the core ideas of analytical psychology and alchemy, then working outwards into psychic instances and cultural analysis. More precisely, of course, the structure of *Psychology and Alchemy* is an amplification moving from psychic image to cultural symbolism. In its circular progress through ideas, it aspires to be the written equivalent of a mandala.

In particular, *Psychology and Alchemy* demonstrates the amplification by analogy from the psychic texts of dreams to the cultural texts of alchemical symbolism. By cultural analogy and amplification, analytical psychology as a discourse is articulated. The course of the volume moves from the modern psyche to history, and thence to alchemy as a cross-cultural phenomenon. Jung explores the multicultural identity of alchemy in the final section by comparing unicorn symbolism in places as diverse as India, Europe and in Jewish scriptures. Here the challenge to Christian hierarchies embedded in alchemy takes on an overtly political orientation. Can amplification across cultures be enacted in the spirit of the web of interanimating symbols? Or, is it to be a colonial appropriation of the matter of an-other's heritage?

I will suggest that the subtle body of alchemical symbolism is a possible mediation *between* cultural difference rather than an attempt to assert western hegemony. Significantly, the multicultural section extends the heteroglossia that is alchemy beyond the centripetal potencies of Christianity. Importance must be attached to the large amount of quotation in *Psychology and Alchemy*. Jung doesn't just describe a past of dialogically inter-animating discourses. Rather he enacts it by incorporating the plural and multiply *located* voices of the other into his work. The result of his dialogical writing is the generation of analytical psychology itself as a *discourse located in history and space* and not detached from its antecedent 'others' (see Chapter 6 for more on this).

So if Jung's alchemy can imply cultural difference as part of a dialogic web, it will be because of two key factors. First of all, alchemy exhibits a greater degree of cultural diversity than more socially elite discourses because it is built by individuals working with the unknown psychic to the extent that they cannot even colonize their own work. Second, Jung's treatment is politically productive because his writing embraces both centripetal and centrifugal dynamics. His vision of archetypes is of sublime unknowable centring energies of the self, activated in dialogue with centrifugal forces inherent in culturally located archetypal images. The substance of culture in image, language and representation is fundamentally heteroglossic because multiple social determinants of a person's history, location, affiliation etc., vitally inform (are centrifugal to) the incarnation of the (centripetal) archetype. In alchemy, Jung finds the 'matter' for his dialogical, socially located psyche. He also finds that it retains, however occluded by Christian bias, an opening to nature and the non-human as part of the continuum of being.

Two other emphases are noticeable in the volume layout of *Psychology and Alchemy* to join the enactment of its amplification. They are the focus on centring self symbols in dreams and in alchemy, together with a stress on the link between alchemy and Christianity in the extensive consideration of the lapis-Christ parallel. Both would suggest that Jung leans towards centripetal cultural forms. In seeking aspirant unitary languages, of analytical psychology and Christianity, he may reveal conservative preferences. Yet his work is far from dominated by attempts to formulate a controlling language of power and/or meaning. Rather the transcendence of Christian doctrine is mitigated by the revelation of its inner 'other', the heteroglossic (subtle) body of alchemy symbols.

It is the inherently dialogic nature of Jung's thinking that calls into being the voices of the other, from the texts of alchemy, and from alchemy's material engagement with nature.

Part I: Introduction to the Religious and Psychological Problems of Alchemy

Forty-three paragraphs of introduction consider the role of alchemy for analytical psychology in a far from straightforward argument. Early discussions confirm the mysterious quality of the psyche and its innate teleology or goal-oriented development towards the future through individuation. Jung is then concerned to link the 'quest' for the 'whole' man with the project of religions (ibid.: para. 6). Without drawing attention to it, Jung notes that the divorce of religion and nature has the consequence of removing serious contemplation of the psyche from religious thinking. The loss of 'Nature' is also the eclipse of psychic 'nature'.

Fascinatingly, this is a characteristically alchemical attitude: that the God is to be found in the matter of nature – here as psyche. To the extent that Jung sees the human psyche as part of nature, human nature as continuous with non-human nature, he is restoring nature to the divine because he here asserts the indigenous religious function of the psyche or soul. The soul has an inbuilt relationship to God in the archetype of the self in the role of the God-image (ibid.: para. 11). It is the refusal of Christianity to cultivate nature in man, the psychological 'other', that has induced its current hollow and brittle quality (ibid.: para. 12).

After describing the psyche's link to the divine, Jung then returns to the impossibility of claiming absolute knowledge of its territories, let alone using psychology to 'prove' the transcendent reality of God (ibid.: para. 15). In a felicitous phrase perceiving a connection between knowledge and power: '[t]he scientist is a scrupulous worker; he cannot take heaven by storm' (ibid.: para. 16).

In fact, Jung stresses the connection between the inability to proclaim transcendent truth and the plural character of archetypal representation, so acknowledging the inevitable heteroglossia of psychic images (ibid.: para. 20). The structure of *Psychology and Alchemy*, even here in its early paragraphs, enacts the oscillation between centripetal drives to make definite claims to knowledge (and power through establishing a meta-theory), and centrifugal realization of the contingent quality of the psyche as manifest. It is the unique character of Jung's writing that he shows to the reader what is at stake in making a 'psychological' argument, structuring a narrative that demonstrates ambitions to be a 'theory', yet has to be generated from culturally situated, personally coloured 'evidence'. Indeed, Jung is notably explicit about the requirement to edit and reposition dream texts in order to describe archetypal dynamics at all (see below in Part II).

However, one advantage of the plural centrifugal pole of Jung's psyche is its compensatory powers *vis-à-vis* Christian one-sidedness. The Christian divorce from nature has elevated its own supreme human image, Christ, away from the irrationality of the human other. As a result, Jung argues, the psychic nature omitted from human culture brings forth a 'chthonic' son, Mercurius, with devilish as well as divine aspects, in the narrative of alchemy (ibid.: para. 26).

In looking at the compensatory functions of alchemy, Jung is alluding to the fundamental narrative structure of the psyche. Individuation is the most obvious 'sign' of Jung's basic conception that story is indigenous to being. Here, he reminds the reader that true psychic expression is embodied in myth rather than intellectual analysis (ibid.: para. 28).

Jung continues to identify the unconscious psyche with nature and strikingly suggests that the discrimination that is characteristic of consciousness is against nature:

> The essence of the conscious mind is discrimination; it must, if it is to be aware of things, separate the opposites, and it does this *contra natram*.
>
> (ibid.: para. 30)

When Jung uses the word 'nature' of the unconscious psyche, he does so broadly in the first two of the three constructions identified by Kate Soper and described earlier in this chapter. 'Nature' is used as a metaphysical category as a distinguishing term from 'culture', for example as here in the 'cultivating' qualities of conscious discrimination. Also, Jung's 'nature' refers to the universal and inescapable laws.

Although less apparent, the third use of the observable natural world as aesthetic does enter *Psychology and Alchemy* in two ways. Most obviously Jung comments on these nature images in dreams and in alchemy texts. *These are regarded as intrinsic components of the human psyche.* Less overtly, Jung employs a few biological figures and metaphors. In turn, such figures may collapse back into alchemical writings as he incorporates 'other' voices into the texture of his thinking. For example, in suggesting a spiral shape to psychic development, Jung's plant metaphor unites both with his psychology of dreams and alchemy's images:

> We might draw a parallel between such spiral courses and the processes of growth in plants; in fact the plant motif (tree, flower etc) frequently recurs in these dreams and fantasies and is also spontaneously drawn or painted. In alchemy the tree is the symbol of Hermetic philosophy.
>
> (ibid.: para. 34)

Interestingly, this metaphor (typically collapsing into actual psychic representation/cultural discourse), is also a template of *Psychology and Alchemy* itself as it moves from a discussion of psychic teleology, to dreams, to alchemy as a cultural work. Additionally, it serves to shift the term 'nature' from the first two to the second two definitions. In figuring psychic development as plant-like, 'nature' (in the unconscious) loses its binary relation with non-nature in conscious discrimination.

Individuation is not always and not simply *opus contra natram*. Only forensic conscious discrimination is simply 'against nature'. Rather, nature metaphors for psychic development provide individuation as a deconstruction of nature and culture in the human soul. Psychic development is a continued negotiation between the 'natural' and the 'cultural' that reveals these terms as continually and contingently constructed throughout daily life. Christianity treats nature as absolute other. Jung and the alchemists seek a differential relationship with traffic across the border.

Of course, Jung's frame, his adherence to alchemy as psychic projection, positions a gap between the 'nature' of the human unconscious and the 'nature' of universal laws and of the aesthetic biosphere. No such gap is envisaged by the alchemists as Jung realizes. Alchemy preserves a bridge to nature as human unconscious and natural world, while the Church seeks to cut nature out (ibid.: para. 40).

Alchemy's eco-logic is assailed on two sides as *Psychology and Alchemy* portrays it. On the one hand its indulgence in Christian analogies exerts pressure to draw the god from matter into the stratosphere. There are moments when it seems as if alchemy is trying very hard to escape from matter and into the Christian story. On the other hand, the second inner pressure comes from Jung's bias towards 'human' nature. Yet, *Psychology and Alchemy* resists an identification of nature solely with the psyche. A margin for eco-logic remains. It is a measure of Jung's respect for the heteroglossia of psychic images that he allows the centrifugal dynamics of alchemy to pull him out of complete reliance upon Cartesian subject/object distinctions and into a nature more largely conceived.

Part II: Individual Dream Symbolism in Relation to Alchemy

Chapter 1: Introduction

The first few paragraphs of the introduction to Part II on dreams are a demonstration of centripetal elements in analytical psychology. Not only does the psyche contain its own centralizing dynamic in the archetype of the self, but Jung proposes to ruthlessly edit hundreds of dream texts in order to make this point (ibid.: paras. 44–50). Indeed the notion of the self is given powerful substance as both centre and circumference of psychic totality (ibid.: para. 44).

However, Jung is actually repeating a structural device of his writing. He asserts something about the psyche as definite (in Part I it was the soul's relation to God), and follows it by emphatic mitigation of any such certainty on the subject. We are told that dreams are, in themselves, part of cultural heteroglossia, meaning that they are not properly analysed apart from their context in their dreamer as an embodied encultured being. Jung is making an exception with this long series of dreams for what we might call generic reasons. Regarded as a series with discernible themes, the dreams offer context to each other, and, are seen to be congruent with other examples of self images from cultural sources (ibid.: para. 50). So therefore this series provides similar, 'generic' images of the sublime self.

The media theorist, Luke Hockley, has made a similar argument for film genres to be regarded as archetypes (Hockley 2001). No ur-film example of any one genre exists; films refer to and are shaped by a (centripetal) yet ultimately unrepresentable form. Such films as archetypal images are culturally and historically located while giving context to each other.

Jung here is faithful to his plural, cultural conception of the psyche by discussing openly the pruning necessary to produce a centripetal dimension to analytical psychology. Such cultivation points to unitary language as never wholly achievable.

Chapter 2: The Initial Dreams

Still in the mode of withdrawing from definitive statements of 'truth' about the psyche, Jung emphasizes experience over understanding. And this preference is innate to the working of *Psychology and Alchemy*. While it would be perfectly possible to boil down the matter of the volume to about ten pages of logical argument, Jung has no intention of doing this. Such a (natural) desire on the reader's part is to miss the point. The repetitive nature of the dreams, alchemy texts, and indeed of Jung's writing *is* the point.

Jung's writing is innately experiential, in particular in its mutating, spiralling, repetitive and oblique characteristics. To read Part II of *Psychology and Alchemy* is to 'experience' something of the cumulative effect of the 59 dreams, taken, we are told, from a collection of some 400 (ibid.: para. 323). It begins by insisting that experience, not intellectual argument, is the key to psychic growth (ibid.: para. 59).

Part II also suggests, early on, that psychic investigation cannot omit consideration of parents and that this particular arena of difficulty was illuminated by Freud (ibid.: para. 81). Later this will be amplified to high-light the necessity for psychic 'earth' (ibid.: para. 148). Now, however, the dreamer's personal parental conflicts are deliberately omitted, in another demonstration of what has been edited out. It is worth remembering just how far Jung owns up to the partial nature of this analysis of dream texts in *not* representing the full, multidimensional approaches that he regards as germane to psychic treatment.

Therefore, it is apparent that this dream analysis will unnaturally bring into prominence the collective and cultural at the expense of the personal and Oedipal. So it is unsurprising that the early dreams introduce Mercurius as a developed protean figure of both spiritual and animal realms. 'He' has helpful properties, yet shares many of the attributes of the devil and can appear as predatory animals (ibid.: para. 84). Despite this unpromising early appearance, Mercurius is not confined to figuring the devil in nature. Nevertheless, it is interesting that this citation puts alchemy into the ambit of the unofficial, semi-heretical aspects of Christianity: its heteroglossia in folk legends of devils in animals.

A more positive manifestation of nature occurs in the dream of a blue flower, regarded as 'like a friendly sign', from the unconscious that har-bours the seeds of psychic growth (ibid.: para. 101). Again, an image, here from a dream, becomes a metaphor, that serves to deconstruct nature and culture as a binary, in favour of them as an alliance. That this is not a sentimental revaluing of nature *above* culture and consciousness, is now apparent. Without individuation 'natural man' would be a mere creature of the 'animal collective psyche' (ibid.: para. 104). The implicit hierarchy of human above animal is both reinforced and problematized by later alchemy texts. Integration with the 'nature' of the unconscious is not regression to it. It requires 'transformation mysteries' for human life to become known, and only by becoming known can it become real (ibid.: paras. 104–5).

Chapter 3: The Symbolism of the Mandala

I. CONCERNING THE MANDALA

Jung starts this chapter by a further self-conscious meditation on his writing. To publish mandalas is a high risk strategy lest readers take his ideas as yet another fashionable fad; the work would become a means of avoiding the truth about themselves (ibid.: para. 126). Such shallow appreciation of psychic images engenders the arresting metaphor of people desperate to dress up in borrowed feathers (ibid.: para. 126). The problem lies in applying such ideas as some sort of external balm rather than submit, experientially, to inner transformation (ibid.: para. 126).

'Nature' here is very much the nature of the gaze, of aesthetic appreciation. It is not something to be added as a veneer over cultural decay. The nature of the gaze is *not itself confined to externals*, to the thin consciousness of the persona. Man cannot re-enter nature through fashion; through dressing up in the newest exotic clothes. That is to treat natural artifacts (psychic nature) as *wholly* cultural by wrenching them out of true context ('borrowed' feathers and plumes). Such facile attempts to appropriate the natural only serves to reinforce the nature/culture binary to the detriment of suffering human nature and the non-human nature it impacts upon. Instead of applying the shallow resources of the collective consciousness to psychic images like mandalas and dreams of clocks, such gifts need to be taken deeply with the element of man's psychological earthiness.

Jung will return to the dream of the clock. Here it suggests to him psychic phenomena surmounting the laws of space and time (ibid.: para. 135). Curiously, it represents yet another shift in the 'nature' of the psyche. Now it has the potential to go beyond the second linguistic use of 'nature' as denoting inescapable physical laws such as those of space and time, and into something new and speculative. There is an emerging sense that a radical reordering of nature, humanity and the cosmos, is built into Jung's intuition about psychic images and the imagination.

Yet, as if the writing needs to beware of 'inflated' ideas, the text immediately pivots to a pronounced examination of man's 'earthiness' (ibid.: para. 148). Not only is human life weighed down by heredity and bad memories, but this very painful dirt is the unavoidable precondition for psychic growth (ibid.: para. 148). To be truly human is to accept the pathologies one is born into, and to assume moral responsibility for the course of life.

The next few paragraphs dwell on the theme of dealing with one's earth by digging deep into it, rather than by ignoring the stench. For alchemists, the source of the desired item, the lapis, lies underground. For the dreamer, the parents need to be considered as parents and then taken deeper; suffused with depth, metaphor, amplification. So father is not only 'fatherland' in the soil of one's birth. He is also the teacher of traditional wisdom (ibid.: para. 159).

A key dream here is that of reconstructing an ape in a ceremonial courtyard. Jung salutes the dreamer's turn to the depths in taking the ape to signify the bestial, 'lower' than human, in another of his hierarchical treatments of animal–human valuation (ibid.: para. 169). Of course, nothing is a simple hierarchy for Jung. Perhaps it is the trope of artifice in *reconstructing* the ape that enacts an animal–human relationship Jung identifies as 'a Dionysian mystery' (ibid.: para. 169). Certainly, going lower is the only means of going on: it carries within it the route to going higher. The divine unconscious exists below as well as above.

Although there is an unmistakable trace of traditional hierarchies about Jung's treatment of the binary animal/human, as with other cultural dualisms what is fundamental to his thinking is its deconstruction. It is worth remembering here that a large section of *Psychology and Alchemy* is devoted to alchemical unicorn symbolism. Alchemy texts certainly do not situate this 'animal' below the human. The unicorn is where animal and divine, Christ, nature and super-nature, meet in the soul of man. Another way of putting it is to regard the unicorn as the space where the centripetal forces pulling the divine into transcendence get bogged down in (folk legendary) centrifugal immanence.

To return to the dream symbolism, Jung asserts that the transforming substance of alchemy was both common, bestial, despised, *and* of the highest value, divine (ibid.: para. 179). Such flexibility gives both alchemy and analytical psychology its potential for subverting cultural norms and, perhaps even exposing them as contingent. Indeed, like Bakhtin, Jung draws attention to the role of medieval carnival in mitigating the heavy-handed dominance of the Church.

> The medieval carnivals. . . were abolished relatively early. . . Our solution, however, has served to throw the gates of hell wide open.
>
> (ibid.: para. 182)

Of course, where Bakhtin regards Dionysian carnival as heteroglossic undermining of an oppressive centralizing language as social power, Jung has a different cultural emphasis. Christianity has become oppressive *psychologically* because it has banished the Dionysian component of religion. The fact that the main western religion can no longer stabilize society since losing its psychological potency is a *problem*. To Bakhtin it would be a very positive development.

Jung's invaluable sense of alchemy as historically located (and therefore informed by its inner 'other' of Christianity as well as other cultural factors) also indicates an awareness of his 'subjective' formulations as coloured by cultural context. An innately conservative appeal to the order provided by oppositions arranged as a hierarchy, is everywhere countered by his sense of profound, human and cultural *need* for the unconscious as the enemy of such rigidity. Consequently, Jung's emphasis on the spiral, circular and centre is designed to bring both what is despised and what is overvalued into a harmonious whole. It is centripetal in figuring Jung's ideas as coherent and persuasive, yet combines powerfully with the centrifugal. *The condition of culture as centrifugal is built into the centripetal drive.*

Therefore such centripetal elements in the writing will never constellate Bakhtin's (impossible) unitary language because they bring in the vulgar and abject *as necessary*, and secondarily make a priority of what remains unknowable. A particularly fertile image for the self's centralizing tendency is a 'mandala garden' in a dream linked to alchemy's 'rose garden of the philosophers' (ibid.: para. 235). Here is Jung's nature: cultivated into a greater signifying, yet what it signifies retains the wildness of what can never be fully spoken.

A few paragraphs later, Jung finds it necessary to underline the experiential rather than doctrinal quality of his dream analysis by discoursing on the provisional characteristics of his thinking. Even the unconscious is a 'mere postulate' and cannot be defined (ibid.: para. 247). 'Self' is a concept whose domain cannot be measured; it is a term of pragmatic rather than absolute use and cannot even be restricted to the individual psyche (ibid.: para. 247).

Such emphasis on the permeable borders of knowledge is a perfect example of Jung's centripetal centralizing writing being at the same time a centrifugal dispersal of claims to knowledge as (ego) power. It is striking that this discourse of the self takes it beyond the subject/object predication of alchemy as projected individuation. Here Jung joins his alchemists in figuring no division between self and world. The personal is the natural, phenomenal and cosmological.

After such spatial expansiveness, Jung moves back to a sense of history. He rebukes narrower definitions of the psyche as merely reactions to stimulus as a materialistic myth (ibid.: para. 249), and detaches the symbolic value of Christ, as a psychic image from the historical person (ibid.: para. 253). Returning to alchemical nature he offers birds or winged beings such as feathered Mercurius and angels as 'fantasies and intuitive ideas' (ibid.: para. 305). As well as bird, the egg is a significant indication of primal chaos and creativity in the psyche (ibid.: para. 306). Yet such incorporation of natural symbolism is quickly matched by a recall of the world clock and of a discussion of the anima. Colour symbolism gives her a tinge of the vertical. She appears in a blue circle as the height and depth of a man (ibid.: para. 321).

The movement beyond the known and concrete in the psyche cannot be allowed to detach itself from human physical and cultural embodiment. Jung's nature alchemy symbols, for example, birds, share the role with super-nature of winged beings; blue sky refers to the feminine other as spirit above as well as earth below – in a welcome figuring of the anima 'above' her usual place when Jung thinks of space as implying hierarchy. Although it must be admitted that the consignment of the anima to above and below, rather than as partner, is a neat illustration of the displacement of the feminine in a patriarchal worldview.

Jung ends his treatment of dream symbolism by drawing attention to the passions of the individual. A scientific attitude hinders natural healing (ibid.: para. 331). Working with the plasticity of dreams requires the emotional and moral judgement of the artist. 'Nature's' healing powers need a discipline prepared to work in partnership, rather than one that substitutes what Jung regards as 'unnatural' language of rational science for the psyche's native exuberance.

Part III: Religious Ideas in Alchemy: An Historical Survey of Alchemical Ideas

Chapter 1: Basic Concepts of Alchemy

The emphasis in both the title and opening paragraphs of Part III is on the historical identity of alchemy. Ancestor of chemistry, alchemy is also here situated by Jung as the antecedent of analytical psychology. The key shift is to unconscious projection as the means of connecting what alchemists did and what modern analysts try to facilitate (ibid.: para. 332).

In effect, Jung is seeking a genealogy for his psychology so that he can establish the cultural aspect of his creation and simultaneously offer it as valid because it is a modern development of a traditional system of working with symbols. Consequently the comparison with alchemy reinforces Jung's sense of the cultural location of ideas and practices, in its difference, and yet validates his epistemological basis, in its likeness. Jung is never a cultural relativist in the extreme sense that all theory and creativity is explainable as the derived product of a particular historical moment. That would be to essentialize historical contingency as the inner essence of every system. Rather, he regards true knowledge of the psyche as possessed through a dialogical relationship between history (as embodied experience) and the unknowable creative sublime. Just as the archetypal image is contingent to culture yet partakes of the sublime energies of the archetype, so alchemy and analytical psychology are differently located cultural versions of psychic verities – each suitable for, and partly dependent upon, their very different cultures.

One of the aspects that alchemy and analytical psychology share, besides similar working with symbols, is the habit of mythic narrative. In this first chapter, after showing how the four stages become the three of blackening, whitening, and reddening, Jung initiates a narrative sense by looking at the conjoining of white and red. This is often envisaged as the 'chymical wedding' of the red king and white queen (ibid.: para. 334).

Chapter 2: The Psychic Nature of the Alchemical Work

Jung begins by noting that the double face of alchemy in chemistry and symbolic philosophy was, to the alchemist, one. They were unaware of their projections. Therefore embedded in alchemy itself was a notion of language as materially and psychically dynamic. Alchemists believed that the mind had a magical power to affect changes in matter (ibid.: para. 366). Here the practice of making analogies is one of cause and effect where the effect is material (ibid.: para. 377). Similarly, Jung recognizes the force of unconscious fantasy, although he sees it here through his trope of projection:

> The psychologist will find nothing strange in a figure of speech becoming concretized and turning into an hallucination.
>
> (ibid.: para. 353)

Jung returns to his 'difference' by restating that alchemists themselves are in an unwitting state of unconscious projection. Then he resumes analysing the alchemist's conception of mental powers by quoting, for example, the belief that the imagination is an inner star (ibid.: para. 394). Glossing 'star' here as 'quintessence', Jung makes imagination an active physical as well as psychic force for the alchemists (ibid.: para. 394). This enables him to be explicit about their rendering of a psychic domain of the subtle body between mind and matter (ibid.: para. 394). These alchemists anticipate ecocritics in regarding the human psyche as part, not only of the ecosystem, but of the cosmos itself.

Meanwhile, physics makes an entrance in its customary role as Jung's prime imaginative pivot (see Chapter 4). It enables him to step momentarily beyond his 'difference' with alchemy as subject imbued with object via projection, and enter into a meditation on a psychic-physical continuum as an animation of subtle bodies (ibid.: para. 394). Such subtle bodies are the native territory of the Jungian/alchemical symbol in denoting neither the real nor the unreal – always both (ibid.: para. 400).

Chapter 3: The Work

It is at this juncture in the historical exploration that Jung adheres to his own principle with respect to symbols, by stressing that they remain, at least in part, mysterious. Structuring another link between alchemy and analytical psychology, he argues that alchemists did not understand each other's symbols, nor always even their own (ibid.: para. 401). In Bakhtinian terms, heteroglossia is innate in alchemy and practitioners proceed by a deliberate centrifugal strategy: they build an individual 'edifice of ideas' by 'boundless amplification' (ibid.: para. 403).

Here Jung draws attention to the parallels between himself and alchemists by describing his method of working with dreams as amplification until they become intelligible (ibid.: para. 403). What Jung does not elaborate upon is the aesthetic quality to the work of both alchemists and analysts in rhetorically moulding the symbol by integrating it with cultural material. Suggestively however, he does refer to the alchemist here as an 'artist' (ibid.: para. 403).

Jung now moves on to the disputed territory of alchemy's complex relationship with conventional Christianity. Clearly, the narrative of redemption, much featured in the illustrations, is common to both. However, where the Church promises redemption *of* man through the intercession of Christ, alchemists position man *as* the redeemer of a deity hidden in matter (ibid.: para. 420). In preserving a tradition of the divine in the material world, alchemy offers a perspective to modern ecocriticism. To the extent that it becomes (centripetally) warped by Christian notions of the divine (and therefore human) transcendence of matter, then its benefit is mainly to reveal some of the heteroglossia of the supposedly monological Christian worldview. Indeed, if alchemy/Christian intertextual relations are reconfigured dialogically, then the Christian legacy of an uninterrupted mutation of logos from god, to science, to technology, may prove to be more complicated. It is possible that *Psychology and Alchemy* provides just such a dialogical innovation.

Chapter 4: The Prima Materia

Unsurprisingly, the problem of comprehending the core substance of alchemy, the prima materia, is not an absence of definition, but an unstoppable proliferation (ibid.: para. 425) Such is the imaginative range of the heteroglossia, that it even finds space for the far more centripetal qualities of the Christian story, without being wholly overwhelmed by its cultural dominance.

Significantly, Jung says that the 'children' of alchemy are chemistry and philosophical materialism, a result of their projection of their highest cultural value, God, onto matter (ibid.: para. 432). In this sense, alchemy joins Christianity in bequeathing the logos to science and technology. I think that the key element in Jung's analysis here is the use of 'highest'. It betrays the hierarchical dimension to Jung's thinking already noted in his treatment of dreams and alchemy earlier in this chapter. Yet it does not take the addition of Bakhtin to show that hierarchy as something static and ordering is neither Jung's theory nor practice.

Jung has a kind of hierarchical habit – particularly pegged to conservative social tendencies – that does not survive his discussion of the nature of the unconscious. While he reveals alchemists as dialogically affected by Christian hierarchy, he also demonstrates their more defining characteristics of a *refusal to separate out* mind, matter, and the sacred. Alchemy does not seek in matter *the truth* (logos) of a God external to the phenomenal world.

Redemption of the God in matter is achieved through a 'treatment' of the divine as immanent in matter, and not by abstracting a 'truth' about it that is transcendent because it exists as separate and prior to its material incarnation. Alchemy ceases to be efficacious, *Psychology and Alchemy* argues, only when it succumbs to (Christian) separation and divorces material practice from philosophical envisioning (ibid.: para. 332). The Cartesian split of self from world destroys alchemy.

This chapter on the prima materia draws to a close with an increasing emphasis on the role of narrative. Alchemical stories tell of a king's cry for help from a sea, which Jung interprets as a signal from the unconscious, and of the importance of the myth of the hero (ibid.: para. 436–7). Myth and symbols engender and emerge from the interaction of conscious and unconscious potencies. In alchemy these are the architecture of the 'subtle bodies' that conjoin mind, matter and spirit.

Chapter 5: The Lapis-Christ Parallel

It is worth noting that this chapter is not the last in the volume. Focusing upon the most obvious instance of the dialogue between Christianity and alchemy in the equivalence between Christ and the object of the alchemist's quest, Chapter 5 is followed by a final section giving a more multicultural framework to alchemy's heteroglossia.

Jung begins by reiterating the common ground between alchemy and analytical psychology in the practice of active imagination and unconscious intervention in subjectivity through individuation (ibid.: para. 448). He then points out that alchemy was unable to collapse into Christianity because it figured redemption differently. In the Christian ritual, the beneficiary of the mass is the human supplicant (ibid.: para. 451). In alchemical ritual it is the human who is the active redeemer. 'He or she is on a quest for salvation, primarily on behalf of an-Other, trapped in matter (ibid.: para. 451). Both of these mythical stories are brought into a narrative, dialogical relationship by alchemy's figuring of the needy god as the king's son (ibid.: para. 451).

On the one hand, the lapis-Christ parallel was not a mere modern analogy, but rather a species of the alchemical material analogy that Jung described earlier. Alchemists, believing themselves to be good Christians, really did think that their redemptive quest could be contained within the orbit of Christian teaching. The so-called 'parallel' is a 'secret identity' between Christ and the philosopher's 'stone' (ibid.: para. 451).

On the other hand, alchemy could never be completely absorbed into the Christian story because alchemists could not consciously accept that they had taken on the redeeming 'work' of Christ (ibid.: para. 452). Alchemy and Christianity remain discrete and dialogically interconnected. In the course of using a few common symbols, the greater power of the centripetal dynamics of Christianity does infect alchemy with its hierarchical positioning of God as above man and matter (after being 'rescued' from it).

So tensions within alchemy through the proximity of Christian discourse inevitably finally drive it into the logos mode of splitting its philosophy off from its material engagement. As Jung insists, disembodied philosophy and materialist science are its heirs. Yet much of the importance of *Psychology and Alchemy* lies in its ability to present alchemy and Christianity in a dialogical relationship, in which alchemy's heteroglossia is a language for articulating *difference* from Christianity, most crucially on the proper incarnation of humanity in relation to the divine.

On two levels, analytical psychology seeks to occupy the differential space between Christianity and alchemy. As an epistemology, analytical psychology provides the framing trope of projection into matter for alchemy and Christianity alike. As myth, Jung composes 'Answer to Job' (1952/1958, CW11), which pivots Christianity by writing a sequel to the Bible in the very alchemical territory that he has framed in the trope of projection. *Psychology and Alchemy* is therefore quite precisely positing an historical location for an 'Answer to Job' that failed to come into being until now. It needed the cultural developments of the modern world to provide the 'answer' to historical questions of early modern religious conflicts (ibid.: para. 452).

Intriguingly, much of the lapis-Christ chapter shows a growing interest in the vernacular as a cultural position for alchemical modes of thought. Before this, however, there is an extended meditation on the wheel as alchemical figure for the opus: uniting notions of the sun god and of the revolving universe (ibid.: paras. 469–72). It brings to mind the persistence of circulation as an image of the ecosystem.

Jung then links a 'naive' translation of alchemy into the language of the Christian mass with the coming of vernacular speech into Christianity through the Reformation (ibid.: para. 489). He does not examine (as doubtless Bakhtin would) the political narrative, as the centrifugal pressures of alchemy on Christianity coalesce with the tremendous splintering of its centralizing power that produces the Reformation. I have described the Christian-alchemy dialogics as one in which the greater centripetal forces of the established public religion must have been largely responsible for alchemy's fall into separation and modern science. Here Jung merely hints at a reciprocal movement of heteroglossia, in mitigating the hegemony of the singular western Church.

Appropriately, Jung follows a recognition of the effects of medieval vernacular with his own example of a popular tale both coherent with, and comically undermining of, his own analytical psychology in centripetal mode. At some length he relates an anecdote from his youth of a domestic cook who obediently kills a chicken only to report back that it had repented of its sins before the axe fell. When told there will be no heaven for chickens, this proto-ecologist persists in his alchemical perspective on animal nature as not separate from the divine *work* (ibid.: para. 494). Jung comments that the cook's theology is a folklore survival of an alchemical attitude in treating redemption as an inner narrative of nature and matter as well as for man (ibid.: 495).

On the surface, telling this story reinforces Jung's argument and bolsters the position of analytical psychology, construed in a very different culture. On the another level, the 'low' comedy of this tale centrifugally undermines the argument's claim to coherence and signifying power. In effect, the comedy of the cook has a 'carnival-like' dialogical relation to the scientific respectability of the Jung persona. In forming part of the dialogical structuring of analytical psychology, this domestic legend is also a comic burlesque of 'Answer to Job' in bringing alchemy, analytical psychology and Christianity into a series of reciprocal exchanges.

Of course, from an ecological point of view, the repentant chicken is also an example of animism. In its dialogues with the non-human, Jung shows alchemy working with a marginalized animism as part of its role in providing an heteroglossia within, and without, the borders of Christian discourse. With less silencing intent than the executing cook, Jung pursues the centrifugal animism of alchemy texts into the avowedly non-human realm. To put it another way, the animism of texts, referred to by ecocritics, is endorsed and promoted by *Psychology and Alchemy* as numerous quotations of an-Other's voices, and Jung's commentary upon them, constitute an explicit and *animated* dialogue.

Here it is possible to argue that Jung's psychic heteroglossia, headed by the anima herself, is placed in the context of a far older tradition of animism. Jung's writing is a bridge between the animism of texts, the animated psyche and perhaps nature as well. For this deliberate cultivation of textual animism as diversity extends to noticing that alchemy's animism includes the non-human. The Christian chicken is a rare moment of Jung mimicking alchemy. He is consciously broadening the dialogue beyond the human. Unsurprisingly he does this in comic mode, suggesting both Bakhtinian insight into the simultaneously subversive and containing properties of satirical revelry, *and* the ecocritic Joseph W. Meeker's proposition that comedy's accommodation with necessity is closer to the ecosystem's (dialogical) web (see earlier in this chapter).

I would stress here that the Christian cast to alchemy is inherently dialogic. Although it reinforces the dominant narrative and registers its tendency to draw *animation* and spirit away from nature, at the same time, alchemy has a subversive function of inserting more diverse voices. Alchemy promotes a trace of nature animism that (centrifugally) mitigates the

Christian construction of transcendent logos as a monolithic utterance. Its Christian symbolism *through* nature maintains a spiritual valuation of it. The public signifying power of the alchemical symbol (in the Jungian sense of pointing to the unknown), is dialogical because it satisfies the demand of collective consciousness as well as allowing representation of the other. For example, images of the green lion and the virgin preserve for Jung a symbolic resonance (and animism) while apparently submitting to collective norms (ibid.: para. 498).

Concluding the chapter, Jung returns to the history of alchemy. Unfortunately the alchemists were unable to develop their technique with symbols. The practice fell into a long decline until, Jung explains, it was rescued by the advent of analytical psychology (ibid.: para. 502). Indeed, Jung cites a dispirited note from alchemist Michael Maier, whose quest for Mercurius and the phoenix resulted only in the feather that was his pen (ibid.: para. 515). Perhaps Jung's repeated emphasis on the decay of alchemy is a warning that the unconscious must be treated through the cultural institutions of the historical moment and not in spite of them. The alchemical projection into matter ceases to be viable. The quest assumes a new cultural form for modernity.

Chapter 6: Alchemical Symbolism in the History of Religion

The dialogical relation with the alchemists becomes more explicitly multicultural in this final chapter. Characteristically Jung illustrates his argument with an image, here a unicorn, to show that different cultures appreciate the symbol forming capacity of the psyche.

As an icon of cultural diversity, the unicorn is fully participant in the centrifugal-centripetal dynamics of the archetype. The centripetal pole is represented by the common theme of the one horned beast; the centrifugal cultural expression is the almost limitless variety of its incarnations (ibid.: para. 518). Inevitably, the unicorn is one figuration of Mercurius. Jung traces him through Gnosticism, into Indian and Arabic alchemy, and the royal arms of England (ibid.: paras. 527–47). He does not forget the Christian symbolism of the unicorn in European alchemy. Here Jung brings out the dialogical difference in that the alchemy unicorn is both Christian and pagan because alchemy cannot reconcile with the Christian notion of God as wholly good. The Christian view of God as pure goodness is 'against nature' meaning against the reality of the psyche (ibid.: para. 547). By contrast, alchemy's divine animals incarnate the propensity of the divine for evil as well as good (ibid.: para. 547).

From alchemy's pagan otherness, Jung describes the unicorn in Persia, Jewish tradition and in China (ibid.: paras. 535–49). In effect, Jung is trying to establish a dialogical relationship between culture that acknowledges cultural difference (the heteroglossia of plural forms of the image) while establishing a paradigm that would allow reciprocal exchange (the previously structured dialogical relation between alchemy and analytical psychology).

It is important to understand that Jung is *not* attempting a colonizing metanarrative that would subordinate cultural specificity to the supremacy of his own ideas. Rather, alchemical symbols are shown as able to function as *subtle bodies between* discrete cultures, as a means of reciprocal dialogics that is an intrinsic part of their own developing heteroglossia.

Three aspects of Jungian practice in *Psychology and Alchemy* aid this multicultural dialogics. First of all, the emphasis on the unknown psychic as the premises upon which all systems of ideas are built means that analytical psychology can never become the kind of theory that colonizes all knowledge. The attention paid to the importance of 'experience' in working with symbols over and above intellectual grasp of them is the methodological counterpart to this principle.

Second, the volume's exhaustive establishing of both alchemy and analytical psychology as conditioned by their historical location (if not reducible to it) has revealed that neither one can be lifted out of their particular culture as a transcendent authoritative schema to be used anywhere and in any period. Third, *Psychology and Alchemy* structures systems of all kinds as *relational*, both to their heteroglossia within and to 'other' surrounding ideas, cultures and religions. No system, discourse, or mode of psychology is wholly discrete to Jung. Just as the individual psyche is caught up in the collective, so cultural forms are moulded dialogically through contact with each other.

In this way a cultural system is like an ecosystem. The small system of exchanges that maintain the living processes of a wood, for example, require, draw on, and in turn affect all the adjoining parts of the landscape and the larger ecosystem. Although far from an avowed ecocritic, Jung's dialogics puts the individual into the cultural system and the cultural system into the ecosystem. He does this by his animation of the 'other' in dream symbols, and the animation of dialogical alchemy that unites textual animism to the non-human.

Conclusion: Jung and dialogical ecocriticism?

Jung, typically, begins his epilogue by countering the centrifugal dispersion of his previous citation of alchemy across cultures. He pivots his argument to emphasize the centripetal pole of his map of the psyche. The psyche offers 'a central position where many lines converge' (ibid.: para. 556). It is therefore possible to be dialogical across time as well as across cultures. The following chapter of this book will explore Jung's historical sense further.

The epilogue reiterates Jung's careful analysis of the paradoxical intimacy between alchemy and Christianity. Although dialogically engaged, ultimately they were irreconcilable. It takes a new dialogics with a third cultural form of analytical psychology to provide both practice and narrative myth that may re-establish, differently, the symbolic function of Christianity and the redemptive role of alchemy.

Jung is not an ecocritic. He records, without regret, alchemy's representation of the non-human in the interests of the human and not for itself. In *Psychology and Alchemy*, the alchemist's god sleeping in matter is overwhelmingly (although not entirely) interpreted as psychic projection; it is not an overt attempt to restore value to nature by reawakening its *animated* spirits. The alchemists' aim to rescue their god *from* matter is one of their inner correspondences to Christian theology: it is part of their pull towards orthodoxy just as their trace of non-human animism is directed away as part of its differential heteroglossia.

Jung is the organic gardener of the human psyche. Regarding the unconscious as 'nature', it is a nature badly in need of the cultivation provided by individuation. Most importantly, the cultivation of the truly developed person has to work in partnership with 'natural' unconscious potencies and cannot simply replace them with an artificial, wholly cultural, edifice. What proves to be 'against nature' in *Psychology and Alchemy* is the attempt to stamp the psyche with one-sided conscious ideals such as the eternal goodness of the Christian God. Truly, the psyche and the process of individuation is where the nature/culture dualism breaks down and is constantly refigured in the dance of subjectivity. Such a cycle of individuation as culture-nature is part of the ecosystem itself when Jung allows himself to speculate upon the psyche touching matter, or as having a dimension beyond space and time.

As a result, *Psychology and Alchemy* offers two related routes to ecocriticism. There is, for instance, the continuum between psyche and matter, and evident in Jung's evocation of 'subtle reality'. Second, there is Jung's profound dialogical sense that does what Bakhtin does not: it goes beyond the cultural and the human.

Psychology and Alchemy generates Jungian psychology in a reciprocal, dialogical relation with alchemy. By means of this dialogue with alchemy and establishing alchemy's dialogue with Christianity, Jung extends the animism of texts into the animism of the non-human. He achieves a phenomenological continuum through textuality as well. By animating the texts of alchemy through dialogically imbuing them with analytical psychology, Jung excavates a discourse that preserves traces of nature's animism that is 'other' to Christianity.

Jung's adherence to hermeneutics is true to its hermetic roots. His textual *treatment* of alchemy breaks up Christianity as a monological cultural phenomenon and inflects it dialogically in the direction of eco logic. True, the fate of modernity is still within Christian logos, long departed from nature, descended via science into a new Christian incarnation of technology. Yet, as Jung demonstrates here, Christianity and its descendants are not grand narratives or unitary languages of such power that they can completely homogenize global culture.

Bakhtin helpfully contributes the notion that pure unitary language cannot exist in social relations since cultural embodiment inevitably entails pollution by heteroglossia. Jung in turn shows the subversive extent of the heteroglossia within Christianity at a crucial moment in the evolution of the logos of science and technology: that subversion is *Psychology and Alchemy*. Just as Bakhtin's unitary language of power cannot exist due to the nature of human society, so to Jung, the psyche's centralizing dynamics can never be fully expressed: the archetype incarnates into heteroglossia, not into the one language of truth.

It is therefore impossible to allege that technology's logos has completely excluded the natural in the human psyche. Logos may be culturally dominant, but it is not identical to itself in social incarnation. It is a unitary language as abstract ideal rather than its living reality. Technology and logos have heteroglossia too: there needs to be a new mediating discourse; an alchemy bringing to consciousness the 'other' of technology and capitalism. That 'other' of techno-capitalism would frustrate the pernicious fantasy of any logos or cultural form that claims to exist as pure power or purely separated from other cultural systems that are embedded in ecosystems.

Ecocriticism could be such an-other of the dominant logos, to do for techno-capitalism what alchemy did to make Christian cultural dominance dialogic and *animated*. Jung's analytical psychology is not such an eco-criticism. It is rather the 'model' for the construction of an ecocriticism by dialogically *animating* the textual *excess*, the heteroglossia undermining the control of the dominant culture. Jung shows the way for ecocriticism to trouble the boundaries of centralizing powers such as capitalist technology.

And it is more than just a textual demonstration. Jung's 'model' for building ecocriticism offers exciting opportunities for recycling some of its parts. In a vision of cultural difference as interwoven and mutually informing dialogical matrices, Jung's individuating psyche is culture *in* nature. Jung portrays the cultural system as part of an animated ecosystem. Nature's animism survives in alchemy, and is dialogically reinvigorated by analytical psychology's engagement with the animated diversity of its texts. Ecocriticism should find in Jung an invitation to enter the dialogue.

History: Time, space and chronotope
Aion, CW9ii

[I]n contrast to the 'Gothic' striving *upwards* to the heights, [there was what] could be described as a horizontal movement *outwards*, namely the voyages of discovery and the conquest of Nature.

(Jung 1951/1959, CW9ii: para. 150)

We will give the name *chronotope* (literally, 'time space') to the intrinsic connectedness of temporal and spatial relationships that are artistically expressed in literature. This term [space-time] is employed in mathematics and was introduced as part of Einstein's Theory of Relativity. . . Time, as it were, thickens, takes on flesh, becomes artistically visible; likewise space becomes charged and responsive to the movements of time, plot and history.

(Bakhtin 1981: 84)

The image of man is always intrinsically chronotopic.

(Bakhtin 1981: 85)

Our ways of narration are limited to four kinds: epic, comic, detective, social realism. . . psychology would do better to turn directly to literature rather than to use it unaware.

(Hillman 1983: 18)

Introduction

The title of volume nine part two of Jung's *Collected Works, Aion: Researches into the Phenomenology of the Self*, indicates ambition (Jung 1951/1959, CW9ii). Here is an attempt to write 'the self', as psychic totality and the goal of being. Characteristically, Jung's book of the self proves to be a work of history. In this chapter, I plan to show how the creative demands of writing the self as historically oriented result in a stunningly experimental work of imaginative literature. *Aion* is a history of the imagination written *from* a particular time and place. It was written *for* the present and future. Indeed, it is the acknowledgement of both its own, and modernity's understanding of time and space that makes up its radical and provocative charge for the twenty-first century.

To begin is to think about the relationship between the psyche and genres of writing. In *Healing Fiction*, James Hillman eloquently analyses depth psychology's patient case histories as embracing a narrow range of literary genres (Hillman 1983: 3–49). For example, there are epic sagas of vanquishing monsters or the detective story where tracking down just one traumatic event will solve, dissolve, pain. He is particularly critical of the epic because of all the persons in the psyche it favours the developing ego. The ego as hero conquers the psyche in a singleness of vision that requires a great deal of re-education before the resulting wasteland can be healed. Alternatively, the territories of the psychic other produce, and are simultaneously produced by, different genres as the expression of an interior world both diversely inhabited and inhabited by diversity.

Given such an attitude to literary style, the notion of the self as psychic totality suggests a need for maximum literary heterogeneity. Of course, the fantastic variety of all kinds of art throughout human history is precisely that: it adds up to the inexhaustible expressions of the self. On a smaller scale, I'd like to argue that Jung heeded Hillman's warning about literary single-mindedness 30 years previously in writing *Aion* as both history and novel of the self (Jung 1951/1959, CW9ii).

For, in M. M. Bakhtin's relentless exploration of the shifting boundaries of the novel in *The Dialogic Imagination*, that genre is the only one that exists by virtue of its heterogeneity (Bakhtin 1981). No other genre *requires* what Bakhtin calls 'heteroglossia', the linguistic multiplicity of actual social experience. As described in the previous chapter of this book, heteroglossia results from the centrifugal dimension of language as its use in a variety of social settings pluralizes its nature. The centrifugal aspect of language operates in tension with the centripetal pole of linguistic homogeneity, which is the activity of power in any society. With heteroglossia as the base metal of the genre, then linguistic diversity is the defining quality of 'the novel'.

Those other literary genres gathered under what Bakhtin calls 'poetry' adhere more to the centripetal dynamic in language and so aspire to linguistic and generic purity. The purity of the desired 'unitary language' is never ultimately achievable in actual expression because once a literary form enters social use, other varieties of language enter into a dialogue with it. So language and the literary tropes made from it are inherently dialogical between centripetal and centrifugal forces. The consequent pollution of the pure ideal form is heteroglossia.

Social and political power works through the centripetal forces in language dialogics in aiming for a 'pure' language of the church, for example, or of 'high' literature. Epic is Bakhtin's prime example of a poetic genre devoted to creating a society of social elites. As a direct response, the novel is the genre that explicitly tries to dismantle epic aristocratic singleness of vision.

Indeed, Bakhtin is so insistent on a dialogic mutually constituting/ undoing relationship between epic and novel his identification of the latter is idiosyncratic. Where novels are conventionally defined as fictional prose works, Bakhtin's 'novel', which can be in verse or prose, is any writing that celebrates heteroglossia and revels in the dialogic imagination. Not limited to fiction, the novel is to be found everywhere and in every time that dialogic language is promoted as open to the other. The novel opposes heroic epic. My argument in this chapter will be that *Aion*'s portrayal of the self is a novelization of epic discourse. *Aion* is a novel in the Bakhtinian sense and not by conventional definition. Bakhtin's prescriptions will allow the radical historical nature of Jung's work to be appreciated as never before.

Bakhtin, history and the novel

Novel versus epic

In specifically contrasting novel and epic, Bakhtin highlights open-endedness as a characteristic of the former. The novel does not close down ideas or images by presenting them as absolute knowable entities. Instead it demands that the reader engage with the material, not as some distanced past ideal, but as meaning that implicates the reader in its formation. The novel is not complete without the reader and consequently must be open to the infinite variety of possible readers.

Therefore a novel is always in dialogue with the present moment of reading; it is part of the construction of the reader's present reality whether the same text is read in the year 1000 CE, 2000 CE or 3000 CE (Bakhtin 1981: 11). Naturally, such vast distances in temporal location will lend themselves to very different readings. *The novel will be a different work according to when it is read, and who reads it.*

Epic, by contrast, is walled off from the present and this, likewise, is one of its determining features. What Bakhtin calls 'epic distance' is absolute and removes the possibility of 'any open-endedness, indecision, indeterminacy' (ibid.: 15–17). Bakhtin's language of the 'walled off' epic recalls Jung's 'fortress' of psychology that he has to leave in 'Psychology and Literature' (see Chapter 1), in order to traverse the alien territory of other disciplines (Jung 1967/1984: 85). Psychology itself suffers from the peril of too much epic heroism. It too needs to embark upon a quest so that it may establish a dialogue with an-other. Not coincidentally, in Jung's essay that 'other' is literature.

Another of Hillman's case history genres, comedy, challenges Bakhtin's epic. Laughter not only brings down the aristocratic solemnity of hierarchy, but also crucially annihilates distance. If we laugh at a character who presents himself heroically, then we are involved in the writing by the (re)construction of meaning. Time itself is no longer sealed off in an absolute past. Rather the present contacts the past in the parodic bringing 'low' of the gods and heroes. Epic travesties are embryonic novels (ibid.: 21–3).

A further characteristic contrast is that between prophecy and prediction. Epics are strewed with prophecies in a lethally powerful form of *containment*, which sees them completed or answered within the narrative. Prophecy becomes another means of absolute distance alienating the reader from a dialogic engagement with the 'time' of the story (both the time of the setting and the time of the reading). There is no dialogic animation of prophecy, whereas there can be for prediction as a mode of orientation to the future. Prediction points towards social processes rather than away from them.

Of course, as dialogically related literary forms, epic and novel need each other just as the 'ideal' of a unitary language and centripetal drives are necessary to limit heteroglossia into intelligibility. Novels contain within them the centralizing forces of epic heroism and indeed work by the dialogical tension between heroic quest of their 'central' characters and the plural voices of other social languages within the work.

Yet the novel has another significant role. What the novel explicitly does for language and for the reader is to incarnate the need for the future. Bakhtin is very close to Jung in believing that the psyche is future oriented because no individual can be 'completely incarnated into the flesh of existing socio-historical categories' (ibid.: 37). There always remain human possibilities unrealized at any moment in time. These possibilities are distilled into a drive towards the future. Hence the dialogic relationship with language is endless and is basic to consciousness.

Reality, to Bakhtin, is continually constructed and remade through engagement with the social fabric of heteroglossia. A need for the future means being impelled towards an impossible satisfaction of all the human possibilities, known and unknown; what Jung would call the self.

Yet however much Bakhtin and Jung appear to generate similar notions of an (impossible to fully realize) transcendent subject, they do differ significantly in their use of myth. While Jung's dialogical psyche needs myth as a narrative mode of inter-animating the other, Bakhtin regards myth as the stripped down form of epic and hence as 'outside' his dialogic language.

For him, myth is a totalitarian form of language with no (dialogic) gap between the word and reality. It is the literary mode of pre-history when human existence was felt to have no culture that was not subsumed in nature. Myth is part of Bakhtin's metaphysics in positing a time before consciousness was mobilized by the dialogical operation of language. His other metaphysical proposition is, of course, the fundamental dichotomy between centripetal and centrifugal powers in language and culture.

Bakhtin's myth is the aspiration of epic to totality and it is a form of totalitarianism in history. Fortunately, such totalitarianism is impossible to ever completely realize today because language cannot be made non-dialogical and heteroglossia can never be entirely eradicated however coercive the state. Neither Hitler nor Stalin could enact pure myth.

For Jung, on the other hand, myth is the way to totality without totalitarianism because to him it is the enabling spine of his 'novel' not its antithesis. *Aion* rescues myth from epic and converts it into novel. It also rescues history and here Jung and Bakhtin are back together. For both, history means a loss of nature; human events are envisaged in a broad dramatic sweep with nature relegated to background rather than a narrative participant (ibid.: 217). In fact, as Bakhtin analyses, history separates out time and space, not absolutely but dialogically. History is events connected in time and enacted in a space that becomes the natural 'other' to history as human culture.

However, history's loss of nature is also a rejection of human individual life sequences. History as a concept lacks interiority and is measured by different standards of value than that defining an individual existing in time (ibid.: 217). Without nature, human nature is also effaced unless a genre can be found attuned to the individual lifespan as opposed to the nation, tribe, the state, mankind. Therefore to Bakhtin, the historical novel has a large duty of reconciling two types of temporal sequencing: the historical and the personal (ibid.: 217).

Just as the novel must overcome the absolute distance incarnated in epic, so it needs to erode the gap between time as history, and time as subjectively experienced. All these characteristics of the novel place it within the larger category of rhetoric (ibid.: 269). To describe language as dialogic is to regard it as oriented towards an answering word. In effect, language is future-directed, like Jung's psyche. The word never relates to an object or to reality in a singular way. It exists in a spectrum of possible language, in the context of the already spoken, and in anticipation of a variety of possible answers (ibid.: 276–80).

If language is always a dialogue between different, socially engaged *positions*, then it follows that the languages and genres of heteroglossia constitute different *points of view*, different perspectives upon the world:

> For any individual consciousness living in it. . . [a]ll words have the 'taste' of a profession, a genre, a tendency, a party, a particular work, a particular person, a generation, an age group, the day and hour.
>
> (ibid.: 293)

We encounter the social other through using language, and this social other has an historical as well as spatial difference. The relationship between time and space in language and literature is now of urgent concern.

Chronotopes and archetypes

A chronotope is a linguistic unity of time and space, a way of expressing time and space together, or one in terms of the other. An example would be the expression, 'the path of life'.

Like Jung, Bakhtin was seized by the imaginative power of Einstein's theory of relativity in, for him, extending the notion of the indivisibility of time and space, the chronotope, to literature (ibid.: 84). Also for Bakhtin, relativity is not entirely a metaphor. Indeed, like Jung, Bakhtin finds the metaphor collapsing as he comes to regard human life as inextricably tied to space-time.

Bakhtin calls the chronotope a constitutive category of literature and says that he will not consider other cultural versions in his book. However, even if an entire human life was spent in suspended animation, it would still have spatial as well as temporal dimensions, so it is unsurprising that chronotopes are to be found everywhere. Typical chronotopes include the notion of a human life as a 'journey', and that ubiquitous mode of modern employment, the 'meeting'. From political meetings, committees and the meeting in the classroom, to religious worship and epiphany, meeting is a contemporary as well as ancient combination of time and space. Indeed, the relation between life and work as a whole is a chronotope, and there is a special intensity to the chronotope that is a work of art (ibid.: 254). The spatial dimension of art is not only the temporal substance of the artist but in turn is part of the individual time of the reader or viewer. Changing historical time is imbued with space, and the space of the work is a dialogue across time.

Of course, a literary work of art is not merely its own chronotope, but also weaves together typical chronotopes of human measurement such as the 'road', the 'threshold', and the 'encounter' (ibid.: 243–8). Roads, thresholds, encounters, etc. in literature are inevitably metaphoric however concrete and literal their appearance, for they are a marking of *time* as well as *ground* (ibid.: 248).

Such specific examples of chronotopes point to wider cultural arguments about language. For although there are abstract elements to meanings that do not rely upon temporal or spatial factors, once language exists as a sequence of signs, inevitably occupying space and time, it has become itself chronotopic (ibid.: 257–8). Even the abstractions require formal expression in writing, and so the chronotope becomes the engine of meaning in human culture.

If language is chronotopic, then it follows that there are a limitless number of potential chronotopes as figures or images of space-time relations. These chronotopic figures will vary according to culture and history and be expressed in any artistic, scientific, political or social organism. Also chronotopes are not necessarily singular or discrete. A chronotope may contain within it other chronotopes, co-exist dialogically with others, oppose or replace each other and enter into evolving complex relationships (ibid.: 252). For example, a novel with the overall chronotopic form, 'the path of life', may dialogically set up a relation within it between the 'meeting' and the 'threshold' as mutually constructing/destructing forms of encounter.

So how do chronotopes actually work in literature? A chronotope is a space-time relation and it is enacted in themes, images and plot elements in the work. What Bakhtin calls a 'matrix' or sometimes a 'complex' is the system of literary motifs that make up the *underlying* chronotope (ibid.: 199–217). So if chronotopes are fundamental to the structure of literary works, they are, naturally, about narrative. Bakhtin describes them as nodes of narrative and bearers of narrative signifying. Chronotopes are the organizing core of narrative events and so are organs of meaning (ibid.: 250).

Crucially, chronotopes also carry emotions and values. Although time and space can be thought of in an abstract way, a chronotope is an embodiment of space-time, always to be found dialogically inter-animated with its linguistic and social context. Chronotopes are thereby charged with emotions and values. They cannot be thought of apart from them (ibid.: 243).

It is suggestive that Bakhtin's chronotopes, as makers of form expressed through a matrix of images, recall Jung's archetypes realized through archetypal images. The resemblances are striking given the way that Jung, particularly in *Aion*, works towards considering space and time as relative in the unconscious psyche. Archetypes do their work by dialogically interpenetrating space and time; by presenting their fusion in psychic and cultural images.

At first glance an archetype such as 'mother' seems unlike a chronotope. Yet, given that archetypes are functional organizational principles of meaning, 'mother' could be considered as a space-time orientation through the body of the other; one that helps to organize consciousness at the start of life. What is helpful about putting the notion of the chronotope next to that of the archetype, is that thinking of archetypes this way does facilitate a realization of them as content free. It removes the tendency to idealize, essentialize and universalize; so, for example, to regard Jung's description of the animus as the natural state for women in all time, rather than a chronotope of sexuality that only acquires content and meaning when dialogically animated with the other chronotopes making up a particular life.

Nevertheless it must be said that Jung and Bakhtin cannot agree on every aspect of archetypes and chronotopes. Jung tended to describe archetypes as transmitted through biological inheritance, while Bakhtin saw chronotopes as carried by language, literature and folklore. For Jung, the association of archetypes with categories of space and time is an underexplored aspect of his thinking; for Bakhtin it is central and fundamental.

Both thinkers saw powerful images in art as traces of the 'other' (chronotope or archetype). For both, such images carried different *points of view* or *perspectives* upon the world. In looking at art and society as a web of discourses, Bakhtin emphasized the dialogical nature of language, Jung, the dialogical nature of the psyche. However, I say 'emphasized' here, deliberately. Although for Bakhtin the other is a social other and for Jung it is a psychic other, these are contrasting priorities rather than mutually exclusive positions. Jung was well aware that the psychic other is often inflected through the social other and Bakhtin writes of the dialogic *imagination*, admitting the psychic dimension to the dialogic word.

While Jung's biological archetypes are not, and never can be, convertible purely into chronotopes, the parallel development of these two twentieth-century theorists is suggestive. It offers a new perspective on Jung to post-Jungians, in particular to those working without the biological conception of the archetype.

Resemblances between Jung and Bakhtin are important, finally, because both Bakhtin and Jung span the divide between art and science in their preoccupation with space-time. When Bakhtin invokes Einstein and mathematics, and calls the chronotope not quite a metaphor, he is pointing to the collapse of art into science as the relativity of space and time is seen as the very breath of human culture (ibid.: 84). From the other direction, Jung moves science into art by describing a rhetorical psyche (see Chapter 4), and by regarding the making of non-causal connections, or analogies, a psychic 'law', so installing aesthetic thinking as fundamental to psychology (Jung 1951/1959, CW9ii: para. 44). In eroding the distinction between science and art, both Bakhtin and Jung celebrate a dialogical imagination.

Jung's chronotopes in *Aion*

Aion is very self-consciously a spatially organized volume. It opens with a section devoted to the ego and moves topologically, via the shadow and archetypes of gender opposites, the syzygy, outwards to the unknown bounds of the self. A later section of this chapter will consider the structure of *Aion* from the perspective of the reader, who necessarily makes a linear progress through the work. This section looks at the range of archetypal chronotopes as expressions of the psyche embedded in time and space.

Intriguingly, *Aion* moves through a number of religious and historical discourses to arrive, near the end, at the scientific intersection of time and space in the atom. Since Bakhtin shows language to be chronotopic and so potential chronotopic figures are limitless, an exhaustive analysis of every possible chronotope in *Aion* would be prohibitive. Instead, my purpose is to examine Jung's treatment of history and the self by means of chronotopic narrative. To this end, I will concentrate upon the major chronotopes in

Aion, which are: atomic space-time, synchronicity, the history of modernity, Pisces-Christ, alchemy, Gnosticism, astrology, horoscopes, psychology: doctrine as medicine, Aion, and history.

Atomic space-time

Towards the end of *Aion*, Jung evokes what he calls the 'marriage quar-ternio' as a repeated form in religious, historical and finally, scientific thinking (Jung 1951/1959, CW9ii: para. 397). Time as a trinity of past, present and future can only truly be understood through the addition of 'an incommensurable Other' that is space (ibid.: para. 397). Conversely, space as height, width and depth needs an-other in the 'shape' of time.

Jung explicitly parallels this structure to Gnostic quaternities and the more familiar Christian trinity of father, son and spirit. To this trio Jung adds Mary or the devil for 'completion' as a quaternio. In acknowledging the category of space-time as fundamental for the perception of physical reality, as archetypal, Jung comes very close to identifying archetypes with chronotopes:

> The space-time quaternio is the archetypal *sine qua non* for any apprehension of the physical world – indeed, the very possibility of apprehending it.
>
> (ibid.: para. 398)

If archetypes are a way of apprehending a space-time relation, then Jung is able to link his psychology to the thinking of particle physics. He makes an analogy between the archetypal rejuvenation of the self and 'the carbon-nitrogen cycle in the sun' (ibid.: para. 411). Jung argues extensively that psyche and matter must touch and interconnect because matter produces psyche and psyche moves matter (ibid.: para. 413).

However, Jung is not suggesting that the atomic space-time quaternio or chronotope is the governing trope of *Aion*. It does not overarch the other chronotopes because Jung is not claiming that atomic space-time is the fundamental truth upon which religious and cultural (chronotopic) dis-courses weave metaphors. Atomic scientific materialism is not the ultimate truth for Jung. Culture and history are therefore not to be thought of as successive mystified attempts to grasp at truth, that finally result in the production of rational science and its 'discovery' of matter and atoms as the root of reality.

Rather, *Aion* demonstrates that the atomic space-time chronotope is woven dialogically into larger chronotopic narratives as *mutually* gener-ating discourses. Scientific materialism is a development out of a matrix of scientific and religious framing narratives, and not an 'objective' practice that is independent of the languages that have dialogically produced it.

Effectively, Jung's self-conscious deployment of chronotopes such as space-time is the narrative structure of *Aion*: Jung's chronotopes serve to position atomic science as *discourse* in a web of inter-animating narratives. So the atomic space-time quaternio is featured as merely one of many fundamentally chronotopic archetypal structures that are repeated in different dress throughout history. The reason that modernity is wedded to the matter of atoms has everything to do with the development of earlier chronotopic discourses.

Before turning to the chronotope of synchronicity, it is worth noting Jung's careful treatment of the way individuals and cultures join together narratives into larger discourses. In effect, Jung offers three mechanisms for amplification as the way meaning is generated by moving from a symbol or an image, to larger myths and cultural forms. Amplification works either by projection of unconscious contents upon the outer world, or by making analogies, or by a strategy of choosing to read in a particular way (ibid.: para. 219).

Jung is stressing here that 'meaning' or even 'truth' is a psychic construct and, moreover, that he regards making meaningful connections as intrinsically human activities. Connecting up different cultural forms and historical events by analogies may not be scientific in the rationalist sense, but Jung in *Aion* shows such a scientific paradigm to be the *product* of a particular history. It is a paradigm incompatible with his beliefs about the psyche, if it is regarded as the measure for his thinking.

Synchronicity

As a consequence of seeing rational science as reflecting only part of human nature rather than able to account for all of it, Jung presents the chronotope of synchronicity. Most significantly, it acts as a kind of reading strategy for *Aion*:

> [W]e must supplement our time-conditioned thinking by the principle of correspondence or, as I have called it, *synchronicity*.
>
> (ibid.: para. 409)

Sometimes expressed as meaningful coincidence across time and space, synchronicity is Jung's formulation of his constant need to assert an aesthetic attitude to reality as no less 'true' and 'necessary' than the scientific one of causality. It is a kind of condensation of his three motors of amplification: projection, analogy making, reading strategy of choosing meaning – into the proposition that mechanical causation is only one aspect of the flow of events.

Roderick Main, in *The Rupture of Time: Synchronicity and Jung's Critique of Modern Western Culture*, provides a comprehensive analysis of Jung's development of synchronicity and its importance to the whole of his thinking (Main 2004). He makes a powerful and cogent case for understanding the difficulties and inconsistencies in Jung's writing on synchronicity as occasioned by his paramount desire to preserve a connection between the domains of science and religion. My far more speculative proposition is to suggest its rhetorical function, which places synchronicity as also an aesthetic attitude. Chapter 7 of this book will apply synchronistic aesthetics further to the topic of gender and culture.

Synchronicity connects events stemming from the unconscious to the wider world in ways that cannot be rationally accounted for, such as a significant dream or a chance meeting that meets a secret need. It is a way of reading reality non-rationally and symbolically, in ways traditionally assigned to the making of art. So synchronicity treats time and spaces as aesthetic components of momentary artistic wholes. It is possible, therefore, to argue that synchronicity is reality in aesthetic (non-rational) mode, or that it represents the human mind 'reading' or 'composing' acausal events into art without being entirely aware of so doing.

Most importantly, synchronicity is a way of *writing*. It 'writes' forms of wholeness or totality without totalitarianism, because of the large role played by the irrational, hence unpredictable and uncontrollable. Synchronicity posits a totality that is fluid, in part unknowable, and to be grasped only aesthetically and momentarily. Myth is the characteristic narrative for organizing synchronistic moments of perception into meaning. Therefore Jung's myths also work as chronotopes.

It is time to look at the chronotopic myth that has produced scientific materialism and modernity.

History of modernity chronotope

[I]n contrast to the 'Gothic' striving *upwards* to the heights, [there was what] could be described as a horizontal movement *outwards*, namely the voyages of discovery and the conquest of Nature.

(ibid.: para. 150)

Aion portrays western modernity's progress as a chronotope of colonial and material *expansion*. Time and space are united in a narrative of political domination and scientific experimentation. Most importantly, Jung links the materialist western chronotope with earlier chronotopic narratives of religious history. The ethereal towers of Gothic architecture are a material dimension to an age's preoccupation with transcendence. A reaction sets in, first with alchemy (see Chapter 5), and then alchemy's turn to matter produces materialist science as both a logical consequence and by bestowing divine powers on matter (ibid.: para. 406). Effectively, alchemy's concentration on the god sleeping in matter becomes matter as god, the only true reality to be investigated. Therefore, far from representing an escape from religion, modernity's fond belief in the atomic chronotope as the underlying truth of existence is yet another twist of religious sensibility.

And the deification of matter extends a dark claw into political modernity, according to Jung. 'Voyages of discovery' are a bland reference to the development of colonialism, but Jung is forthright about the evils of his own Europe of modern slavery and labour camps (ibid.: paras. 273, 368). The devil that Christianity, Jung alleges, refused to take seriously, resurfaces in modernity as the dark aspect of materialism's religious energy (ibid.: para. 235). Modernity's chronotope is a conscious spatialization of time in a rhetoric of conquest; the conquest of the Earth and the conquest of Nature in rationalist science that claims to 'know' with all the exhaustive confidence of the heroic ego.

Modernity reinstates epic as the heroic engine of the pursuit of power (see Chapter 7 for more on the ego-hero of culture). It even penetrates the citizen in both the development of individualism itself, in the priority given to reason, and in all the cultural devices for strengthening ego expansion at the expense of the other. To counter the dark gods of materialism, Jung tries to provide a chronotopic narrative to undermine the contemporary illusion that the current state of the world and its materialist beliefs are necessary and true. It is the mission of *Aion* to take science, politics and cultural norms out of the realm of the self-evident 'given' and to resituate it as discourse (in his terms mythically structured). *Aion*'s chronotopes unite religion, history and science, in a grand project to remake modernity; to offer a dialogue of salvation.

The Pisces-Christ chronotope

A large part of *Aion* is devoted to the exploration of fish symbolism and its long association with Christ. Jung is at pains to point out that Christianity coincides with the astrological aeon of Pisces, usually represented by twin fishes. Christ was born at the very end of the aeon of Aries, and so images of shepherds and sheep gather around him. He inaugurates a Christian era dominated by an underplayed dualism. Jung believes that the dark twin or the devil is never sufficiently integrated into Christian theology and so around halfway through the Piscean period, about the year 1000 CE, instability sets in with passionate new heresies.

Such an embrace of religious extremism leads eventually to schism and Protestantism, the flowering of alchemy, and the turn from Gothic heights to horizontal expansion into colonialism, and scientific materialism. The Christian west arrives at the end of the Pisces aeon in thoroughly anti-Christian mood (the dominance of the dark twin) as witnessed by the Nazis' assertion of pagan symbols.

Particularly significant in the Pisces-Christ narrative is that it is more than a myth for western history. As an astrological symbol, Pisces is a spatial as well as temporal form. The linking of Pisces with Christ implicates the cosmos in the man and the man in the cosmos: each is enabled to stand for the other (ibid.: para. 177).

Christ as a spatial category is already to be found in the Gospel parables where he refers to symbols for the kingdom of God such as the grain of mustard seed, the hidden treasure, the pearl of great price (ibid.: para. 346). Jung argues that the saviour and his kingdom are identical in meaning (ibid.: para. 346).

So Jung is deliberately casting the Christian story as a chronotope where the time of Christ, his life story and then that of his Church, is simultaneously manifest spatially in symbols. Space is hereby made dynamic and fluid since the grain of mustard seed is God's kingdom and the starry cosmos speaks of one lifespan.

Moreover this particular chronotope is a form of history since the whole orientation of *Aion* is to regard the Christian era as a time-contained structure underpinning and motivating historical change. As Pisces-Christ dialogically engages with the chronotope of the history of modernity, the chronotopes also participate in present realities. So *Aion* opens itself to the time of its reader. Whatever the epic striving within modernity, Jung is writing a novel in the Bakhtinian sense.

Naturally the characteristic structuring within the Pisces-Christ chronotope is synchronistic rather than causal. Jung refuses to accept that Christian enthusiasm for fish symbolism is *derived* from study of the signs of the Zodiac (ibid.: para. 177). Rather the psyche spontaneously produces fish symbolism in a way that suggests a relationship of star patterns to human culture beyond what is rationally known of the interpenetration of time and space.

Alchemy chronotope

As described in Chapter 5, alchemy has a dialogical relationship to Christianity since it both concentrates upon what Christianity explicitly excludes, in the divine status of matter, while being itself deeply influenced in its material theology by the Christian narrative. *Aion* stresses the chronotopic nature of alchemy in its realization of an interior microcosm matching astrological thinking about the cosmos (ibid.: para. 251). Alchemy too is a mobilization of space beyond the inert. In investigating space as matter, alchemy materialized the psyche through projection. A materialized psyche is conceived necessarily as spatial, perhaps sponsoring the topological metaphors of contemporary psychology. Yet the psyche is inevitably temporal as well as spatial, expressed most strikingly here as alchemy as the *mother* of materialist science (ibid.: para. 368).

'Mother alchemy' is a fascinating narrative construction because it recalls the excluded fourth of the Christian trinity: the mother of God and the devil. Alchemy as mother represents alchemy's marginality *vis-à-vis* Christianity as both inside, and that which has to be excluded in order to formulate (masculine) transcendence. In effect, mother alchemy is Christianity's other: its abject.

Alchemy is the chronotopic mother who sought to nurture as one, both religion and science. In Oedipal terms she is a challenge to masculine transcendence, whether in the form of the Christian God or in 'his' resurrected descendants of Enlightenment science and contemporary technology (see Chapter 5).

Astrology and horoscopes as Gnostic chronotopes

Alchemy is joined by Gnosticism in *Aion* as another parallel intersecting discourse with Christianity. Gnosticism appeals here because of its portrayal of a dark ignorance within the divine. Space precludes elaboration of Gnostic mythology in this book. I refer readers to Robert Segal's excellent *The Gnostic Jung* (Segal 1992) and Paul Bishop's scholarly commentary on 'Answer to Job' (Bishop 2002). It is unnecessary to deviate into Gnostic narratives here since my purpose is to examine the way *Aion* weaves the dialogical encounters of different religious discourses into its own 'novel' whole. *Aion* is both itself a work of *discovery*, a commentary, and most crucially of *construction*, a creative work.

Therefore Gnosticism, like alchemy, takes on some of the darkness downplayed by Christianity, in its ignorant demiurge; a divine being unaware of greater powers. It is also used to build Jung's chronotope of alchemy's profound mutation into the myth of modernity. Jung explains that alchemy as 'mother' of modern science enabled its exploration of the dark side of matter (ibid.: para. 368). Such an evolution in discourse is a reoccurrence of the Gnostic myth of Nous, who was so transfixed by his reflection in the depths that he dropped down and was devoured by Physis (ibid.: para. 368).

Astrology and the making of horoscopes are also acknowledged by Jung as chronotopic practices in their own right as well as contributing to Gnosticism and the Pisces-Christ narrative. This points to the creative tension in *Aion*, mentioned above: that between *discovery* of chronotopes in historical culture, and of Jung *constructing* them out of his own dynamic readings. Of course, 'discovery' and 'construction' are themselves dialogically implicated. The 'novel' or new chronotopes that Jung puts forward of Pisces-Christ, doctrine as medicine, Aion, and 'his' idiosyncratic history, are generated out of close readings of cultural material.

Jung presents his overall chronotopic history in *Aion* as the latest emerging myth in a series of typological versions of the human psyche (see Chapter 2 for Jung's 'radical typology'). *Aion* is an historical novel that problematizes the distinction between history's claim to 'discover' and art's claim to 'create'.

Both astrology and horoscopes are maps of time in space and space in time. Intriguingly, when discussing horoscopes Jung stresses its spatial aspect in treating it as a planetary map that works for the individual psyche (ibid.: para. 212). Conversely, astrology is highlighted as a mapping of time in the Piscean identification with Christian history and in identifying cosmogonic myths with the dawning of consciousness (ibid.: para. 230). From an appreciation of 'discovered' material in astrology and horoscopes as cultural discourses of the psyche, it is now worth turning to the 'creative' end of the continuum in the recasting of Jung's own analytical psychology as chronotope.

Doctrine as medicine chronotope

The entire drive of the *Aion* novel is to reposition Jungian psychology as a chronotopic myth. It achieves this by dialogically presenting it as structured with, and through, the other chronotopes of the 'history of modernity', Pisces-Christ, etc. Consequently Jungian psychology is presented as a form localized in the time and space of western secular modernity. It is not a grand overarching theory, nor a truth that underlies all the metaphorical elaborations of Christianity and Gnosticism, etc.

Like the presentation of scientific materialism, Jungian psychology is shown as a myth contingent upon a particular history and, in his opinion, as the product of specific mythological narratives that inform history. Unlike scientific materialism, it is his own construction.

Jungian psychology is chronotopic because it explicitly treats the psyche as a node of space-time: a person inhabits a particular social and cultural space, has a unique personal history, is temporally implicated in larger histories. It is also overtly chronotopic in being presented as the product of a specific space of western secular culture at a unique historical moment. Jung offers his psychology as what cultural theorists call 'discourse', or what he calls myth – one without essentialist, universalist or foundational pretensions.

Most importantly, the Jungian psychology chronotope is medicinal. It is a treatment for the toxic extremities of the chronotope of the history of modernity and *as such* is part of the larger chronotopic structuring of Jung's understanding of history. Hence, like Christianity and alchemy before it, Jungian psychology aspires to heal the soul. The narratives of Jungian psychology do more than describe the need for healing; ideally, they enact it (ibid.: para. 249).

Of course, the requirement for a psychology to become a chronotopic myth leads to issues with language. After all, the excessive reliance upon rational concepts is part of the poison of modernity. Conventional scientific language is that which needs to be augmented. Almost any science can be pursued 'with the intellect alone except psychology' (ibid.: para. 61). Here

Jung is characteristically expanding the domain of his science to accommodate 'value-feeling' or non-rational, religious and aesthetic practices (ibid.: para. 61).

If it is through value-feeling that a person comes to have a true sense of reality, then like Bakhtin's chronotopes, writing with sensitivity to the presence of archetypes is bound up with emotions and values. Therefore, Jung argues, children need fairy tales, and adults need religious ideas in order to engage with the irrational parts of the mind (ibid.: para. 259).

So it is unsurprising to find the anima described in transcendent poetry of 'mystic awe. . . the star crowned woman whom the dragon pursues' (ibid.: para. 22). Poetic treatments of the anima are demonstrations of 'affect' as an intrinsic element in psychic reality. The mythical anima and animus are neither 'real' nor 'unreal': they are psychic instances of irrepresentable factors.

Of course, in *Aion* the best demonstration of the Jungian psychology chronotope is the idea of the self as enacted in the image of Christ. For the Christ image functions both to signify and generate wholeness in spatial dimensions as well as temporal. Indeed, Jung argues that he represents three kinds of time. He is first personal time in that as a real historical being he lived a personal life. Second, he is time as prediction since he came to fulfil oracles. Finally, he is time as eternity since he is one with the divine (ibid.: para. 148). So when Jung suggests that it is reasonable to describe the call of the self archetype as the 'will of God', the psyche is posited as multidimensional, needing non-rational as well as rational notions of space-time (ibid.: para. 50).

In effect, *Aion* provides three characteristics of Jungian psychology as chronotope. First, his dividing up of time and space relations enacts a chronotopic 'quaternity'. Time in three ways is personal (ordinary, everyday experience), is predicted (somehow revealing an underlying order), and is eternity (pertaining to lasting things beyond an individual life). This trinity is joined by its absolute other – space, which is indispensable to its realization. A spatial dimension to time will enable its multiplicity in any key image or event to be psychically absorbed if not rationally understood. Synchronicity is, of course, the Jungian method of aesthetic (affect-laden) reading, which holds the chronotopic Jungian quaternio in his psycho-therapeutic understanding of human existence.

The second chronotopic characteristic of Jungian psychology is the representational dimension of the first. Religious, poetic and mythological discourse is *necessary* to engage with, and live out, the quaternity of the three types of time united through space. Such language is not an essentialist truth about any one point of the quaternity so it is not a religion in aspiring to be an exact verbal equivalence to the divine. It is not a colonial fantasy either, in purporting to wholly represent space in an act of verbal conquest. Rather, Jung's religious, poetic and mythological language is a discourse in four dimensions: it attempts to be a vehicle for psychic reality of an individual in dialogue with the cosmos.

So Jungian psychology as chronotope is *a particular kind of writing* for which Jung uses the term 'symbol' and rejects 'nothing but' language (ibid.: para. 279). Symbols point to what is not yet known or knowable while 'nothing but' language is the triumph of rational illusions that deep truths can be completely exposed in consciousness. Christianity's creed is supposed to offer a 'symbolum' yet has become too focused upon rationality (ibid.: 270).

So the third characteristic of Jungian psychology as chronotope is that it adopts the role of symbolum vacated by modern Christianity. For if the psychology is itself a symbol, then the Jungian chronotope is itself a healing act; it is a doctrine as medicine: a system of ideas and images that itself is healing:

> Thus the doctrine. . . is at the same time the instrument whereby the object of the doctrine or theory can be freed from its imprisonment in the body.
>
> (ibid.: para. 249)

The healing efficacy of the discourse – for its right time and place – is germane to all the chronotopes of *Aion*. Unsurprisingly, it becomes a defining characteristic of Jungian psychology, as it is the energizing purpose behind its chronotopic quaternity.

The Aion chronotope

In *Aion* Jung devotes very little space to explaining the work's title. Nevertheless it provides a chronotopic image for the whole volume. While the opening line of the foreword informs the reader that 'Aion' is the Greek for 'aeon', so signifying immensely long periods of time, the term is only noticeable later when it recurs in personified form (ibid.: ix). In the section on Gnostic symbols for the self, Aeon makes an appearance as a god:

> [T]he ageless Aeon, eternally young, male and female, who contains everything in himself and is [himself] contained by nothing.
>
> (ibid.: para. 298)

Like *Psychology and Alchemy* (see Chapter 5), *Aion* draws upon quotation as the voices of the 'other' in the text. Appropriately here, Jung is demonstrating his argument about religious discourse embodying the psyche as chronotope-quaternio. For Aeon is not just the self experienced as god by the Gnostics. Edward F. Edinger, in his detailed analysis of the work, shows that an aeon can also stand for a human lifespan (Edinger 1996: 15–17). This is self as eternity witnessed within human temporal life. In the everyday sense of an aeon as an enormous expanse of time, the title refers to the Christian aeon under the astrological sign of Pisces, now drawing to a close.

The Aion chronotope is therefore another quaternio consisting of human life, Christian-Piscean history, and the self as god of time, joined to the fourth spatial dimension. Human life unites time and space. Christian history is also its material, spatial culture and the self as an icon of eternity requires spatial thinking. Using the Greek word 'aion' ensures that aeon is not misread as simply a long time. It also substantiates Jung's sense of many cultures as other to each other. 'Aion' stands for his chronotope as one located in, and dialogically engaged with, the chronotopes of the Christian era.

'Aion' therefore signifies that the dialogic psyche is one of dialogic time or, more precisely, a dialogic quaternio of time as personal, as predicted, as eternal, realized through space. The work *Aion* is also, in the Bakhtinian sense, a novel, since it dialogically implicates the reader. Just as aeon is time as personal and collective, so Aion is a literary chronotopic figure within Jung's argument and is also *Aion,* the entire work. As symbol (Jung's language) and novel (Bakhtin's), *Aion* cannot be wholly understood, for that would be to bely its essence by translating it into rational terms. Rather, *Aion* offers chronotopic images in a reciprocal, dialogical structuring of a relationship with the reader. Above all, it is a novel designed to produce a chronotope of history.

The chronotope of history

Jung ends *Aion* on what might appear at first glance to be an unnecessary note of modesty with words like 'sketch', 'hypothesis', and even 'the risk of making a mistake' (ibid.: para. 429). The motif of his ideas as an 'hypothesis' runs throughout all his writing and is fundamental to his position that not only is part of the psyche not subject to rational knowledge, but also that personal and cultural constraints condition what can be asserted at any one moment. Therefore writing as 'open' to argument and modification is a founding principle. It is a consequence of a belief in, and is an enactment of, the dialogical psyche.

From the point of view of Bakhtin, Jung's 'open' text places his oeuvre as novel rather than epic. In particular, *Aion* is an historical novel because it restores the time of history to the time of the individual reader. Nevertheless, *Aion* is far more ambitious than most historical novels as Bakhtin would conceive them. Jung's surpasses Bakhtin's formulations in producing an historical novel as a *model* for thinking historically. He produces what Bakhtin could not imagine being actualized: a totality without totalitarianism.

What do I mean by this? To Bakhtin the novel is the one literary form that celebrates multiple voices and otherness in embracing the different points of view incarnated in the heteroglossia. If it were possible to overcome the dialogical structuring of language, then totalitarianism would result as there would be literally no space or time for the other. Such a time of totality for Bakhtin is one where myth structures society as bound in a continuum with nature. As the one literary form that delights in heteroglossia, the novel has a political dimension in counteracting the stratification of society in social classes. The novel's virtue is that it mixes things up without homogenizing them.

Jung, on the other hand, is able to use myth dialogically as the narrative mode of his psyche. Therefore for him, totality is not confined to the remote past; although like Bakhtin Jung asserts that totality cannot be fully realized in language. Jung makes myth work as the shaping narrative of his 'novels', whereas Bakhtin sees myth in novels as an archaic remnant of little value. Essentially, Bakhtin is hampered by an allegorical view of myth as producing 'fixed' truths while Jung manages to see it as radical typology, as an engine of narrative without closure or foundational pretensions (see Chapter 2). Therefore for Jung, myth incarnates totality without totalitarianism as it explicitly structures a space for the unknown, unknowable 'other' as part of the narrative.

Aion is therefore history as totality, and the reason that it is not totalitarian is in its use of mythic chronotopes. By dialogically inter-animating chronotopes such as alchemy, Pisces-Christ, Gnosticism, to produce Jungian psychology as chronotopic and under the chronotopic image of 'Aion', Jung locates his mythical narrative *in history and as history*.

It is history as totality because it unites the discourses of the psychic past with images of the psychic present (that are also future-oriented). In so doing, *Aion* creates a new discourse (in Jung's language – a myth) of the psychic present-in-touch-with-psychic-past-and future. Jungian writing becomes a fourfold affective embrace of time and space. What totality without totalitarianism means, then, is a sense of wholeness predicated upon the contingent moment.

Aion is history as a map of the psyche in four dimensions of space-time. It is an attempt to offer history as a form of psychic energy. The rest of this chapter will look more closely at the texture of this ambitious chronotopic tapestry.

Aion: Researches into the Phenomenology of the Self (Jung 1951/1959, CW9ii)

Chapters 1, 2, 3: The Ego, The Shadow, The Syzygy: Anima and Animus

Aion has a simpler structure than most volumes in the *Collected Works* with 15 chapters, the last one merely headed 'Conclusion'. As previously noted, it is spatially arranged, beginning with the ego and moving 'outwards' to the esoteric images of the boundless self. Prefacing the chapters is a fore-word that stresses the psychological 'attitude' of the work. Neither religious confession nor tract, *Aion* is to seek 'forerunners' of archetypal images of wholeness in history and explicitly view them from the perspective of today's conscious needs (ibid.: para. x). This is to be an understanding of the past rooted in the present.

The two chapters following on the ego and the shadow reveal a charac-teristic combination of language. Jung moves from succinct summary of the complexities of the ego to the insistence that such psychic theorizing can be no more than an hypothesis. Then he enters the more demonic register in the intimations of the shadow (ibid.: paras. 3–9). The shift into mythical language is explained as standing for psychic realities beyond the personal.

Similarly for Chapter 3 on the syzygy, in weaving the heightened register of divine myth with explanatory prose, Jung performs in writing his argument that the archetypal psyche is a realm of emotion, fantasy and narrative, which can be experienced, while not being wholly comprehensible to scientific reason. Anima and animus are fatal gods, initiators of tragedy and wielders of fate (ibid.: para. 41). They are linked to two psychic qualities since Jung aligns anima with Eros as emotion, connectedness and relationship, and animus with Logos as reason, discrimination and cogni-tion (ibid.: para. 29).

Unfortunately, although Jung states that he does not want to give too fixed an account of Eros and Logos, he suggests unhelpfully that women's consciousness is Eros-oriented while masculine consciousness possesses the valued capacities of reason and discrimination (ibid.: para. 29). Naturally the unconscious of each gender takes on the inferior function so female 'rationality' is consigned to the irrational animus. Ironically, Jung puts himself in a position of a man faced with an animus-ridden woman and reveals the *male* potentiality for extreme irrationality.

> Often the man has the feeling – and he is not altogether wrong – that only seduction or a beating or a rape would have the necessary power of persuasion.
>
> (ibid.: para. 29)

I have dealt at length with Jung's treatment of gender in Chapter 3, and Chapter 7 will consider Eros and Logos. Here it is important to remember that *Aion* is all about context. Jung's cross comment, undeniably misogyn-istic, is overtly the speech of an-other – the man who is not altogether wrong. It also reveals the perilous aspect of the embrace of rhetoric, the writing for 'affect' as well as logical argument. It is worth noting that the comment is about a man's 'feeling' and not about his action. It is about the extremities of emotion in lived experience. As rhetoric it needs to be considered in the repeated context that Jung is writing an 'hypothesis', is acknowledging the subjective element, as he starts to build a culturally situated chronotopic myth.

More consequential than the emotive comment on male irrationality – Jung does not say that the man is *right* to 'persuade' the woman in that way – is the conceptual gendering of Eros and Logos. The fact that Jung insists in the very act of expressing this position that these concepts are merely 'aids' and will go on to undermine the universal validity of any psychological 'concepts', needs to be borne in mind. *Aion* is an historical novel first: it does violence to its rhetorical nature to petrify it into a succession of psychic 'facts'.

Chapter 3 ends with the first hint of the coming of the quaternio as anima and animus are joined by their expanded 'self'-implicated forms: the wise old man and the chthonic mother (ibid.: para. 42).

Chapter 4: The Self

Chapter 4 on the self is the last before the turn to history. Taking the themes established in the earlier chapters, of the limitations of rational language, the imperative to respond intuitively and experientially to the psyche, and the function of religion and myth in channelling the irrational, it opens the question of the desire for wholeness, and its correspondingly overwhelming claims upon the subject. Treating the experience of the self as 'the will of God' is appropriate psychologically and does not require metaphysical belief (ibid.: para. 50). To live with the self is to live with history understood as the psychic interior of past cultures. Since the self is a function of unity, totality and highest values, its images cannot be distinguished from the god-image (ibid.: para. 60).

Rhetorical emphasis on self as the most potent energy-image in the psyche is accompanied by a further warning against conceptual language as truth-bearer. Concepts are 'intellectual counters', in a reference that chimes with the high mythical tone in conjuring up an image of the gods dicing for human fates (ibid.: para. 60). In fact, the intellect is supreme for all sciences except psychology, which demands additionally 'feeling-tone', 'values' and 'affect' (ibid.: para. 61). Concepts have meaning and use only insofar as they stand for 'experience' that cannot otherwise be communicated to readers (ibid.: para. 63).

Another referential dimension enters this chapter in the integration of contemporary events. The unconscious world of monsters became terrifyingly literalized in Nazi Germany (ibid.: para. 67). *Aion* is a history of the present; a novel that aims to install history as a component of psychic being within a moral framework.

Chapter 5: Christ, a Symbol of the Self

Christianity features in *Aion* as the narrative structuring of an historical era. A chronotope, Christianity is a portrayal of a culture evolving through time and constructing material, intellectual, social and psychic entities in space. Indicatively, the huge attention given to Christianity in *Aion* begins with a portrayal of the Christian chronotope in grave crisis with the fears of mass violence. This is history as a direct intervention into the present, for the 'Luciferian' development of science and the destruction of the Second World War all too obviously recall the Christian myth of apocalypse (ibid.: para. 68).

Aion will convert that 'comparison' into mythical narrative, fortunately developing a redemption myth (in Jung's own chronotope) for the modern world (see my Chapter 2).

With great urgency, we are given a sketch of the linking chronotopes of *Aion*: the mystic marriage of Christ and Church becomes the alchemical wedding of hermeticism, and finally the chemical combinations of post-Enlightenment science (ibid.: para. 72).

Also quickly, the core problem of the Christian era is outlined, the 'problem' that is the drive behind the chronotopic mythmaking, which is of Christ and God being overidentified with the good and light to the exclusion of the evil and dark (ibid.: para. 74). If Lucifer is expelled from heaven then he makes mischief on Earth. Here too, *Aion* embraces a spatial understanding of history as the Gothic striving for spiritual heights is converted into scientific and political expansion horizontally (ibid.: para. 78). The Luciferian present is marked by concentration camps; a demonstration of the imperative of addressing concrete embodiments of evil at large today (ibid.: paras. 96–8).

Psychology offers the perspective of good and evil as opposite energies, knowable not as absolute essences, but in relationships and social functioning (ibid.: para. 97–8). God and evil constellate each other. The Christian impulse to expunge the reality of evil from its theology is a cultural extension of the human moral impulse to give increased energy to good and decrease the bad (ibid.: para. 98).

Fortunately for the possibility of psychic health, Christianity has always possessed marginalized discourses acknowledging the reality of the demonic. For example, a 'natural' expression can be found in Gnostic-Christian Clementine Homilies, which states that good and evil are the right and left hands of God (ibid.: para. 99). From this image of divine morality presented as human anatomy, it is easy to reverse the representation strategy and discuss the human figure of Christ as a sign of the unconscious self. Christ as self embodies time as multidimensional. As an historical person Christ lived a human lifetime; as an aspect of God he is timeless and eternal (ibid.: para. 116). Christ is therefore both the essence of human individuality and also a boundless divine being. Yet, the collision of Christ and self is an imperfect fit. For Christ is wholly good and the self must encompass all human possibilities; the highest is compensated by the lowest and most dark (ibid.: para. 116).

History and psychology are now united in a single narrative chronotope. Although *Aion* will continue to struggle with the role of darkness, much of its narrative proliferation is devoted to seeking out the repressed history of the dark other in the marginalized discourses of astrology, alchemy and Gnosticism. Just as a psyche emphasizing the good will undergo an enforced encounter with the power of evil, so the cultural striving for the light invokes the prince of darkness.

In the weaving of chronotopic myth from religious culture to psychology, there can be faintly heard a narrative answer to the awesome finality of apocalypse. *The texture of Jung's writing is itself an answer.* For the religious, mythical, poetic, and aesthetic powers need to be rewoven into everyday living, and into the rational languages of science and technology. In rationalism lurks a materialist demon. His poison can only be treated by a wholeness of culture that must invoke the potent languages of feeling-value in myth, poetry and religion. *Aion* the novel is not just *about* healing a wounded world; it is itself an attempt at such a balm.

The rest of the chapter on the self is devoted to the mystic significance of matter in the historical narratives and to the importance of individuation in a cultural as well as individual sense. The question of the relationship between Jung's psychology and the religious discourses is brought to the fore. Is Christ a self symbol or is the Jungian term itself a version of the Christian hero (ibid.: para.122)? *Aion* opts for Christ as self-image, we are told. This choice is crucial in positioning Jung's psychology as an explanation of Christianity. However, the fact that the alternatives are so plainly put before the reader, and the way that the whole volume of *Aion* defines Jungian psychology as both *continuation* and *product* of its historical chronotopes, significantly mitigates the possibility that Jung is here offering his ideas as a foundational truth.

Chapter 5 ends with an exhortation to modern man to set about individuation with attentive seriousness (ibid.: para. 125). Advising people to take care when descending into a pit is a good example of Jung in the vernacular, and of *Aion* as (Bakhtinian) novel (ibid.: para. 125). The reader's contemporary consciousness is artfully embedded in the web of religious-historical symbols.

Chapter 6: The Sign of the Fishes

With the first chapter title denoting historical phenomena, *Aion* sketches the astrological Pisces-Christ chronotope. In an extended parenthesis, Jung reminds his readers that a symbol stands for something unknown and at least in part, unknowable (ibid.: para. 127). Here, he specifies that a doctrinal series of statements can also be a 'symbolum' (ibid.: para. 127). Symbols are not confined to simple or single images. They can be more complex cultural artifacts like a myth or a religious creed.

To introduce Pisces we are told that Christ is said to have been born in the Zodiac sign of the twins at the time of a triple conjunction of the fishes (ibid.: para. 130). Pisces, as Jung will point out, is denoted by *two* fish so the twins attribution hints at the consanguinity of Christ with his dark antithesis: the Antichrist. This astrological measurement of time is, of course, a chronotope; it binds cosmos to history. It is a very important move in that it undermines the separation of nature from history, the cosmological from the cultural. It also undoes the separation of transcendent and eternal from immanent and transient. Human life is mapped onto the cosmos and religious myth becomes a narrative shaping of human history, not to be regarded as abstractable into timeless truths.

Also significant is the way that Chapter 6, focusing upon the Pisces-Christ chronotope, refuses to stick only to that topic. Symbols mediate between different cultural traditions. No discourse, to Jung, can or should be purified of its other, or how else can the wealth of what is unknown be signalled?

The Pisces-Christ aeon of 2000 years reaches a crisis point midway through when the dark sign starts to manifest itself (ibid.: para. 140). Unfortunately, the anti-Christian Piscean era will unloose devils in the contemporary world such as 'idealisms' and 'doctrinarianism' (ibid.: para. 141).

Chapter 6 draws to a close with an insistence upon a multiple understanding of time, and a downplaying of causal historical explanations. There is no proof of the origin of Christian fish symbolism in astrology. Rather there is a simultaneous occurrence that, if not collapsed into 'causes' of each other, offers a notion of time as threefold, personal, predicted and eternal (ibid.: para. 148). Time is the personal experience of the historical man, Christ, while also being a predicted moment, and eternity. This threefold perspective on time is a device for constructing meaning in human life; for regarding human life as personal, historical and atemporal.

So the chapter ends by emphasizing the reversal of opposites in the Christian era; the 'enantiodromia' (ibid.: para. 149). Where the 'second fish' starts to influence the Renaissance is a movement that will be consummated in secular modernity.

Chapters 7, 8 and 9: The Prophecies of Nostradamus, The Historical Significance of the Fish, The Ambivalence of the Fish Symbol

Notwithstanding the title of Chapter 7, Nostradamus's 'prophecies' are presented as what Bakhtin would call 'predictions'. They are a linking of history to present consciousness rather than being events completed in a zone of the absolute past. In particular, Nostradamus is shown to infer a reorientation of chronotopic history, as the Gothic striving for spiritual heights is replaced by horizontal expansion into material science and colonial excursions (ibid.: para. 150).

Chapter 8 begins on the intertwining of Christian and pagan symbolism as the Aries era overlaps Pisces. Both Christ and the pagan Attis are suffused by Aries symbols of shepherd, ram and lamb. Indeed, the two can combine in ritual as Jung cites a pagan celebration of a Virgin birth of the god as Aeon (ibid.: para. 164).

From the interweaving of religious discourse it is a short step to the most culturally diverse New Testament text of Revelation. Here is to be found the Aries motif of a seven-horned ram and a vital warning of the necessity of integrating the Christian shadow (ibid.: para. 167). The focus of this chapter on 'historical' significance is emphatically interpreted to mean 'history of the present'. Jung's history is the historical novel that predicts consequences for *now*. Humanity is threatened with extinction while Christianity fails to enlarge its domain to deal with devilishly explosive tendencies (ibid.: para. 170). In a depiction of the Church as materially implicated in space-time, there is sadly 'no thought of building onto their house and making it roomier' (ibid.: para. 170).

The house of God is articulated by Jung here as a chronotope: it needs to measure time as well as space by adapting to different historical conditions. And the time it needs to measure is not merely eternity, for that would be to elevate the 'house' into a transcendent realm disconnected from history. Instead, the house of God must accommodate time as personal, historical and cultural as well.

The chapter goes on to bring together the duality of Christ with the core duality of Jungian psychology. Christ as man corresponds to the ego, and as God signifies the self (ibid.: para. 171). So although consciousness can never truly know the whole, the self may be unconsciously present in the ego. The rest of Chapter 8 concentrates on history by looking at the fish symbol in cultural discourses. As Jung explicitly states, symbolism of this kind extends narrative into the 'other' as other cultures (ibid.: para. 172).

Also Christ is represented as both the fisherman and the fish that is eaten in the mass (ibid.: para. 174). Jung circles back to the question of the 'origin' of the fish symbol and asserts again what he tentatively proposed earlier, that there is no evidence that Pisces-Christ was *derived* from astrology (ibid.: para. 177). He promotes the hypothesis that astrological and Christian coincidences are spontaneous simultaneities – an argument that anticipates discussion of synchronicity.

However, unlike the earlier speculation on symbolic simultaneity, here the chapter amplifies the narrative parallels between astrological Pisces and the Christian story: each contains a cross, moral conflict, a dark–light duality, son of a virgin, mother–son tragedy, danger at birth and a saviour who brings healing (ibid.: para. 177). The fish also encompasses its monstrous variation such as the Old Testament leviathan. These specific forms record stages in the history of consciousness as Old Testament monstrosity becomes the 'human' fish of Christ. For Jung, history is the history of consciousness, and is not one of inevitable linear progress. He is haunted by contemporary monsters of consciousness as the Churches fail to contain the darkness of the psyche.

To set the scene for the next chapter, alchemy is reintroduced as a Renaissance attempt to counter the over-perfection of the Christ image. In particular, alchemy tried to rethink sacred geography through paradox. A portrayal of divine love burning in the flames of hell is a direct attempt to revivify the chronotope (ibid.: para. 191). God and the abode of the Anti-Christ cannot be permanently separated for that would be to release the enormous energies of opposition into psychic splitting and apocalyptic catastrophe. Space and time must be thought of together, lest space be petrified into dead matter and time be separated out so that history is forever divorced from eternity and cosmos. Against such tendencies, Jung seeks out the sacred geographies of pre-Christianity, such as the association of the 'north' with hell and as the dwelling place of the highest gods (ibid.: para. 192).

Chapter 10: The Fish in Alchemy

Alchemy also has a fish symbol to stand for Christ. The fish is one of the plural images for the stone or lapis that Jung associates with the self (ibid.: para. 194). Here Jung describes a dream of a jellyfish by a student trying to decide on a path of study (ibid.: para. 207). Although the dream is unattributed, it would appear from its appearance in *Memories, Dreams, Reflections* to have been Jung's own (Jung 1963/1983:104–5).

Again the dream is a (Bakhtinian) novel device in linking the cultural history of the past with revolutions in current consciousness. It is accompanied by an expansion of the topos of the end of the previous chapter of the revolutions of space. The ambiguous north and divine love shining out of hell becomes a vision of the north pole as hell (Jung 1951/1959, CW9ii.: para. 209). Jung treats this as a mandala projection. Together with the dream it represents the spatial element of the psyche.

From the mandala, spatial dimensions are amplified into consideration of spheres and wheels as psychic and cultural forms. Amplification is, of course, intrinsic to the production of Jungian narrative: he both uses and advocates it. Alchemy texts enable the soul as sphere (mandala) to be analogously linked (amplified) to the spherical cosmos, and to the cultural practice of horoscopes as psychic maps of the individual (ibid.: para. 212).

The chapter now pauses to offer a psychological examination of the idea of totality. Everything exists relationally except absolute totality, which is a sublime notion: its reality is unimaginable, an image cannot be found to encapsulate it. Only a symbol pointing to its unknowable nature will do. For man, existence depends relationally on some 'other' (ibid.: para. 221):

> Even the loneliest meteor circles round some distant sun, or hesitantly draws near to a cluster of brother meteors. Everything hangs together with everything else. . . This is undoubtedly the same as the idea of an absolute God. . . But which of us can pull himself out of the bog by his own pigtail?
>
> (ibid.: para. 221)

The language here is delightfully representative of *Aion*, combining high seriousness and vernacular comedy. There is something both Dantean and Bakhtinian about Jung's style in *Aion*: divine comedy meets earthly Rabelais. Here the cosmos enacts brotherly harmony and the sublime notion of absolute totality is contrasted to a very human and muddy predicament.

Such flexible style performs Jung's further point about totality; the self as unimaginable whole is both the smallest fish, and is also the sea of awe-inspiring vastness: it makes space mutable (ibid.: paras. 222–3). Cosmos here is both space and theme, topos and topic. Cosmogonic myths, we are told, represent the dawning of consciousness and correspond to alchemical symbolism, which often makes explicit use of creation stories (ibid.: para. 230). The concentration of space into smallest/greatest is thereby accompanied by the similar complication of time. The vast periods of the creation story are simultaneously viewed as cultural and personal acquisition of conscious development.

Jung returns to the historical node of alchemy by citing the synchronistic rise in the middle of the Pisces-Christ aeon, of religious agitation. Psychic disturbance heralded the coming of alchemy itself, of Protestantism, and those demonic 'isms' of the modern age (ibid.: para. 235). Throughout *Aion* Jung repeats this condensed narrative: that modern materialism and rationalism is a direct development of the Pisces-Christ chronotope. Again, this repetition appears to be a technique of rhetorical familiarization, much used in Jung's characteristic form of argument (see Chapter 4).

Chapter 11: The Alchemical Interpretation of the Fish

Although *Aion* might be considered to have already covered a lot of fishy 'ground', this chapter does have a specific task. It explores 'interpretation' as something more than intellectual explanation. Such interpretation is explaining without explaining away. It is interpretation as a psychic act that reaches for more than just rational cognition. Alchemical interpretation or 'secret teaching' is itself a medicine for the soul (ibid.: para. 239). The 'interpretation' or teaching is interchangeable with the healing substance:

> The 'doctrine' or 'theory' is personified. . . sometimes Mercurius is a substance like quicksilver, sometimes it is a philosophy.
>
> (ibid.: para. 240)

The doctrine is substance and interpretative theory. Moreover, the doctrine is also the instrument whereby its object can be grasped (ibid.: para. 249). So the doctrine is both 'the precious secret' and the treasure that is supposed to be the object of the alchemist's efforts (ibid.: para. 249). For this Jung gives the explanation of 'projection' whereby the arcane matter is to be found both within and without the alchemist. Truly, alchemy seeks an annihilation of subject–object distinctions, although Jung tries to preserve a trace of Cartesian dualism by preferring the paradigm of projection. Yet the notion that theory and substance (to be found within and without) are one, suggests something more radical than the interior self painted upon the cosmos. For the alchemists, inner being and the spirit in matter were united (see Chapter 5).

A major part of the design of *Aion* (its intention and structure) is to seek out the voices of the other through historical religious discourses. Hence Jung's concentration upon, and adoption of, the terminology of theologians and alchemists. Here he takes the standpoint of the alchemist by evoking his sense of an interior cosmos or microcosm – *he uses historical language to draw upon the psychic other* (ibid.: para. 251).

However, he also 'translates' alchemical language into his own terms of ego and self as a bridge to the modern reader. Jung writes from the territory of the other, but is careful to move back into the familiar lands of the same, so that the connection between the modern ego (the contemporary *position*) and the other is maintained.

Such a representative strategy is laid bare further on in Chapter 11 when Jung shows how different kinds of narrative enable the limited ego to experience something of the vast alien territories of the other. For although, the ego needs conscious concepts for material to be absorbed into understanding, for so much of psychic reality such concepts are unavailable (ibid.: para. 259). So children should be told fairy tales and adults require religion because both work as psychic symbols (ibid.: para. 259). *Aion* is itself a model of this strategy. Jung constantly explores the religious symbols of the other. He aims to make sufficient links to rational concepts so that the reader's comprehension is engaged without annulling what is alien and mysterious.

Chapter 11 concludes with a moving portrait of alchemy as 'mother' of modern science (ibid.: para. 266). Such a gendering is both traditional in picking up on the long association of woman and matter, and is part of the architecture of *Aion*, since the feminine, matter and the devil all make up the hidden fourth disastrously excluded from the Christian trinity. If alchemy is mother, then she needs to return.

Chapter 12: Background to the Psychology of Christian Alchemical Symbolism

'Mother' alchemy spans the chapter divisions, for, in one of Jung's characteristic family reversals (see Chapter 2), 'she' was once daughter to Gnosticism. To Jung, Gnosticism was an attempt to synthesize a vision of human culture as whole, in which physical and mystical were harmoniously integrated (ibid.: para. 267). Had the project succeeded, the modern world would not be characterized by psychological, cultural and political fission (ibid.: para. 267). Again, *Aion* is crucially an historical *novel* (not epic), in seeking to renew modern consciousness through contact with the thinking of the past.

The Gnostics are important for Jung because they include the psyche as a source of knowledge (ibid.: para. 269). Christianity has a highly refined treatment of the God-image or self, but has omitted the study of nature (ibid.: para. 270). Consequently, Christian discourse has structured another throughout the ages (alchemy), devoted to the study of psychic and non-human nature (ibid.: para. 270).

In considering the significant omissions of Christianity, the chapter moves to the 'earth' of the psyche in cultural and political senses. Whereas it is possible to learn a great deal from civilizations such as India, Europeans of Jung's time are rooted in a Christian past and so should pay attention to their own discursive-psychic structuring (ibid.: para. 271). However, Christianity replaced polytheism in Europe – in some areas, relatively recently. Paganism has returned, in Jung's diagnosis, bringing with it brutality and slavery (ibid.: 273).

Twentieth-century issues recur in *Aion*, the historical novel, in two repeated forms. They are either devilish intellectualism and materialism or political savagery with special reference to Nazism. The two modes of citation of modernity rhetorically stamp Jung's unique sense of history as ideology (derived from the reigning chronotope) in practice. They represent *Aion*'s mission as an urgent intervention into the present.

What Jung and *Aion* are against is singleness of vision. For example, biology as the mechanics of life is a necessary form of understanding, yet is only one in a spectrum of perspectives important to human existence (ibid.: para. 279). By invoking biology, Jung stresses the importance of the origin of the psyche in the living being. It is a counterpart to his similarly emphatic insistence upon cultural origins in connecting European Christianity to its pagan predecessors. For Jung, man is essentially a social being.

Origins go beyond those of the body to the interior sculpting of the soul. Consequently, the pressing concern of modernity is, paradoxically, history (ibid.: para. 282).

Aion tries to mobilize the psyche by reinvigorating historical religious discourses. The book is a psychic instrument. Its main structuring device is to trace out Jungian psychology as a chronotope embedded in the interlinking chronotopic myths that underpin modernity. Throughout the temporal course of the religious discourses, the Christ image was absorbed into a 'psychic matrix' in language that recalls Bakhtin (ibid.: para. 283). Of course, Bakhtin uses 'matrix' for elements of the chronotope discernible in literature where Jung is situating it in the psyche. Nevertheless both thinkers are operating a structure of fundamental temporal-spatial shaping (archetype/chronotope), revealed through images (or elements of languages) that embody the viewpoint of an-other.

The fish symbol concludes Chapter 12 as a bridge between Christ as historical figure and the psyche as constellated through discourses such as astrology (ibid.: para. 285). Connecting discourses via symbols such as the fish refigures boundaries between them as negotiable spaces. Gnosticism and alchemy, for example, are given in *Aion* as influencing each other (dialogically) while belonging to different cultural locations.

Chapter 13: Gnostic Symbols of the Self

As other religious systems, Gnosticism is an attempt to think from the standpoint of the other, or to Jung, the self (ibid.: para. 296). Gnosticism gives other names for totality as divine absolute. He is the 'Autopator' or 'ageless Aeon', showing a Gnostic interest in the nature of time (ibid.: para. 298). Totality as the God of Time adds imaginative space to the rather too human Judaeo-Christian characterization of authorized scriptures. If Christianity will not build more rooms onto its doctrinal house, then *Aion* as novel of the modern psyche will do so.

Jung is interested in Gnosticism as an example of psychic structuring through myth. So he is quick to notice that the traditional signs of earthly power in the insignia of kingship correspond to a cosmic portrayal of man as Anthropos (ibid.: para. 310). Gnostics too possessed an image of man as both painted on the cosmos and abiding within; an image by which one may know God (ibid.: para. 336). So it is unsurprising to learn of reciprocal exchanges between the images of the Gnostics and those of the established Church (ibid.: para. 336).

Christian-Gnostic parallels, we are told, enable the reader to sense the mentality of the early Church when both systems were evolving in the same cultural space (ibid.: para. 337). Both chronotopes in themselves, Gnosticism and Christianity also shape history as chronotope in being the design of an historical period in specific places. Yet again, 'theoretical premises' must be hooked into the present peril by warning that the psychic sophistication of Christianity today is under grave threat in the contemporary inflation of reason (ibid.: para. 346). By such concrete, urgent repetitions, the chronotope that is *Aion* is firmly embedded as the novel of modernity's crisis.

Chapter 14: The Structure and Dynamics of the Self

This chapter title signals a change in direction as the desire to incorporate the reader becomes ever more acute. *Aion* tries to convert its readers into allies in the great project to redeem a disastrously split materialist world. By now the reader should understand that it would be a travesty of the entire volume if the title was taken as a retreat to the security of the modern language of psychology. *For modernity can only be redeemed through history*, taken as a multiple symbolic understanding of time and space. Chapter 14 tries to write the Aion chronotope in Jung's most daringly imaginative reordering of the essential structures of the history of religion.

The chapter opens with a series of analogies in which self-images are evoked from the geometrical circle and quaternity through alchemy's stone and its vision of cities, castles, vessels, astrology's star maps and horoscopes, to animal symbols in modern dreams or landscapes, and even to sexual phallic images (ibid.: para. 352–7). Freud, unsurprisingly, is caught in the web of sexual imagery as his work represents a compensation to the former devaluation of sexuality on rational grounds (ibid.: para. 357).

It is entirely apt that Jung begins the penultimate chapter with a series of images as the list serves as a non-rational, non-linear summary of the preceding historical religious narratives. Images work here as a form of citation that highlights their irrational, non-intellectual function in the discourses of which they form the prime ingredient. Again, Jung's method of writing enacts his psychological position.

Also, the analogous movement from image to image demonstrates in miniature the thesis of *Aion*, which is that cultures operate dialogically with the psyche and with each other through symbols. The mutually implicated religious discourses make up a web that informs the historical experience of any aeon. From mathematical signs to architecture and the apprehension of nature, self symbols embody a sense of totality by linking psychic and cultural experience to what cannot be wholly known. Chapter 14 is itself a small scale model of this argument as it opens in a shower of potent images and closes with an expression of their implied pattern of order; that there is a psychic law behind the cultural structuring of analogies (ibid.: para. 414).

Moving into the heart of the portrayal, Jung outlines his attempt to discover meaning in the interweaving chronotopes by setting out their development as a series of arrangements in four parts: as quaternios. He organizes the temporal progress of Gnosticism and alchemy into four quaternios that he calls successively: the Anthropos (or Moses) quaternio, the Shadow quaternio, the Paradise quaternio, the Lapis quaternio (ibid.: paras. 381–401). These are all additionally named 'marriage quaternios' because they offer the greatest formation of the vast territories of the self by including gender differences. It is specifically stated that a quaternity without gender difference, such as 'Horus and his four sons', would not serve the purpose (ibid.: para. 383).

Therefore Christianity becomes a marriage quaternio with the addition of Mary/the devil as the farthest, most alien 'other' to the masculine trinity (ibid.: para. 397). To denote the self, darkness and what Jung characteristically calls 'the antagonistic feminine element' is required (ibid.: para. 383).

Two typical aspects of *Aion*, and indeed Jung's writing as a whole, are also basic to the discussion of quaternios: the link to the modern psyche by referring to dreams, and the acknowledgement that this specific arrangement of cultural symbols is to be regarded as a useful paradigm (ibid.: para. 383). It does not claim to be an immutable truth.

So far I have stressed the dual nature of the *Aion* novel. First, it portrays culture and history as a chronotopic *dynamic* web of symbols, and second, that Jung is enacting in *Aion* a flexible schema by which to both construct and discover meaningful patterns of order. It both reads history and teaches us how to read history. Crucially, Jung's 'schema' is not a fixed grid of rational concepts, although conceptual language is part of its repertoire. Jung's schema, the 'how to read' bit, is itself presented as an historically generated chronotope that seeks to heal by activating the psyche: it is itself a malleable culturally located form.

So, in order to develop the quaternio aspect of *Aion*, the occult and baroque languages of the Gnostic-alchemy quaternios need to be opened up to contemporary cultural absorption. For this reason, the quaternio is considered through the prism of twentieth-century preoccupation with base elements: matter, energy, time and space (ibid.: para. 395). Jung offers a space-time quaternio, which is the realization that the three aspects of time as past, present, and future, can only be successfully measured by the addition of their antagonistic other, space. It also works the other way round for the measurement of space as height, width, depth through the addition of the fourth dimension of time. Where alchemy proclaimed as base a quaternio of four elements, today's discourse of physics uses the paradigm of the quaternio of space-time. It is, of course, the contemporary model of all chronotopes, or, as Jung puts it, the fundamental archetypal organization of the perception of matter (ibid.: para. 398).

Space-time is the psychic quaternio for apprehending the physical, so it represents, as the rest of the chapter elaborates, an expression of modernity's prime myth of materialism, rather than the apex of the pyramid of knowledge. Gnosticism's personified quaternios are *continued* in different cultural form in modernity's deification of matter that regards the space-time quaternio of the physical world as fundamental (ibid.: para. 405). *Aion* does not portray it as *necessarily* fundamental for that would be to fall into the embrace of Physis (as god) and to offer a novel only to the ego's love of rational, causal explanation.

In showing modernity's space-time quaternio (chronotope) as merely another mode of a recurring mythical structuration, *Aion* refuses to close off the expanses of the non-rational psyche it has mapped via religious discourse. *Aion* fulfils its promise to be a novel of the self, rather than merely the ego.

As Jung argued earlier, everything exists relationally except sublime totality. One of the major achievements of the *Aion* novel, *for* modernity, is to describe the contemporary dominance of materialism and rationalism in relational, rather than absolute terms.

So, in drawing to a close, *Aion* highlights the need to incorporate the non-rational in methods for constructing a picture of reality. Of prime importance here is synchronicity (furthered considered in Chapter 7). To allow a sense of psychic wholeness into thinking, logical causal connections should be supplemented by those of meaning. Significantly, Jung points out the role of synchronicity as a way of overcoming a one-dimensional approach to time (ibid.: para. 409). Synchronicity involves a multiple notion of time drawing upon the *Aion* chronotopes: time is more than linear past, present, future, it is also time as personal, predicted, eternal – and united with space.

So the simple *material* space-time quaternio will not do. Synchronicity is a quaternio of archetypal perception (chronotope) that employs a fourfold perspective of time-space in which psyche and matter are wed. The material space-time quaternio of modernity assumes the physical world to be separate from the mind and falls down at the level of quantum mechanics, *Aion*'s mythical space-time chronotope sees a connection between mind and matter beyond the rational eye of the ego. So meaning is not just a construction of the human psyche; it inheres in its reciprocal relation with matter. Synchronicity, in its fourfold bloom, is another of Jung's 'models' for glimpsing the unexplainable sublime limitlessness of the self (ibid.: para. 413).

Aion works out modernity's myth of materialism by working through it. The self as both form and dynamic process resembles the rejuvenation of carbon atoms who have their own chymical wedding with nitrogen in the sun (ibid.: para. 411). Physics and psychology can come together in the preoccupation with atom and archetype, and all this 'purely speculative construction' is prefigured in the earlier discourses (ibid.: paras. 412–14). So Jung is emboldened to claim that making analogies is a law that regulates psychic functioning (ibid.: para. 414). The paradoxical 'truth' that Jung asserts is that human cultures are irredeemable mythmakers; the search for meaning constructed by drawing analogies is *Aion*'s only universal.

Chapter 15: Conclusion

A short concluding chapter completes *Aion* with three points of emphasis. In the first instance, human morality requires a social context (ibid.: para. 423). Good and evil appear to be necessary for the development of consciousness. To ascribe metaphysical absolutes to them would be to deprive them of meaning by taking them out of the realm of human social relations – the means by which consciousness is wrought (including engaging with the unconscious). Jung is not saying that good and evil do not exist outside the psyche. Instead he says that to define them *solely* as extra-psychic is to eradicate morality as immanent to human life: responsibility is diverted elsewhere to transcendent deities. Such a situation would inhibit the evolution of consciousness by stifling moral struggle.

Second, the conclusion refers to *Aion*'s historicizing of the psyche in suggesting that notion of anima and animus correspond to a culture of polytheism, and the self to monotheism (ibid.: para. 427). This implies a developmental model, yet Jung is firmly associating it only with western religious discourses by immediately citing Christianity and Gnosticism.

Third and finally, the very end of *Aion* is another note of caution about taking its narratives as foundational truths. With the chronotopic presentation of its argument as 'uncertain ground' Jung admits the dynamism of uncertainty into his mythical treatment of history (ibid.: para. 429). *Aion* remains a novel; a text 'open' to more than one reading and designed to dialogically inspire modernity.

In *Aion* Jung offers history as psychic energy. By showing how the religious discourses surrounding Christianity are liminal to each other and construct culture through chronotopes, Jung's is also the dialogic imagination. Most pertinently, *Aion*'s portrayal of myth as chronotope is simultaneously a creation of Jungian psychology as a doctrinal medicine. Jung is always seeking out the word with the power to heal through its appeal to more than the narrow requirements of the ego.

Religion and art are repositories of symbolic forms that nourish the whole psyche. Believing western modernity's soul to be starved, Jung in *Aion* turns to the (Bakhtinian) novel as a means of nourishment through restoring intuitive resources once freely available, now consigned to past and marginal discourses. By conceiving of archetypes as functions of space-time (not confined to the materialist space-time quaternio), as chronotopes, this novel connects the symbolic constructions of the past to present consciousness.

History is re-imaged, re-imagined as the spatial and temporal expanses of the psyche as self. History is a map, whereby the self is imaged in discourses that work dialogically with each other and with the psyche. The self dreams its being into totality; one whose ultimate nature and bounds cannot be known. Jung called it Aion.

Chapter 7

Culture: Ethics, synchronicity and the goddess

'Synchronicity', CW8, 'Kore', CW9i, 'Trickster', CW9i

[Experiment] makes conditions, imposes them on Nature, and in this way forces her to give an answer to a question devised by man. She is prevented from answering out of the fullness of her possibilities.

(Jung 1952/1960, CW8: para. 864)

We could therefore say that every mother contains her daughter in herself and every daughter her mother. . . This participation and intermingling give rise to that peculiar uncertainty as regards *time*.

(Jung 1941/1959, CW9i: para. 316)

Even [the trickster's] sex is optional despite its phallic qualities: he can turn himself into a woman and bear children. . . This is a reference to his original nature as a Creator, for the world is made from the body of a god.

(Jung 1954/1959, CW9I. para. 472)

Introduction

This chapter will look at the way Jung uses writing about archetypes and archetypal images to represent the psyche and culture. By additionally considering his essay, 'Synchronicity: An Acausal Connecting Principle' (hereafter 'Synchronicity'), the chapter will look at how conventional science is reoriented in the direction of hermeneutics and aesthetics (Jung 1952/1960, CW8). Such remodelling is both apparent and obscured in the two archetype essays, 'The Psychological Aspects of the Kore' (Jung 1941/1959, CW9i), hereafter 'Kore', and 'On the Psychology of the Trickster Figure', hereafter 'Trickster' (Jung 1954/1959, CW9i).

Previous chapters of this book have argued that Jung evolved an 'aesthetic science' in his characterization of the psyche. My approach here is to suggest that his direct expositions of synchronicity are his attempts to explain and justify such a radical reworking of the conventions of scientific writing. Synchronicity is the topic where Jung is most open about his epistemological stance of giving adequate weight to the psyche and the unconscious in describing reality.

Jung regarded conventional materialist science as underpinned by simple causality. One role of the essay, 'Synchronicity', is to portray such causality as merely relative, not fundamental. Drawing upon then new discoveries of the 'irrational' behaviour of quantum particles, and using his basic trope of analogy, 'Synchronicity' aims to bring the connective power of meaning to challenge the picture of a wholly mechanical universe. Of course, Jung is careful to insist that making simple causality relative does not diminish it as a potent explanatory force.

Such a perspective has a crucial effect on Jung's native ground, the archetype. If causality does not govern the psyche and archetypal dynamics are embedded in synchronous events, then archetypes themselves are not to be regarded as only causal energies. Archetypes should be understood as inhabiting the domain of meaning rather than that of determination.

In addition, 'Synchronicity' suggests that the phenomena of meaningful rather than causal connectedness may reside in the body–mind relationship, hence removing causality as the sole directing force between psyche and body. Elsewhere Jung has always been careful to insist that the body–psyche continuum does not mean that either the body or the psyche controls the other. 'Synchronicity' offers an explanatory architecture for that delicate relationship.

Culture and gender?

Both 'Kore' and 'Trickster' are expositions of the presence of archetypes in modern culture; they explore the role of archetypal images in the dance of the contemporary world. What is most immediately striking in a comparison of these two essays is their polarization of gender.

'Kore' is built on the ancient Greek myth of Demeter and Persephone as it pertains to the modern feminine, which significantly applies to both the psyches of women and the unconscious anima in men. At first glance, there is something perverse about Jung's insistence that the myth and its cult must have been mainly the product of the female psyche because it concentrates on mother–daughter bonding. It is even said to be characteristic of a matriarchy where man is 'indispensable' yet merely a 'disturbing factor' (Jung 1941/1959, CW9i: para. 383). Given that the myth turns on the abduction of the kore or maiden by the Lord of the Underworld, Jung's downplaying of these aspects of the story is striking.

Moreover, the mono-gendered treatment of 'Kore' has the consequence, explored earlier in this volume in Chapter 3, of using the feminine to mark the limits of representation and culture. 'Kore' links the feminine to unconsciousness, the body, and especially time. Its main mode of psychic manifestation is the dream sequence. Approximately half the essay concentrates upon women, where Demeter-Kore signifies self or 'supraordinate' images. Although Jung the healer regrets the lack of 'psychic hygiene' in modern culture that does not readily provide such feminine symbolic structures (ibid.: para. 317), the women's dream sequence ends when the images arrive at the destination of the Christian Church. Thereafter the feminine becomes the anima in language insisting upon her shimmering, illusory qualities.

'Kore' inscribes a version of femininity using a myth from a distant culture and ends by referring to matriarchy as a long-lost condition (ibid.: para. 483). It fuses the feminine with time in the peculiar odour of immortality of the anima and in the time of bodily generations as mother begets daughter. So the essay feminizes time as circular and reproductive as bearing children signals a return in a woman's life to maternity in which her own birth is also encapsulated. Consequently the feminine here maps the limits of knowable culture as the distant past, as dream, body, unconsciousness and time.

Given this push of the feminine to the margins, *as marginality itself*, it is not surprising to discover that 'Trickster' is marked by the masculine signifying culture, space and history. Where 'Kore' uses dreams as psychic representations, 'Trickster' uses other cultures, in a move that seems designed to align the feminine with elusive time and the masculine with inscribable space. Indeed, where the feminine as anima resists intelligibility as a glittering empty being, the masculine as trickster works as an analogy, parallel or reflection of something protean but also *readable* in psyche and culture.

In Chapter 3 of this book I suggested that there was something both structural and personal about Jung's persistent resort to gender as a polarity. Gender became the means of positioning a dialectics out of a multiplicity, and hence the construction of the very territory of psychological theorizing. In later chapters, I argued that when Jung links his ideas to culture and history through religious narratives and alchemy, the dialectics of gender gives way to a dialogical psyche of archetypal representation through forces of centring and dispersing.

So it appears that there is a tension between the desire for gender as a simple opposition, and the more complicated range of positions out of which that opposition is momentarily constructed. This tension is mobilized into the notion of individuation as a perpetual challenge to fixed positions. The discourses of history, in the areas of religion and alchemy at least, figure polarity as a dialogical exchange. So the very *ground* of Jung's writing is made up of a constant shifting between a 'play' (as in play of a rope), between Jung's dialectical ideal and a dialogical encultured psyche.

'Kore' and 'Trickster', each dealing with the psychic-social range of a particular archetype, are neither the texts focused on individuals considered in Chapter 3, nor the general psychological argument of Chapter 4, nor do they aspire to the 'objective' cultural and religious narratives considered in Chapters 5 and 6. Operating in a hinterland between Jung's scarcely acknowledged drive for gender polarity, and his adherence to a culturally situated psyche, these essays, together with 'Synchronicity', demonstrate the role of gender beyond the personal and theoretical: they illustrate the function of representation, intelligibility and gender in what I will call for the purposes of this chapter, 'the project'.

The project

'Synchronicity', 'Kore' and 'Trickster' can best be read as a response to three problems that Jung perceived as germane to modernity. The first of these is the problem of material science. Established forms of scientific methodology, such as the experiment, or the formulation of an hypothesis before trying it out, have significant difficulties when it comes to the psyche. There can be no real 'objective' knowledge when the instrument of knowing, the psyche, is also the matter to be studied. For this reason, the model of objective knowledge, the 'truth' that exists apart from the material of reality and accurately describes it, such a model needs to be questioned.

The second problem follows on from the first and is that of modernity itself. The exaltation of rational knowledge above all other, has resulted in psychic impoverishment as the religious symbols of western religions lose efficacy. Not only is feminine signifying absent from such religious culture, but even the masculine signifying of a father god is seriously weakened. It is to Jung's credit that he sees a connection between these two conditions. If his core project becomes the shoring up of masculine signifying of the psyche, then at least he asserts that the feminine can no longer be ignored (even if, to him, it remains of secondary importance).

The third problem haunting 'Synchronicity', 'Kore' and Trickster' is the inadequacy of the hero myth as a basis for modern identity, and even as a basis for Jung's modification of it in individuation. The hero, with his final triumph over the territories of the (unconscious) other and his winning of union with the feminine as a prize, fuels the decay of modernity rather than healing it. Too easily, the hero is co-opted as the narrative of masculine rationality whose success is measured by conquest of the other.

Jung, of course, is ambivalent about the hero and it is easy to see why. 'He' is such a potent icon of masculine representation that Jung is loath to lose him. So Jung does not explicitly do away with the hero as a template for individuation. It fitted rather too well with an early twentieth-century mentality that regarded, for example, mother–daughter bonding as having little to do with men or fathers. However, these three essays do contain serious challenges to the ego as hero. For example, 'Trickster' demonstrates mythical models of identity to be culturally situated. Arguably, the whole tenor of 'Trickster' is that the days of western heroic triumphalism are numbered. Moreover, the 'hero' is not at the forefront of Jung's cultural project, which is the healing of the western psyche through a reinvigoration of traditional, mainly Christian, symbolism.

The essays 'Kore' and 'Trickster' reveal complications and even contradictory impulses in Jung's own methodology for what I am calling 'the project'. The refusal to challenge outright the hero myth of individuation enables its implicit presence to disrupt some of the radical implications of mythical narrative for both essays. Indeed it is the hero as a meddler where he does not belong that leads to a tension between image and narrative itself, which will require further examination.

Yet what 'Synchronicity', 'Kore' and 'Trickster' also demonstrate is the potent presence of the 'margins' to representation itself. All three essays, in different ways, illustrate the use of *the frame* as a figure for both structuring and complicating the relationship of 'inside' and 'outside' in culture. It is now worth turning to 'Synchronicity' for its expansion of the frame-*work* of science.

Synchronicity and the problem of scientific methodology

As Roderick Main has so cogently argued in his comprehensive treatment of Jung's synchronicity, it is 'indeed his boldest response to the one-sidedness of science' (Main 2004: 125). Main shows how the difficulties in the synchronicity texts may be accounted for by the grand design of making a space for science and religion to meet (ibid.: 91–114). My purpose here is to explore the concealed role of gender in one synchronicity essay as it relates to the wider cultural project, and ultimately to the tensions in Jung's work between aesthetic narrative and plural forms, versus oppositional, conceptual and dialectical representation.

The essay 'Synchronicity' addresses the problem of scientific method when it is regarded as separate from its subject, which is impossible when investigating the psyche. Such a mode of science ignores the reality of the psyche, for Jung the guiding principle of his work. In a way that barely surfaces in the writing, 'Synchronicity' counters the problem by a return to the goddess:

> For [experimental science] there is created in the laboratory a situation which is artificially restricted to the question and which compels Nature to give an unequivocal answer. The workings of Nature in her unrestricted wholeness are completely excluded.   [W]e need a method of enquiry which. . . leaves Nature to answer out of her fullness.
>
> (Jung 1952/1960, CW8: para. 864)

This evocation of reality as feminine Nature is probably the closest Jung gets to bringing the mother goddess into his thinking. For here Jung is not analysing goddesses as archetypal images or as stages in consciousness. It is a vision of reality from within his depiction of the psychic quality of Eros, the 'feminine' function of relationship, as opposed to (inevitably) the 'masculine' Logos principle of conscious discrimination. So Nature is to be investigated because and *by means of* the human psyche that is part of it. True knowledge here is that which takes account of the psyche. By contrast, rational ego-led enquiry is a form of 'knowing' that is constructed out of the repression of relating to unconsciousness; it is knowledge as separate and transcendent of the matter to be investigated. Logos knowledge relies upon the hero myth as the sole arbiter of what is to be valued as 'science'.

As part of the ecocritical argument of Chapter 5, I looked at the history of the construction of logos knowledge out of a Christian transcendent father-god and into the paradigms of modernity's science. Animism, the divine voices of the living and inanimate things, is one alternative structure. What lies behind animism is an alternative creation myth to the sky-father gods who 'artificially' make the world and remain above it, unchanging and eternal. Sexual creation myths stem from an earth mother from whom all things emerge and to whom, dying, they return. Reality in the goddess myth is erotic. It is what Jung called Eros, the function of relationship. In making both the Logos function of rational spirit and the Eros qualities of relation important in individuation, Jung is fundamentally trying to reconcile two opposing, gendered, myths of creation.

The 'Synchronicity' essay is, of course, a kind of cultural individuation. It seeks to bring the Eros principle into science, the motherlands of Nature or chaos into the fatherlands of logical reason and causality. Interestingly, Jung does not convey his love of opposites into his challenge of causality. Synchronicity is when two events, or an event and a psychic state, occur separated by time, or by space, or by both, in ways that resist conventional notions of causality for explanation. They are therefore linked by meaning not mechanism, and this form of connection is an additional principle to causality, not its opposite. Roderick Main shows how synchronicity fits into that other recurring Jungian pattern: the quarternio, as a fourth explanatory principle in addition to time, space and causality (Main 1997: 19). The quaternio model seems to be a late attempt by Jung to literally *square* the tension in his work between dialectics and plurality.

The idea of synchronicity makes possible a 'whole' judgement because it is a response to the wholeness of nature of which human unconsciousness, and even human consciousness, is a part. Whereas there is an underlying acausal archetypal ordering in the psychoid, synchronicity is an ongoing phenomenon of creation. Archetypes are not the causal origins of synchronous events. Rather they are factors structuring their meaning. So synchronous events are *'acts of creation in time'* (Jung 1952/1960, CW8: para. 965).

George Bright has described the 'Synchronicity' essay as an hermeneutical exercise (Bright 1997). Meaning in the domain of synchronicity, he argues, is both subjectively 'made' and objectively 'found'. Pure, objective meaning in psychoid reality can never be known. Once knowability comes in, then the subjective ego is involved. Rather, meaning in the terms of 'Synchronicity' is a mutual activity between the ego and the objective psychoid nature of matter, which is touched by the invisible border of the human unconsciousness as it abuts both body and world. To put it another way, in the language of Jung's 'whole' judgement out of the 'fullness' of Nature, synchronous meaning (unknowable purely objectively in psychoid matter, knowable only through realization in subjective ego) is a function of relationship with psychoid matter; mater, the mother goddess.

Crucially, Jung justifies the argument of 'Synchronicity' neither in the language of scientific logos, nor in terms of the myth that he is inhabiting. Instead there is an overt call for 'neutral' language that might structure a 'unity of being' and that may overcome the gap between the observed and the observer (Jung 1952/1960, CW8: para. 960). He insists that it is not a philosophical proposition but an 'intellectually necessary principle' in order to take account of 'empirical' evidence of synchronous events (ibid.: para. 960).

As an 'intellectually necessary principle', synchronicity is a daring attempt at a frame to bring the mother goddess, with her Eros relating and generative ongoing creation, into the Logos regions of modernity in order to heal the arid contemporary mindscape. However, 'Synchronicity' struggles with the two types of language and the goddess remains obscured.

As with Christianity, Jung aims to bring feminine relatedness *within* masculine territory rather than challenge the necessity for the ego to be marked so strongly by rational Logos as its most prominent faculty, 'Synchronicity' seeks to give the ego an '*intellectually* necessary principle', after all. Its so-called 'neutral' language is careful to marginalize the prominence of the feminine in favour of the 'project' of resituating masculine signifying. It is the intellect as hero who masks the face of the goddess. The hero myth is granted another victory over his ancient adversary, the goddess of complete (Jung's word, 'fullness') being.

Perhaps the 'Kore' essay contains a near admission of the gender politics of 'Synchronicity'. For 'Kore' characterizes science in two ways. Science as cutting up a dead object, as 'anatomy' or dissection (Jung 1941/1959, CW9i: paras. 307, 318), versus 'natural science' of classification and description, which is appropriate for the psyche (ibid.: para. 308). The goddess hidden in the word 'natural' is discernible through the lens of the 'Synchronicity' article. Jung's evocation in 'Kore' of the necessity of treating psychic material as fundamentally *alive*, rooted in its context in the individual and the moment is, on one level, the most radically gendered argument in the entire piece.

'Kore' and feminine consciousness/anima

It is important to remember that the 'Kore' essay, concentrating upon 'feminine' images, devotes about only half of its space to women. A dream image of the death of a maiden is the pivot used to shift the essay onto a man's anima. At least the death of the maiden is described as revealing the limitation, for women, of their supposed role of standing for the masculine 'other'. To be trapped into embodying a man's anima is recognized as harmful to female individuation (ibid.: para. 355).

Where in 'Synchronicity' the 'intellectually necessary principle' functioned as a frame to make the 'wholeness of Nature' (the goddess) partially visible, here it is the Demeter-Kore myth that is used to make the feminine psyche partially readable. There is a problem, which the essay only lightly touches upon, of the disjunction between the structures of this pre-Christian myth and the symbolic resources of contemporary culture. Demeter-Kore as a narrative works simultaneously to bring the feminine inside, to render it visible, and paradoxically, to mark it as 'outside', in particular with the characterization of the anima as 'empty' (ibid.: para. 355). So the feminine as woman and anima becomes aligned with time. For women it is a bodily and reproductive time through the mother–daughter bond; for the unearthly anima it is immortality. Female psychic orientation through the body looks suspiciously like archetypal dynamics simplified into bodily causality. Jungian hermeneutics again appears to be limited when it comes to gender.

By giving the 'Trickster' cultures and history, and the 'Kore' dreams, these two essays represent variations on the tension in Jung's work between the narrative aspect of myth and the imagistic quality of Jung's psyche. The next part of this chapter will look at the structure of the 'Kore' essay to examine the workings of the myth as a frame for feminine signifying. In simultaneously making visible and bracketing off, a frame may well become a 'frame up'. Why does this Demeter-Kore myth have the mysterious addition of Hecate and the omission of the Lord of the Underworld? Does the suggestive attention given to the chthonic mother have anything to do with the brief, yet surprisingly powerful treatment of the animus?

'The Psychological Aspects of the Kore' (Jung 1941/1959, CW9i)

Jung's opening on the Demeter-Kore figure as maiden, mother and Hecate alludes to a 'problem' (ibid.: para. 306). The issue proves to be the dual nature of the myth in producing self-images for women, and displays of the anima for men. However, as an opening sentence it is particularly artful for it smuggles in a stranger to the myth, Hecate, referred to later as the 'chthonic mother' (ibid.: para. 312). This figure is an object of fascination for the first part of the 'Kore' essay. Associated with blood, sacrifice and the moon, the 'Earth Mother' is emphatically assigned to *women* (ibid.: para. 312).

Jung is sensitive to the charge that 'she' is not proper to classical instances of Demeter-Kore. The dark presence of the chthonic mother is a symptom of the problems of modernity. The very different circumstances of modern culture produce different psychic needs in women. When the myth was part of a shared symbolic system of society, its cult must have been 'rejuvenating' for women, while today's 'lack of psychic hygiene' means the absence of such sustaining psychic experience (ibid.: para. 317). Hecate as Earth Mother enters Demeter-Kore images today because of the paucity of numinous images of the feminine. A certain darkness inhabits the psyche when symbolic resources for manifestation are missing from religion and society. 'Trickster' will pursue this notion under the rubric of the shadow.

In recognizing the scarcity of powerful feminine images in culture as a problem, Jung is being both radical and conservative, as was his wont. By inserting the Earth Mother into a myth that he insists is primarily about mother–daughter experience, Jung positions the absence of a goddess image as a problem only for women, not for the culture as a whole. 'She' is at once brought into, and marginalized from, modernity. By such a move, Jung's assertion in the 'Kore' essay of a 'relational' science of classification and description is left vitally obscured as to gender.

It almost seems a consequence of the weakness of feminine cultural representation that women are here assigned psychic realization through a reproductive connection to time:

> We could therefore say that every mother contains her daughter in herself and every daughter her mother. . . which brings with it a feeling of *Immortality*.
>
> (ibid.: para. 316)

Women's access to the numinous is here focused through their reproductive capacity. It is a more 'expansive' treatment of women's psyche than Jung gives elsewhere, but is also strikingly 'vertical', condensed to 'time' as opposed to the intelligibility of cultural space.

Another structural problem for Jung is hinted at early in the 'Kore' essay when he describes manifestations of the unconscious as possessing 'types of *situations* and types of *figures*' (ibid.: para. 309). He then goes on almost exclusively to discuss figures, first of all his individuation 'collection' of shadow, wise old man, mother, child, anima, animus, and then treats the Demeter-Kore myth itself as a succession of figural representations. Of course, downplaying narrative in favour of regarding a myth as a succession of images enables Hecate to be inserted in the first place as the dark other of Demeter, the good mother. Yet it is also what enables the Demeter-Kore narrative frame to be placed both inside and outside modernity. It allows images to be meaningful while the framing narrative provides as little as possible disruption to conventional structures of representation. In the second part of the essay Jung analyses a series of dreams by women, mostly in terms of image or 'figure' rather than 'situation' or narrative.

Treating the myth imagistically, as a structure for understanding images, enables Demeter-Kore to become *meaningful* and so part of the modern psyche. The living tissue of the dream, as rooted in psyche, body and culture, can be read for meaning constructed out of an interaction between personal and collective, if images are regarded as in a dialogue with a narrative frame.

On the other hand, the insistence on the different functioning of the myth/images for women and for men restricts the myth, the story, to the margins, so that it cannot threaten the pre-eminence of the myth Jung wants to shore up, the Christian 'masculine' one. Once made marginal, Demeter-Kore operates to bracket off feminine representation as outside contemporary culture, and so represents time as vertical, as unconsciousness.

Therefore it is unsurprising that Jung ends his dream sequence of *women* with two motifs which suggest that the function of representation for modern (as opposed to ancient) woman is masculine. First of all, in a dream of pictures painted by an important man, Jung highlights the role of the animus in making representation possible for the female psyche. 'He' may appear as a painter, cinema operator or gallery owner (ibid.: para. 350). In this usefully non-toxic Jungian portrayal of the animus we could discern an optimistic note about women, representation and technology.

In the final woman's dream quoted, however, a girl in a red dress hangs on a cross in a Christian church. The frame of the myth, has succeeded in inserting feminine signifying into the Christian narrative and there, suggestively, Jung's depiction of women's psychic representation rests. What is potentially liberating about Jung's attitudes here is his sense of gender restricted only by cultural context. There is nothing innate about women's marginalization from symbolic culture. Rather, the female psyche suffers and struggles because of the lack of sufficient symbolic 'space' in modernity.

What is less progressive is that Jung is not really interested in doing anything about it *for* women. He sees a promotion of feminine symbolism as necessary for the rescue of modernity as a whole; the peculiar plight of women is of secondary importance *and he sees no real connection between what he posits as two issues.* Jung's strategy is not the grand project of feminism, which in some senses has tried to heal modernity by shifting symbolic and literal power into a more equal relationship. His project is to make use of the feminine other to recuperate traditional masculine signifying, in particular that of Christianity.

The sacrificed maiden on the cross is an image that becomes the pivot of the essay as Jung goes on to discuss the feminine who belongs to man, the anima. Symptomatically, where sacrificed maidens, powerful mother and animals in *women*'s dreams lead Jung to draw upon powerful, if pre-Christian myths, the *anima* as animal, shape-shifting, mysterious woman, does not lead anywhere so imaginatively rich. Anima animals stand for the less than human rather than for ancient, mysterious cultures. Indeed, the anima's representative powers in the rest of the 'Kore' essay consist of the less than human (animals), popular romantic fiction (Rider Haggard, inevitably) (ibid.: para. 356), a romantic red-haired countess (ibid.: para. 375), or pure banality as in the lavatory attendant or a 'petite bourgeois' (ibid.: paras. 367–8).

The anima possesses psychic potency with little intelligibility. The 'Kore' essay displays her lack by insisting upon her emptiness that is paradoxically an over-fullness. She is 'empty and merely glitters', an 'illusion' (ibid.: para. 355), yet all possible meanings glitter in her (ibid.: para. 370) and for men, the 'shimmering' anima experiences are enduringly powerful (ibid.: para. 382). Here truly is the feminine that evades signifying: the absent 'presence' of the Jungian unconscious.

The 'Kore' essay ends with a firm demarcation of genders translated into historical vision. The psychology suggested by Demeter-Kore indicates a long-past matriarchal world where man is necessary yet disturbing (ibid.: para. 383). There is something almost self-satisfied here about polarizing gender so far apart as to denote different aeons! Matriarchy and the mother goddess are 'framed' by the myth as *outside*, *before* the modern world. Even so, by teasing out a dialogical relation between images and narrative (where the one gains meaning from relationship to the other), Jung manages a limited insertion of feminine representation into contemporary culture. That is, he manages it as *limited*, since a full-blooded feminine *narrative* of the numinous would prove far too much of a disruption to the Christian framework of Jung's modernity.

Taking images and narrative dialogically, enables 'Kore' to 'frame off' the feminine by assimilating it to time with only the most marginal of signifying space in the psyche. Myth in the form of Demeter-Kore is therefore used as a frame by which to make the feminine psyche and even feminine symbolic representation *visible*. However, the mythical frame of visibility simultaneously brackets off or marginalizes feminine symbolic structures from cultural *space* by Jung's insistence upon its intrinsically pre-Christian matriarchal identity. Hence the feminine here stands for time with a very limited thickening of the image into space.

The Demeter-Kore frame makes the feminine visible, but it fails to make it intelligible. The essay's funnelling of the feminine into the 'glittering' anima is an expression of this underlying assumption.

To put it another way, Jung is not trying to promote the cause of women making their own meanings, just as he is not trying to replace a rational Logos modernity with goddess relatedness and Eros. Rather he is trying to individuate modernity by bringing Eros and Logos into a mutual codependence. Yet since he is aiming to rejuvenate Christianity rather than to replace it, the role of the goddess and feminine signifying must be subordinated to the greater project of shoring up the masculine.

And this is not just Jung's gender preferences at work. Acutely aware of the importance of context, the other lesson insisted upon is that goddess consciousness is too foreign to modernity to be capable of healing it. That Jung suggests that this attitude is the perspective of only half of modernity's citizens, that is, men, does not detract from the fact that what is a marginalization of women is also a recognition that the symbolic resources of the 'other', here a pre-Christian ancient society, cannot simply be co-opted for today's needs.

In order to bring goddess relational Eros consciousness to cure modernity's angst, it is necessary to seek out the other who is already present, within and without the margins of the monotheistic west. Another frame is required. The emphasis shifts from otherness of time, to that of space and other cultures. If women are too 'foreign' (!), then there is another mythical frame that can serve to make visible and even perhaps intelligible the unconscious psyche. Goddess consciousness is 'framed' within and without modernity by the trickster.

Trickster goddess

Oliver Davis has explored the problem of Jung's emphasis on images at the expense of narrative (Davis 2004). Such a priority is particularly evident in the use of myths:

> Jung never actually makes clear how the static images are related to the extended narratives. . . Either way, the archetypal images or symbols have ontic and epistemic priority over the myths that they suggest and constitute, for it is only by means of the archetypal images that myths are anchored in the collective unconscious and thereby acquire their significance.
>
> (Davis 2004: 67)

Davis is correct to draw attention to the 'gap' between images and the narrative dimension of myths as something not overtly examined by Jung. However, I think he overlooks the *functional* value of myth, for Jung, in elucidating archetypal meaning. Hence my argument in this chapter that in relation to images and symbols, myths are for Jung a frame that enables images to be 'read' as part of a contingent individual, cultural, historical text. The framing work of myths gives to archetypal meaning a local habitation and a name.

It follows, therefore, that far from being an embarrassing disjunction in Jung's writings, the 'gap' or absence of an explanation of the relation of image to narrative in the treatment of myth is often *productive* of a textual weaving of cultural difference (more evident in 'Trickster' than in 'Kore' as I shall show).

In 'Kore' the preference for images allowed a limited amount of feminine symbolic representation into modernity as the narrative myth 'framed' dream images as meaningful, yet both inside and outside culture. Although the disjunction image/narrative remains in 'Trickster', it is, I suggest, more productively handled as a mediation of difference between cultures. I argue that Jung preserves a 'gap' that positions image/narrative as a dialogical relationship. Image is only something dynamic with potential for meaning if it has a connection to narrative (or words). Narrative without images is drained of affective or embodied feeling. Regarding images and narratives as mutually constitutive yet distinct, is also a version of the assumed image/word dichotomy. Yet as David L. Miller has persuasively shown, images and words are not a dualism, but a dialogue between two different and related aspects of thinking (2002).

The 'trickster' essay is more complex in structure than the binary mirroring of 'Kore': the feminine for women pivoting onto the feminine for men. What begins in 'Trickster' as a reading of Native American myth against modern European culture is mediated into a subtle weaving of cultural space in the layering of history. Even Jung's preferred model of the hierarchical-implied layering gives way to something more like a (goddess) web of being. Cultural space twists into historical space, generates Jung's contemporary image of the 'shadow', and becomes the means of portraying Europe as a land of witch doctors and high speed transport.

Jung has a nuanced reading of what is for Native Americans a delightful *myth* of the Trickster, and for medieval Europeans the cathartic ritual of the Fool, is, for the modern European the comparatively thin yet powerfully black *image* of the shadow. Here the disjunction between myth as narrative and comparatively static image has explanatory force as part of the atomizing of the modern western psyche.

On the other hand, this persuasive cultural diagnosis is also a means of retaining the hero myth for individuation. Implicitly rather than explicitly here a counter to the ego-hero's lofty pretensions, the shadow as image rather than as trickster narrative permits the irredeemable course of his story to be subtly modified. Where the trickster cannot be cured of his amorality, the shadow can be left behind. Behind the shadow 'hides' the anima and behind her the wise old man (Jung 1954/1959, CW9i: para. 485).

By concentrating upon *image*, the trickster *narrative* can be diverted into the upward trajectory of the hero. The 'hero' suggests a linear course of moral improvement, and a simple story of conscious development through a life's *time*. Elsewhere in the essay, the trickster narrative is shown to frustrate such comforting assumptions.

Ultimately, it is Jung's love of opposites that allows him, however tenuously, to bring the hero and the trickster into a relationship in the essay by means of images and cultural history. An oppositional relationship of hero and shadow needs both the trickster and the hero narrative to resolve tensions in the interests of Jung's project for modernity. The trickster is the nearest the modern European can get to goddess relational consciousness; that is, relational to the 'other'. Or at any rate, the goddess as trickster is Jung's means of retaining the project: the rejuvenation of monotheistic symbolism. For the project to succeed, the goddess must energize the European psyche. Yet she cannot be allowed to do that in a way that would so revolutionize masculine symbolism that monotheism itself is challenged – Jung wants the 'one' to continue to be privileged over the 'many'. Hence the trickster; his devious dance inhabits the realm of the signifier as well as the psyche, for Jung.

So the trickster, appropriately enough, stands for Jung's double-edged attempt to reconcile the deficiencies of masculine monotheistic signifying with a basic conservative desire to retain it. So the contemporary European can only get close to the trickster through the shadow image, which entails a better comprehension of the otherness still alive *within* modernity. Symptomatically, the trickster essay ends with Jung's favourite mechanism for reconciling the rational ego with the unruly unconscious: enantiodromia, the conversion into the opposite permits the ego-hero to relate to the shadow and vice versa (ibid.: para. 488). That transforming energy, as Jung has just shown, is native to the trickster in all his cultural incarnations.

The Native American trickster myth is a frame, making possible a postcolonial examination of European cultures and psyches. It enables goddess consciousness to be discerned *within* the multiple layers of social practice, both as past history in the medieval Church and in present cultural space in the folk rituals of today. Such practices inform images in the psyche. Where the mother goddess was the fertile source of both genders, the trickster is similarly marked by her generative power. 'He' is equally capable of feminine incarnation and is indeed a version of the creator god(dess):

> Even his sex is optional despite its phallic qualities: he can turn himself into a woman and bear children. From his penis he makes all kinds of useful plants. This is a reference to his original nature as a Creator, for the world is made from the body of a god.
>
> (ibid.: para. 472)

Most striking here is that the trickster is a creator out of whose *body* the world is made. In the goddess creation myth it is the earth mother's body that is the source of life and to whom all life returns as opposed to the more 'technological' or artificial creation by a sky father. As I argued in Chapter 5 for alchemy, Jung discerns the other within, the marginal within cultural forms, as a possible way of cultivating better health for modernity.

Consequently, the divorce between image and narrative in the divergence between trickster myth and shadow image is part of Jung's argument about the spiritual poverty of his age: it is both his criticism and part of his counter-strategy. By taking another culture as a frame, the 'Trickster' essay mobilizes the myth itself as a second frame that can work to negotiate cultural otherness between Native American and European. The myth as frame can also mediate the symbolic otherness of the European past and present, to make visible and intelligible a psychic other within the contemporary. Jung then chooses to exploit the more static value of images in order to use trickster and shadow to recuperate the ego-hero myth. His individuation of modern culture is in the interests of maintaining traditional symbolic structures through rejuvenation. A greater emphasis on narrative would risk revealing the trickster's greater intimacy with the goddess than with the upright hero.

Another aspect of Jung's sophisticated treatment of image and myth in 'Trickster' is his recognition that the narrative aspect of myth has a vital social function. The trickster story works by keeping the inferior and outgrown aspects of the psyche before a society. It does by means of story what Jung has to do in his essay by means of history: remind the present of the unpleasant aspects of the past *so that they remain past* and do not become incarnated again in social dysfunction. History is the modern world's trickster narrative. It works by enabling the past to remain past, by keeping it before consciousness as a possible present: that is how conscious discrimination works.

It is therefore important in 'Trickster' that causality is criticized if it represents a claim to understand the psyche as a simple progressive mechanism. Jung draws attention to the overtly colonial assumption that modern Europe has abandoned its trickster myths because it is so far ahead of Native cultures as to be able to forget the part-animal, part-divine forms of consciousness they signify. Using history to deconstruct the European assumption of superiority, Jung posits a dialogical relation between image and narrative contained in the living quality of the myth for other cultures. Far from being merely a 'primitive' survival, it is actively developed by consciousness as the best way of criticizing the shadow (ibid.: para. 474).

Where the myth is an active social phenomenon it is a structure by which the individual psyche is dialogically engaged with the collective. Such a dialogical relationship develops collective consciousness by its very participation in the collective unconscious. Mythical narrative without the internal image would appear comparatively uninvolving and meaningless. Meaning is both created and found, here in the interaction between 'inner' image and 'outer' narrative structure. The strategy that Jung adopts for his

'Trickster' text, that of the frame, is how he regards the individual psyche as working in the collective space of a social group: myths, powerful narratives, 'frame' and make 'intelligible' inner contents through dialogical relationship.

Indeed, 'Trickster' shows much more precisely than 'Kore' how such framing works – by hermeneutical devices of analogy, parallel and reflection. Of course, the essay itself has an ideological direction: it aims to interpellate western consciousness into the trickster myth by means of analogy, parallel and reflection of the shadow. 'Trickster' reorients the European historical sense to function in the same mythical/ethical mode as the trickster myth does for the Native American.

So this is not just an essay about trickster/goddess consciousness, it is also an exercise in it, designed to incorporate the reader. Therefore it is unsurprising that the most urgent address occurs in the middle. If the trickster is a means of coming to terms with the modern shadow then it becomes a matter of ethics. Without the self-consciousness only possible through individuation with the inner 'other', the outer 'other' may be subjected to devastating 'mindless' violence. Jung evokes the modern soldier who does not know how to subject his orders to ethical scrutiny (ibid.: para. 479). With such a horrifyingly persistent product of modernity, it is worth looking closely at the structure of the 'Trickster' essay to see how 'goddess consciousness' becomes ethical relating.

'On the Psychology of the Trickster Figure' (Jung 1954/ 1959, CW9i)

Jung's opening sentence 'frames' the essay as a dialogue of cultural space and historical time:

> When I first came across [the trickster myth]. . . I was struck by the European analogy of the carnival in the medieval Church. . . still continued in the carnivals held by student societies today.
>
> (ibid.: para. 456)

Analogy pivots the topic of the myth onto, first, a focus on the European past, and then second, to its present with a telling note about the past's survival in social rituals on the margins. Immediately, space and time are mutually implicated as the other located in space (the Native American culture) analogously cites the European other within European cultural space: history, and its continuities in the present. The next seven paragraphs elaborate the historical parallel in medieval rituals. These are revealed to be permeable to pre-Christian symbolic systems. For example, as a marginal cultural continuum, the Feast of Fools contains within it Roman Saturnalia (ibid.: para. 458).

Even the Old Testament Yahweh exhibits trickster motifs, as do the phenomena of poltergeists, shape shifting, shamanism, medicine men (ibid.: para. 457–8). Three substantial paragraphs are devoted to a medieval ass festival in which the whole congregation made animal noises (ibid.: paras. 461–3). Officially a celebration of the holy family's flight into Egypt, Jung describes the ritual as risking a symbolic equation of Christ with the animal (ibid.: para. 463).

These opening paragraphs concentrate on collective religious practice as a matrix of past and present myth. The essay changes direction after noting that once banished from church precincts, the European trickster reappeared in the theatre. Jung then picks up the hint of pre-history, even pre-culture suggested earlier in Mercurius as older than Hermes (ibid.: para. 456). Apparently a survival of undifferentiated consciousness close to animal level, the trickster is an indication of a very ancient past in the evolution of culture and consciousness (ibid.: para. 465).

Here Jung pivots entirely characteristically to reject the biological causal explanation for the trickster as sufficient for 'his' potency for the individual and the collective. The trickster is not just a quaint reminder of human evolution. Causal approaches answer the question of origins without revealing anything of his significance for culture (ibid.: para. 465). In order to have meaning, one must have purpose in Jung's teleological psyche (ibid.: para. 465). Indeed, where the causal explanation for the trickster suggests an unimportant survival from a pre-cultural past, this would not 'satisfy' the Native American Winnebagos for whom the myth is still a delight requiring no more justification than the European Christmas tree (ibid.: para. 467).

Cultural pivoting enables Jung here to displace biological causality as a governing trope for explaining the trickster. In a sophisticated postcolonial move, the essay uses the cultural *difference* of the Winnebagos (collectively valuing the trickster myth) to marginalize the explanatory power of biological mechanisms, and so return to European cultural space under a trope of functional value. Native Americans provide the frame by which European attachment to irrational customs can be reoriented.

So far the 'Trickster' essay has concentrated upon a collective narrative made concrete in social practices. Now it starts to mediate between the personal and the collective by positing a dialogical relationship of image and narrative. Although modern carnival customs are a remnant of a collective figure, European culture has become too fragmented to sustain them as anything more than fringe activities. Instead the trickster has been relegated in two directions: to folklore, and mainly to the personalized image of the shadow in the modern psyche (ibid.: para. 469).

Before developing the theme of the personalized shadow, the essay pauses to draw out some of the fascinating and paradoxical qualities of the trickster. Subhuman and superhuman, 'he' is bestial and divine, is without bodily unity, can be a woman and give birth, was originally a creator god (ibid.: para. 474). Such a development of trickster qualities is a preparation for the insistence that the trickster is not just about looking back. Constant retelling of the myth must have therapeutic properties for it would not occur if it did not tap into living imaginative energy (ibid.: para. 474).

Jung reintroduces the shadow as a 'legitimate parallel' from individual psychology, yet significantly, struggles to bring together the European shadow and the Native American myth (ibid.: para. 474). Whereas the shadow represents something disagreeable and repressed *now*, the trickster stands for a *past* condition of consciousness and is far from repressed as its retelling is collectively encouraged. Unable to completely identify shadow with Native American trickster, Jung returns to the trope of functional value that he set up several paragraphs ago. The myth works because it serves to keep the shadow visible and intelligible to the native culture. Although there appears to be a gap between 'conscious criticism' (of the shadow via the trickster narrative) and the 'delightful' qualities of the stories, the development of consciousness will deplete the entertainment value of the myth (ibid.: para. 474).

Ultimately, Jung will negotiate the disjunction between Native American trickster and European shadow (a disjunction he is conscious of as cultural difference that cannot be wholly assimilated) by bestowing the narrative role of the trickster myth on the western discourse of history, a 'frame' that makes the shadow images of modernity all too visible. The 'gap' between narrative and images works to articulate cultural difference, and dia-logically as critique of the western psyche. Of course, it is also a means of retaining the hero myth, although as one of a series of images that are also placed in a web-like dialogue.

So it is significant that the essay does at least notice the discrepancy between the other culture's use of the myth and Jung's own schema of his psychology contained in the notion of the shadow image. The discrepancy has a structural importance in this text because much of the essay refers to the *European* delight in its own trickster figure in past carnival customs, now merely marginal survivals. So it is notable that the rest of the essay will problematize the simple colonial equation of European past parallels Native American present, with a deepening sense of European *regression*. For Jung, conscious development and cultural evolution may have a linear spine, but it is never merely linear. In fact, 'other' cultures are also a mirror of *present* psychic conditions as well as a frame by which to read history.

Indeed, Jung's complex weaving and unweaving of the trickster and the shadow is designed to challenge the complacent western assumptions of linear developmental 'progress' that is also the structure of its colonial pretensions. In announcing that apparently 'civilized' westerners have for-gotten the trickster, Jung embarks upon a sustained cultural criticism of modernity that links psychological impoverishment to the perpetration of atrocity. By forgetting the trickster, the modern European pays no attention to the shadow. What is only faintly perceptible to him in 'fate playing tricks' is completely unintelligible to him as personal ethical responsibility (ibid.: paras. 478–9).

The trickster myth has a sophisticated dual function for Native Americans: it signifies a desire to leave a more undifferentiated state of consciousness and at the same time to remember it *as an ethical psychological process*. The myth literally re-members an earlier state of consciousness for its society (ibid.: para. 480). Conversely, the European is comparatively simple minded in his blundering assumption that his vestiges of ritual practice in Christmas trees represent nothing essential in the psyche. At this moment, the mirror of the European mindset is to be found in the Africans of Mount Elgon who similarly refuse to admit their credence of ghosts (ibid.: para. 481).

Jung then cites an extraordinary example of cultural layering. Once in *his* native land he watched a 'sort of local witch doctor' exorcizing a stable while an international express train sped past (ibid.: para. 482). The 'frame' of the cultural other deconstructs the boundary between 'outside' and 'inside' as a European 'witch doctor' works beside an icon of technological modernity. As an intensifier of this challenge to fixed notions of inside/ outside cultures, Jung links his own (colonial) depiction of the polarization of primitive and civilized (postcolonial in this context), to his adherence to the reversibility of opposites as their defining characteristic:

> The conflict between the two dimensions of consciousness is quite simply an expression of the polaristic structure of the psyche, which like any other energic system is dependent on the tension of opposites. That is also why there are no general psychic propositions which could not just as well be reversed; indeed, their reversibility proves their validity.
>
> (ibid.: para. 483)

Coming directly after the vision of the witch doctor beside the railway line, the two dimensions of consciousness here are trickster (mythological goddess) consciousness and rational modernity: the ingredients of Jung's cultural individuation for 'the project'. In fact, this is an excellent example of Jung working hard to distil dialectical reasoning from narrative ground (here trickster myth) in the psyche (see Chapter 3). At the level of myth itself, Jung's dialectics are visible here as the two opposing creation myths: the father-god who begets Logos, and the Eros-embodied earth mother. The next part of the essay describes how mythological consciousness works through the fascination with the autonomy of mythological figures (ibid.: para. 484):

The figure works, because secretly it participates in the observer's psyche and appears as its reflection, though it is not recognized as such.

(ibid.: para. 484)

The image acts as a *mirror*, a 'reflection'. The shadow is always active. If it has not the collective resources of a myth, then it may be projected on other social groups and peoples (ibid.: para. 484). Again 'figure' is abstracted from the narrative aspect of myths and is used to extract 'images' for the individuating psyche, as in the 'Kore' essay. However, here it is explicitly the spiritual weakness of modern Europe that means that this myth is found primarily as shadow *image* and only secondarily as folklore myth and ritual. Jung's preference for image over narrative in myth is revealed here as part of his cultural diagnosis, not a perverse idiosyncrasy.

Yet, the cultural raison d'être of the primacy of images is also a structural opportunity for the hero. For if the trickster is paralleled to the shadow image, then the progressive trend towards conscious meaning in the narrative can be used as a justification for the trickster image being placed in a cycle of meaningful replacements (ibid.: para. 485). 'Behind' the trickster is the anima and behind her is the wise old man. 'Image' becomes the means by which the trickster myth is replaced by the hero narrative in the form of the 'progression' of modern man in individuation.

By trying to convert the trickster into the hero, Jung is aiming to reconcile goddess consciousness with post-Christian modernity by favouring the heroic symbolism of the latter. In an engaging end to the 'Trickster' essay, it closes in both success and failure to recuperate the 'masculine' signifying of Christianity, as the most visible and intelligible. Such is the painfulness inflicted by the trickster, that he represents a hint of a saviour; he is the *need* for a healing Christ who 'can undo the tangled web of fate' (ibid.: para. 487).

Here the pivot from trickster *myth* to shadow *image* is overtly onto Christian ground. After this moment, the essay offers three more arguments: on the level of the individual the problem of the shadow is answered by the anima as relatedness; that consciousness is the most important aspect of the history of the collective as source of light and liberation; that as myth and image, the shadow contains within it the possibility of conversion into its opposite (ibid.: para. 488).

The shadow's tricky reversals betray its legacy of goddess consciousness in relating both positively and negatively to the irrational psyche. By bringing 'the saviour' in as one who unpicks a web, Jung provides Christian heroic consciousness undoing the goddess-trickster's relational web of the universe. The function of relating in consciousness is feminized and relegated by being assigned to the anima; it is essential, yet positioned as serving the succeeding figure of the wise old man/monotheistic self in the heroic narrative.

Nevertheless the final note about the persistence of psychic reversals is yet another twist in the analogous, reflective, slippery parallel game of culture being read through an-other. The trickster-goddess is still in the frame.

Conclusion: Culture and representation

Early in this chapter I suggested that 'Synchronicity', 'Kore' and 'Trickster' should be read as responses to three problems: that of science, of the sickness of modernity, and of the myth of heroic consciousness. The main method of response has been the device of the 'frame', that which makes content visible by marking it as inside or outside. The frame converts psyche and culture into a readable text. Whether the making visible amounts to making intelligible, and whether the 'inside' is permeable to the 'outside' as these terms define each other; this is what 'Kore' and 'Trickster', in particular, explore.

The 'Synchronicity' essay brings Jung, the practical worker with the psyche, into the arena of the definition of 'science' and 'scientist'. Unsurprisingly, it is an attempt to 'individuate' science by adding the creativity of the unconscious to the rational mode that relies exclusively (to Jung) on mechanical causality. By complementing causality with meaning-making acts of creation in time (synchronicity), Jung aims for a 'wholeness' of vision. It is a vision of Nature as fecund and an active participant in the human psyche. Meaning is both created and found by *realization* of the goddess.

Jung then needs to translate this healing of science into the amelioration of modernity, or at least its western, unhealthy incarnation. Crucially, his preference is conservative. He wants to rejuvenate the modern world by reconnecting traditional symbols with the psyche using myth as a language of psychic relating. On the one hand this has the merit of working with material *inside* the frame of modernity, of looking at the other *within* culture in ways that is made explicitly ethical. It largely resists appropriating the cultural resources of another. Moreover, it seeks to mobilize what Jung believed to be integral to psychic functioning, the historical residue found in archetypal symbolism that connects unconscious powers to cultural discourses.

On the other hand, this conservative evolutionary approach produces it own methodological problems. If traditional symbols have lost their collective potency, then their restoration is not necessarily the most desirable outcome, seen from the perspective of individuation. Can modernity be healed by, in some sense at least, standing still? There is a political tension in much of Jung's work between a conservative wish to hang onto the past (a forceful drive in archetypal theory), and a literally *revolutionary* sense of psyche and culture as a *process*. Such tension is made visible by, and refracted through, his desire to regard gender as a polarity. Whether the urge to polarize gender feeds the cultural conservatism or vice versa, it remains an essential part of 'the project' of rescuing traditional western symbolism that the feminine be simultaneously foundational and marginalized.

In the dialogue between the one and the many that runs through Jung's writings, his political preference is for a self archetype aspiring to the 'one' of patriarchal monotheism, rather than the 'many' of a pluralistic, web-like goddess-relational psyche. Consequently, the gendered invocation to Nature as goddess, must be obscured in the text by the heroic intellect as synchronicity is described as an 'intellectually necessary principle' (Jung 1952/1960, CW8: para. 960). Such terminology defines synchronicity as a frame by which goddess-relational consciousness is both made perceptible and pushed to the margins.

Feminine signifying undergoes a similar process of 'framing' in 'Kore'. Here a pre-Christian myth of Demeter-Kore frames the feminine as both inside culture in images, yet 'outside' for the lack of a living myth to sustain them. The dichotomy between images and narrative is here overtly in the interests of marginalizing feminine signifying. Indeed the anima's presence as glittering evanescence and banality should perhaps be read largely as a *cultural* poverty, rather than, as Jung does, a stage in maturity for both women and men to outgrow. Still, his positive opinion that women should cease to 'be' the anima for men is not unhelpful. Men, of course, are encouraged to move on from the glittering anima to find their heroic destiny in the wise old man, even if the anima can never entirely be forsaken. Either way, in 'Kore', representation as visibility and spectacle is feminized, as intelligibility it is masculinized. Myth here is a frame that serves to exclude more than include.

Therefore it is not surprising that causality is used prominently in 'Kore' to link the feminine to the body via reproductive capacity. For in 'Synchronicity', Jung links the repudiation of causality as sole mechanism, with the assertion of *meaning*. If the feminine is not wholly intelligible, because of a lack of feminine symbolism within culture (that Jung does not intend to assuage), then, of course, women for Jung will be more aligned with causal explanations; their psyches shaped causally by their reproductive involvement with other generations.

Jung has made a significant separation between the 'feminine' goddess Nature, sponsor of synchronicity, and women in his modernity living under the sign of bodily causality. This separation is perhaps another version of his polarization of image and narrative in 'Kore', so that the feminized is framed as inside yet marginal. The revolutionary possibilities of feminine religious narrative are subordinated to traces, just as Nature plays such a tiny role in the psychic politics of 'Synchronicity'. So it is entirely in keeping that 'Trickster', devoted to masculine signifying through culture and history, will challenge causality in the name of purpose and meaning.

'Trickster' unites both subject matter and form in its tricky, sinuous, refracted, mirroring, doubling back, repetitive, contradictory and humorous argument. The essay delights in vivid portrayals of earthy rituals and vignettes from Jung's own experience. It provides three frames by which it tries to shore up masculine psychic symbolism and render it intelligible.

First of all, there is the frame of the other culture, mainly, but not exclusively Native Americans. Here, as with other frames, it serves to mark inside from outside. Yet the characteristic of this frame is that it makes the border between cultures as liminal, such as the moment when African practice mirrors Europeans so permitting a vision of a European 'witch doctor'; a making intelligible of an irrational darkness in western identity. The appropriation of the African in order to make this point is, of course, a colonial narrative act.

The second frame is that of the trickster myth that operates to make readable both the challenge to causality (in the myth serving an ethical *purpose* for Native Americans), and by doing so makes history readable. The myth makes intelligible and ethically dynamic, European history of carnival and its surviving remnants in folklore. Together these two frames constitute another: of 'history' as a psychic myth with an ethical loading. They structure history as a story that must be remembered in the psyche, as a form of consciousness, if it is not to be repeated unconsciously. Without 'history' as European modernity's own trickster myth, its repetition will be without ethics as modern man loses a sense of his inner other. The 'Trickster' essay's dances and mutations of meaning are an incorporation of history into the cultural representation of the body of modernity. The essay interpellates the European reader (less directly the western reader in general) into an ethical structuring of a relationship to the irrational psyche. In re-membering the trickster for the reader as *history*, Jung makes 'him' our own.

This trickster history is, of course, a version of goddess consciousness gone native in modernity. However, the tension between Jung the social conservative and Jung the fearless diagnostician of modern ills, remains. If trickster is a smuggling in of the goddess via other cultures and myth, his gender fluidity is significantly downplayed. There is a trade-off between making him intelligible through the link to traditional Christian practices that are in masculine guise, and 'his' revolutionary feminine qualities. Ultimately for Jung, the trickster must be incorporated into the hero myth rather than vice versa.

The hero haunts both 'Kore' and 'Trickster' as a privileging of the ego through the representative resources of masculinity and rationality. Since these resources have been conflated in both religious tradition and Enlightenment modernity, even finding expression in the Jungian ideal of gender/ psyche as dialectical, the writings continue to polarize the feminine under visibility against the masculine as intelligibility. For the 'opposition' that

Jung struggles to set up between two gendered myths of consciousness, that *very duality,* is a product of the same masculine reason that Jung is trying to displace as paramount, in the cause of saving it from disintegration in apocalyptic chaos.

So the trickster and the hero myth continue their battle in Jung's writings on alchemy as the trickster-devil asserts his (goddess-relational) intimacy with the culturally heroic Christ. Yet on the smaller scale of the 'Trickster' essay, the text demonstrates the role of the *present other,* the other within the cultural imag[e]ination, as the essential frame of cultural representation. It is the present other as a treatment for modernity's sickness that Jung shows to be an ethical enterprise. Through the frame of the present other, culture can be read as an ethical act.

The trickster's synchronous activities secrete goddess consciousness back into modernity as a necessary ethical process. There may be a conservative emphasis in Jung's preference of the one over the many in the dialogic psyche, but whenever he reaches for the net, or the web, the rhetorical, the interdependent, the numinous, the unknowable, the relational, the endlessly narrative, he records not the logocentric 'presence' of the rational and knowable, but behind and within, another kind of 'presence' altogether. The kind of intelligibility that Jung's frame of the present-other institutes is not that ego-centred presence that underpins materialist science and rational philosophy. Rather it reveals the logocentric presence of masculine signifying to be dependent upon a relation to the other. It destabilizes rationality, presence and logos as sole harbingers of truth, presence and meaning.

In Chapter 6, I described synchronicity as an aesthetic form of reading reality. Here in Chapter 7, we see the mythical structuring of Jung's revision of the science/art dichotomy. Synchronicity as the union of a masculine 'intellectually necessary principle' with feminine wholeness, provides a form of knowledge as the child of both. Mythically, masculine heroic conscious-ness quests for meaning by relation to/by means of, the goddess. 'She' also nurtures art since, as Jung puts it: '[t]he creative process has a feminine quality. . . from the realm of the Mothers' (Jung 1930/1950/1966, CW15: para.: 159). After the 'art' of the alchemists split so that material experi-ment no longer went hand in hand with the practice of making symbols, modernity was ever more torn by the divorce of science from aesthetic practices. In mythical form, the male logos god of science represses the goddess art of wholeness. Jung wants a new practice of psychology that will put art and science back together again.

In showing meaning to be a function of a relation to the other (goddess-consciousness), Jung rewrites the script of modernity. 'Synchronicity' demonstrates reading for meaning in a dialogical relation between subjective understanding and objective, unknown reality; a relational mode of meaning dependent upon the other. 'Kore' and 'Trickster', despite the gender polarization, show the accretion of meaning as a function of dialogue between inner content or image and outer narrative frame (myth, other cultures, history). This accretion is the activity of culture and it is the ethical work of the goddess. Culture is weaving and unweaving texts that knit psyche into the collective by revealing meaning as dependent upon *relating* to the other.

Jung understood that his culture was built on structures of exclusion, and that this was a sickness. He tried to put back together the rational science derived from religious premises with ethical relating to the (unconscious) other. Mythically these are represented by the transcendent father-god of monotheism and the relational web of the Earth mother-goddess. While Jung's texts are limited by his own prejudices, his writing is yet to be fully appreciated as an experiential *process* of cultural healing. In the urgent task of addressing a world still haunted by apocalyptic narrative, now in the form of environmental crisis and global terror, Jung's aesthetic-science is a resource *in the writing*.

Epilogue
Hamlet and Psyche

Critically examined, can kinship libido be socialized, that is, understood in broad terms as holding social organisms and political forces together? If so, different facets of kinship libido, different kinds of incestuous sexual fantasies, will be involved in the emergence and destruction of different political forms. At one point, Jung hints that kinship libido helps to hold 'creeds, parties, nations or states together' (Jung 1946/1954, CW16: 233).

(Samuels 2001: 67)

[Y]et English Seneca read by candle-light yields good sentences as 'blood is a beggar', and so forth: and if you entreat him fair in a frosty morning, he will afford you whole *Hamlets*, I should say handfuls of tragical speeches.

(Nashe 1578/1994: 17)

Introduction: Literature and political forms

When Jung wrote his evocative account of reading James Joyce's novel *Ulysses* (see Chapter 1), he presented a literary work as a form for the transformation of consciousness (Jung 1932/1966, CW15). For him the novel was a cultural document as an active intervention in an ongoing history.

Jung's essay, 'Ulysses', drew on the vernacular of the present age in order to detect the novel's saturation in medieval sensibility. He saw a work of art as drawing upon the presence of the past in a contribution to a future revolution in consciousness. Great artistic works are goal oriented and meaningful in synchronous ways that complement and go beyond causal and autobiographical genres of criticism. If Jung's depiction of 'psychological' art is that it evokes what is contemporary and known in the work's cultural context, then 'visionary' signifies that it is imbued with what is not yet known, what may never be 'knowable' in rational terms, and what is potential in the culture. A visionary work may detect the obscure traces of what is yet to come.

The eminent theorist, Andrew Samuels, has developed Jung's thinking on kinship libido in the realm of cultural politics (Samuels 1993, 2001). Whereas Freud concentrated on sexuality as a personal matrix in the individual, for Jung, incest fantasies did not have to be regarded as primarily literal. Incestuous desire does not always signify sex. Rather incest images and narrative could operate at further levels of meaning as part of the psyche's teleological drive for future development. Samuels sees in Jung's concern for meaning in the relationship between the individual and the collective a germ of a theory of politics that does justice to the psychological make-up of its practitioners.

So, if kinship libido drives the structuring of political forms as part of the teleological framework of the human psyche, then perhaps literature (and art in general, of course), is one of the cultural spaces where political forms are debated, conflict, and the new struggles to be born?

This book has analysed Jung's writing as he struggles to find an art to undo the exclusions of modernity. Notably, he described the European Renaissance, the time of the flowering of alchemy and of Shakespeare, as a key turning point. So to illustrate some of the possibilities of Jung as a writer *for* modern ills, I am going to use his work as a frame to look at the play *Hamlet*'s diagnosis of the early modern condition. My argument is that Jungian and post-Jungian ideas can do more than just comment upon a work of art. Rather they are a means of intervening in the dialogical web of culture, ethics and politics. How can Jung help Hamlet speak to us today?

Not a Jungian reading of *Hamlet*

One way of taking a look at Shakespeare's play, *Hamlet*, is to see a hero myth in endemic crisis. Young Hamlet, the hero, has serious anima problems. Unable to move on from his first anima model in his mother, Gertrude, to his proper anima destination in his bride, Ophelia, he seems stuck in a Freudian destiny. The discovery that his mother has not only committed technical incest by marrying his father's brother, Claudius, but that she is also wed to his father's murderer, sends poor Hamlet insane. The situation is even more Oedipal if the play is read as Hamlet fantasizing that the man in his mother's bed has got there by killing his father. In removing Hamlet's father and taking possession of the body of his mother, Claudius is acting out Hamlet's repressed incestuous fantasies. No wonder Hamlet finds it difficult to kill him.

His delay is psychologically fatal because it leads to the death of his true anima figure, Ophelia. Eventually he carries out his heroic task in killing Claudius, yet the lack of a connection to life results in a wider extinguishing of possibilities. In the slaughter of the whole family, Gertrude, and Hamlet's simpler shadow 'other', Laertes, also die. The hero fails to restore health and plenty to his land by completion of his mission. As Hamlet dies, his land is taken over by an alien invader.

Hamlet is, in this reading, the hero myth interrupted. Perhaps that is a definition of tragedy: a failure of the hero narrative to be realized in action, with disastrous consequences for the well-being of a whole society. The difficulty of getting beyond Freudian dynamics here should alert us to serious problems in this reading from a Jungian perspective. From the vantage point of Jung's own writings, reading *Hamlet* as a failed hero myth has two flaws: it treats the play as a myth rather than a text (and Jung was well aware of the difference), and it assumes that the hero myth itself (about which Jung exhibits ambivalence even in his own age), is the only myth of individuation or consciousness for any period in history.

Hamlet: Myths in texts

Simply assigning the myth of the hero to the play is to assume that it is 'about' the character called 'Hamlet'. The play follows the failed individuation of the protagonist as if the growth of the individual was as much of a focus of the play's own age as it was for post-Romantic Jung, and for today. In fact, the contemporary title of the play we call *Hamlet* suggests that it is not concerned with a private individual at all. In the play's first printing in 1603, the title reads: 'The Tragicall Historie of Hamlet, Prince of Denmark' (Holderness and Loughrey 1992). It is a play about a prince, a politician.

Jung was careful to distinguish between myths as narratives that may occur in different places and epochs, and texts, which if mythical, are the precise realization of that myth in a particular cultural context. In order to find the right mythical language as the *frame* to make a text readable in Jungian terms, it is necessary to look for the *present* other.

Composed in an era of religious conflagration that was simultaneously on the cusp of a new dawn of science and colonial expansion, Shakespeare's *Hamlet* requires consideration of its material origins. Produced at the very end of the reign of the last Tudor monarch, Elizabeth, *Hamlet* was first performed less than a kilometre from a court looking to a new dynasty, and beyond that, quite soon, to revolution and civil war. The play is saturated with a mood of political crisis. As the Virgin Queen gives way to autocratic King James, *Hamlet* is less concerned with a hero myth than with a political myth.

In *Shakespeare and the Goddess of Complete Being*, Ted Hughes has described the present 'other' of Shakespeare's major plays as two intertwined myths (Hughes 1992). In the Venus and Adonis myth the great goddess is rejected by a chaste young man who is killed or sacrificed to her wrath. Often this killing is performed by the goddess herself in animal form. In the rape of Lucrece myth, a male goddess-destroyer wreaks havoc. These sacred narratives, Hughes argues, are respectively the myths behind renaissance Catholicism in its adherence to its goddess, Mary, Queen of Heaven cradling her dying son-lover, and of reformation Protestantism's goddess destroying god. 'He' is determined to crush the sacred eroticism, the network of the essential relatedness of living things, which goddess sexuality stands for. Puritanism is the cultural outcome.

Hamlet, like the other major plays, is framed by the living myths within the tortuous (sadly, literally so) cultural processes of sixteenth and seventeenth-century religious and political turmoil. Prince Hamlet fulfils his mythical destiny in being the means of destroying a court dominated by the transgressive sexuality of his (goddess) mother.

Undoubtedly, in his splendidly persuasive work, Hughes has succeeded in identifying the myths of Shakespeare's plays, both from internal evidence and cultural context. However, his reading of *Hamlet* makes no claim to explore the play as a process by which the myths are transmuted into political forms. He makes explicit his choice to tease out the myth, not to reveal the plays as text, where the myth is also a political and cultural space (Hughes 1992: 35–8). Nor does he consider the play teleologically. More work needs to be done on the Jungian model of the plays as texts in which the framing activity of myth makes visible political pressures within psychology itself.

Hamlet and political forms

Prince Hamlet seems modern to us. He is a university graduate, introspective, and has to learn politics the hard way. In particular, he experiences consciousness as a burden. Time and again, the Prince is caught in a gap between his capacity to reflect and discriminate, and the action his inherited social role demands of him

Hamlet's personal tragedy is that the play's events spur his consciousness into developing a greater ethical dimension, making his traditional role more and more untenable. What the mythical frame makes visible here is that the play is about an unbearable tension between an increase in consciousness and ancient social practices. It is 'about' the painful transition between past and future political forms: sacred kingship, in which family structures are indivisible from government, is fracturing under the pressure of a growth in discrimination that seeks to disentangle family, government and religion. In effect, this microcosm of society is *dying* to individuate, from its undifferentiated 'primitive' identification of family, rule and the divine.

KING: But now my cousin Hamlet, and my son.
HAMLET: A little more than kin, and less than kind. (I, ii, 64–5)

This verbal muddling of relationship in the King's address to Hamlet is a signal early in the play that what was formerly unified in sacred kinship is now just chaotically mixed up.

Prince Hamlet's starting position is one of relatively straightforward grief at his father's death and mother's remarriage, which has entailed – in a way that would be obvious to Shakespeare's first audiences – his displacement from his 'natural' succession to his father's crown. His mental breakdown, and by extension the annihilation of the entire royal family at the end of the play, is both a result of the unbearable growth in consciousness fragmenting old forms, and is itself a decisive forward-looking break with the past. Another kind of government, the military takeover of Fortinbras, enters the stage in the final moments. Therefore the end of the play leaves the audience with two incompatible images: a military state, and much more idealistically a kind of horizontal anti-hierarchy symbolized by Horatio, who clasps the dying Hamlet in his arms and swears to keep faith with him. A Jungian reading needs to see both possibilities as harbingers of a potential future.

On the one hand, the play *Hamlet* represents contemporary fears of constitutional breakdown as the 'magic' reign of the Virgin Queen gives way to a male family line. On the other hand, it is directed towards the history to come in which sacred kingship will indeed be prised apart in a period of Civil War and subsequent military rule. Secreted within its fraternal images in the one relationship of Hamlet's that lasts beyond the play, one might discern some of the utopian 'brotherhoods' of the Diggers and the Levellers that came to the fore in the Civil War. Of course, in a longer trajectory of cultural development, *Hamlet* shows the transition between the myth of sacred rulers to the myth of the politician. In Hamlet's feigned madness and disposal of one-time friends Rosencrantz and Guildenstern by a ruse, there are the mythical lineaments of the trickster.

However, to be more precise, I am not arguing that the true subject of the play is simply the growth of Prince Hamlet's consciousness. More aptly the play records the evolution of consciousness *of the whole court*. And the court is a metonym for an entire society. Arguably, Prince Hamlet develops *as a result* of the increase of consciousness around him. If that were the case then the real heroic figure is not Hamlet at all, but Gertrude.

Gertrude and the Ghost

As the play begins, the action turns on two previous events, only one of which required an increase in consciousness. Old King Hamlet has died and Queen Gertrude has married his brother, Claudius, who is now king. Gertrude has acted upon her desires and has paid a familiar price for breaking with custom: guilt. Her increased consciousness takes the form of transgressing her society's prohibition on marrying a dead husband's brother under the bar of incest. She has achieved this self-determination by reactivating a structure prior to the rules of patriarchal sacred kingship (where father gives way to son); one of matriarchal sacred rule. Sometimes the psyche leaps forward by looking back at its history.

In the myth of matriarchal monarchy the Queen exerts power in the name of the great goddess. *She* chooses her consort who is ritually killed by his successor. As to be expected in a significant leap forward, Gertrude has acted instinctively, in touch with her unconscious, and the cultural unconscious of divine monarchy. She only intuits that Claudius has fulfilled the older myth by executing his rival. It is this sensing of the ancient mythical framework that enables Gertrude to shape her desires as something comprehensible to her ego: it enables her to act against the conventions of her age.

Gertrude's increase in consciousness takes the form of a transgressive deed. Her activation of the unconscious synchronously provokes an archetypal response: the Ghost walks. It is helpful to think of the whole play as an individuating psyche; a metonym for the collective culture. The Ghost will not cease haunting the battlements (the fringes of consciousness, the last defences of the ego), until he has succeeded in telling his story to the one element to whom it will be most disturbing, Prince Hamlet.

The Ghost of the Father suggests an archaic form of the self, particularly in a patriarchal age. We know that he is archaic because he is dead, and because he is the shade of the immediate past, the sacred king who is gone. So unsurprisingly, the Ghost represents the present-past of sacred male kingship, the patriarchy of father-right demanding punishment of the pair who have deviated by harking back to the long vanished era of the goddess. Prince Hamlet's invocation to the Ghost stresses the indivisibility of paternity and rule.

> Thou com'st in such a questionable shape
> That I will speak to thee. I'll call thee Hamlet,
> King, father, royal Dane: Oh answer me. (I, iv, 33–5)

Significantly Hamlet is calling on a protean figure also called Hamlet. The suggestion of something erupting from Hamlet's unconscious is overwhelming. Prince Hamlet calls to a Hamlet who is dead, who was King, who is his father and the role – the identity – his culture has prepared for him. Prince Hamlet is looking at both the future he was bred to expect and the immediate past. Even time is unindividuated.

Significantly, this is not all about Prince Hamlet, the individual. Given that it is not only the bereaved son who sees the dead king, the Ghost may signify a collective attempt to regress to an earlier state of warrior sacred kingship, for remember, the Ghost demands action. Only Prince Hamlet hears the Ghost's story, however, suggesting that the collective will be transformed only through the tragic journey of one element. It also indicates that increased social consciousness is a tortuous uneven process in which individual social dysfunction is likely. Fortunately, collective regression, spearheaded by a warrior Prince, is not what happens next. Prince Hamlet resists being entirely engulfed by this (unconscious) apparition because he starts to apply conscious criteria. He questions the Ghost's veracity. Can he trust this story from the unconscious?

> The spirit I have seen
> May be the Devil, and the Devil hath power
> T'assume a pleasing shape, yea and perhaps
> Out of my weakness, and my melancholy,
> As he is very potent with such spirits
> Abuses me to damn me. (II, ii, 594–9)

Prince Hamlet, having started to think for himself, now has three choices. He can dismiss the Ghost's story as a fiction, he can believe it and refuse to act as the Ghost wants, or he can submit unthinkingly to the Ghost's direction, becoming its tool for revenge (the way of regression). The third option of regression is already marked by the play as the past. In either of the first two ways Prince Hamlet cannot escape a growth of consciousness in weighing and evaluating the Ghost's potent narrative. It is a measure of the development of *political* consciousness that Hamlet decides to test the evidence. For, under the myth of warrior sacred kingship he *should have already acted* in eliminating Claudius, even before the Ghost arrived to spur him on. That is, in sacred patriarchy Prince Hamlet should have seized control from the usurper who has denied his filial succession; there is no need for a murder story. In the gradual detaching of politics out of religious practice, crime fiction as a genre is a by-product! *Hamlet* demonstrates that crime fiction is closely related to political consciousness.

Hamlet decides to test the murder story by having a similar tale performed at court. In effect, a *repetition* of the monstrous accusation will *dramatize* the increase in consciousness of one individual and transform it into a collective event. *Prince* Hamlet's own individuating psyche plans to magnify the process outwards into the state. He thereby shows that drama's claim to be a representation of power is more properly here an exercise of power. What Prince Hamlet does is to make the play into a political arena in which political forms mutate. On one level a straightforward device of consciousness raising is, on another level, a visionary demonstration of politics as dramatic ritual. The play marks a political/sacred space in the material and cultural environment of the court. Overtly displaying politics in the temenos, the sacred arena of transformation, drama's rules and practices are a means of acting out and so transforming conscious and unconscious processes in the state:

> The play's the thing
> Wherein I'll catch the conscience of the King. (II, ii, 600–1)

Indeed the play is the crucible in which the conscience, as heightened consciousness, of King Claudius is forged.

Audiences on stage: Claudius, Ophelia, Laertes, Polonius

Prince Hamlet's sponsorship of 'the Murder of Gonzago' is successful in penetrating the royal complacency of King Claudius and Queen Gertrude. They leave hastily. Shortly afterwards the audience hears Claudius's confession of murder as he attempts to pray. The speech exposes Claudius's and the state's particular peril: sacred rituals of governance have failed in the face of political and dramatic rituals. Instead of a confessor hearing Claudius and absolving him, the audience does. Claudius is barred from seeking absolution elsewhere because he is not prepared to give up his ill-gotten gains, his crown and his wife. So the audience is explicitly positioned in the role of the sacred; a role unable to be fulfilled in its traditional manner.

Concealed in this pregnant dramatic moment is a very modern idea: that a government is legitimated only by the will of the collective (audience). It is an even more powerful idea if we reflect that in this potentially democratic sanctioning of Claudius is sought absolution for murder. In the relationship of crime fiction and politics lurks the dark side of the democratic contract: the implicit licensing of the government to kill on the people's behalf.

This moment of a king on his knees, witnessed only by the audience, is a laying bare of the spiritual structuring of political forms. The old mould is displayed as untenable. What will come forth when the sacred dimension of governance is invested in the people, rather than the body of the monarch (as the crying of the impotent old Ghost indicates)?

From this point, Claudius can no longer impersonate the sacred king, precisely because it has been revealed as an impersonation. Drama as a cultural form has emptied the drama of Claudius and Gertrude's grandeur of its ritual potency, and left only consciousness structured upon self-awareness that they are 'acting'. Claudius's crime, like that of Gertrude, has granted him an increase of consciousness framed as guilt. On the surface level of the play, Claudius is guilty of murder. At the level of deep (political) form, the crime is an engine of increased consciousness that is driving political changes.

For Claudius, being forced to face his guilt is to know, and simultaneously to present to the audience, a complete divorce between divine comfort and human politics:

May one be pardoned, and retain th'offence?
In the corrupted currents of this world,
Offence's gilded hand may shove by Justice,
And oft tis seen, the wicked prize itself
Buys out the law; but tis not so above, (III, iii, 56–60)

Claudius as king is cut off from unconscious healing by his refusal to atone. By clinging to an archaic ritual sacrifice because it satisfied his greed, Claudius cannot individuate into the present by remaking his identity on ethical grounds. His decision confirms that regression to goddess/matriarchal rule is not viable for this society since it has resulted in a painful separation of conscious and unconscious energy.

Ophelia is another member of the court who is part of the on-stage audience during the 'play'. Previously wooed by Prince Hamlet, she is now doubly put in a position where dramatic ritual increases her consciousness and precipitates her own pain. For as well as enduring Hamlet's lewd remarks during the play, which are designed to heighten its transgressive sexual content, Ophelia has already become an actor herself. In a further unfolding of the transition of the court from ritual to play acting, Ophelia was enlisted in an apparently harmless deception. Her role was to aid her betters in discovering the true state of Hamlet's disorder. She believed that she is 'acting' for Hamlet's own good and is entirely 'unconscious' of the King's far more sinister motives for being one of the concealed audience. Realizing the plot, Hamlet rejected Ophelia as one who is engaged in linguistic *substitution* for what had once been her potential to incarnate the goddess for him:

HAMLET: That if you be honest and fair, your honesty should admit no
    discourse to your beauty. (III, i, 107–8)

His speeches to Ophelia dwell upon her beauty and brutally strip her sexual allure away from the sacred. In '[g]et thee to a nunnery', we have another instance of the divorce of religion and state (III, i, 121). Here decisively ends the possible union of sexuality and sacred in the divine marriage of king and queen as Ophelia and Hamlet. For now the continuation of the sacred state is *dramatically* repudiated. Symbolically, Hamlet's rejection of Ophelia's well-meant advances is a dismissal of her attempt at increasing consciousness by invoking the goddess as sexuality as active relating.

Hamlet has his Protestant goddess-destroying moment in his cruelty to Ophelia. It is a rehearsal for his more extended indictment of his mother (goddess) for her ancient consciousness-raising rite of marrying her husband's killer. Ophelia's fate is sealed. Her consciousness is too marginal to survive the blows to her function of relating, inflicted first by rejection, and second by bereavement. For her, the adoption of the goddess mode in reaching out to Hamlet in love is not enough to free her from patriarchy in her attachment to her father, Polonius. When Hamlet kills him, her fate is to fall into the mythical unconscious.

Victim of the struggle between father-god and mother goddess, without being able to individuate a separation from their unconscious energy, Ophelia goes mad. At one level, Ophelia is Hamlet's feminine self and destiny. 'She' is rubbed out in a political world on the move from sacred masculine dominance to political masculine dominance. So Ophelia becomes the feminine forced back into the collective unconscious. She ends as the mouthpiece of the goddess as nature:

OPHELIA: There's rosemary, that's for remembrance. Pray love remember:
  and there's pansies, that for thoughts. (IV, v, 173–5)

It is possible to hear in these words an appeal for Jung's Eros, for goddess-consciousness, which is also love, to be remembered in this masculine world. Unfortunately for women, the one moment of embrace between a man and a woman in the play is when a banished prince raises a dead woman in his arms out of her grave. However, Eros does return, in fraternal mode, in the play's dying moments.

Ophelia's brother, Laertes, determines to revenge her suicide and his father's death on Prince Hamlet as author of his wrongs. Mourning the untimely demise of a father and dishonour of his female relative, Laertes is a sort of parallel or shadow Hamlet for the second half of the play. Unlike Hamlet, Laertes chooses the way of least consciousness. He wishes to be all action and no reflection. His aim is to go back to the political form now visibly withering at court: the sacred state with its warrior princes. Yet as with Claudius, this warrior identity is signalled as outdated by showing it to have lost its real connection to the sacred/unconscious. Claudius asks Laertes to prove himself a warrior son in a patriarchal state, in ways that go against the previously assumed connection between the divine, state power and personal honour:

CLAUDIUS: Hamlet comes back: what would you undertake,
  To show yourself your father's son in deed,
  More than in words?
LAERTES: To cut his throat i' th' church.
CLAUDIUS: No place indeed should murder sanctuarize;
  Revenge should have no bounds. (IV, vii, 123–7)

In choosing deeds above words, Laertes is not only downplaying the increase in consciousness that to Prince Hamlet has been enacted through the exercise of words above all, he is also seeking a return to political ritual determined by body and action, rather than words and discourse. Of course, Laertes' father Polonius has amply demonstrated that a rich diet of words is no guarantee of increased self-awareness. Profoundly ignorant of the true situation, Polonius's verbosity is yet another example of an ego so out of touch with the inner other that words have little meaning.

The struggle between Laertes and Hamlet is on one level the contest between politics as ritual action and politics as ritual discourse. Nevertheless, if the new political form shifts emphasis to the word, this development in the signifier still requires ritual connection, via the body, to the body of the state. The sacrifice of Polonius's body, killed unseen by mistake for the king, indicates a vital struggle between the body as sacred harbinger of power in divine kingship, and, the danger of a divorce between signifier and that which is signified in the new political discourse.

Polonius is killed *as a signifier* of the king; as a sign of unjust rule. Hamlet thinks he stabs Claudius hiding in his mother's room. In that dramatic moment, Polonius's death *pre-figures* the English Civil War 40 years later. In those battles, as in Shakespeare's play, the killing of king-signifiers (soldiers) will not prove sufficient. The king's body still has ritual potency; he too, must die.

So the death of Polonius is yet another rehearsal in a play devoted to the presentation of drama as the new cultural space of politics. Hamlet will finally kill Claudius and evade becoming an actor in a murder story by the very self-conscious regression of the whole court into archaic ritual; the setting up of ritual combat between Hamlet and Laertes. Before this can happen, Prince Hamlet has to complete his political education in ways that amount to collective political evolution.

Early in the play, Prince Hamlet decides to 'stage' his persona as madness in order to conceal his genuine condition of psychic invasion by the archaic form of the self in the Ghost. Unfortunately, the 'antic disposition' proves disruptive of the court system of signification and Polonius dies for Claudius. Sent to England, Hamlet on voyage ceases to be torn apart by the psyche/Ghost and achieves temporary integration with his 'antic' personality by becoming a trickster. He succeeds in having his friends executed instead of himself, demonstrating both the amorality of the trickster and the instincts of a politician.

Hamlet as trickster demonstrates that even operating at the level of tricky discourse (all he does is *substitute* a letter) can be lethal. Yet on return to Denmark, Hamlet is forced to re-encounter his brush with words and death, not as blithe trickster, but through a renewed function of Eros-relating. Having twice delivered death through the signifier, he literally enters and inhabits it *bodily* in the graveyard.

Arriving just before an unnamed funeral, Hamlet and Horatio are intro- duced to a skull, that of another trickster, the clown, Yorick.

HAMLET: Let me see. Alas poor Yorick, I knew him, Horatio, a fellow of
infinite jest. . . Here hung those lips, that I have kiss'd I know not
how oft. . . Now get you to my Lady's chamber, and tell her, let her
paint an inch thick, to this favour she must come. Make her laugh at
that. (V, i, 178–89)

So far in this scene the extinction of Hamlet as trickster is staged twice.
First, Hamlet is told of his own madness and does not claim it. He does not
admit to being the mad banished prince. Second, the beloved clown is very
definitely dead, as we see Hamlet holding up his skull. Hamlet's most Eros-
like love scene is with the dead skull of a trickster. Now looking beyond the
archaic vengeful self as the death-demanding Ghost, Hamlet begins a new
connection to the numinous, and a new Eros: with death rather than the
feminine. So it is not surprising that when Ophelia's funeral begins
Hamlet is able to utter words of love only in a past tense: 'I Lov'd Ophelia'
(V, i, 264).

His true Eros is now, as it has always been in this play, with death. Yet it
is no longer death as bearer of sacred patriarchal vengeance. Death as
numinous contains positive political energies for the future as well as overtones of civil war. So Hamlet's self as vengeful Ghost gives way to a new self
image as 'fate', a numinous connection to death.

HAMLET: [T]here is special providence in the fall of a sparrow. If it be now,
'tis not to come: if it be not to come, it will be now: if it be not now
yet it will come; the readiness is all. (V, ii, 215–18)

Consequently, in the final scene, which Claudius sets up as an overtly old-
fashioned ritual murder of Hamlet, the protagonist's elimination of the
corrupt king is far from a fulfilment of the Ghost's command of warrior
revenge. Rather it is a ritual cleansing; a sacrificial act as Hamlet embraces
his own end in the very moment of striking. It heralds the death of sacred
monarchy and the instating of new political forms. Hamlet's numinous
connection to death is also a bringing into being of the future.

The final scene

For the last scene Claudius sets up ritual combat between Laertes and
Hamlet in order to finish off the latter. Should Laertes fail in his stated plan
to kill Hamlet rather than to respect the rules, then Claudius has provided a
poisoned cup for his refreshment. Fatally, Gertrude drinks the poison by
mistake. Dying, she reveals the treachery in a final, suggestively verbal,
embrace of her son rather than her husband.

GERTRUDE: O my dear Hamlet,
    The drink, the drink, I am poisoned. (V, ii, 315–16)

Even dying Laertes manages to catch something of Hamlet's numinous Eros. At last he shows some sign of individuating away from his kin(g)ship libido regression and reveals that Hamlet has been poisoned by his blade on the king's orders. So when Hamlet stabs Claudius, it is as much an act to remove a dangerously out of control killer as it is to avenge his father (who is not mentioned).

Prince Hamlet's final action is, typically, designed to increase the *collective* consciousness by the furtherance of his *story*. At the same time he explicitly forbids civil war by legitimating the new invader, Fortinbras, whose soldiers are now on stage. Horatio, a constant figure of Eros between men in loyalty to Hamlet, offers to die with him. By forbidding Horatio from instinctively copying his example, Prince Hamlet prevents his own numinous embrace of death from becoming a collective surrender to unconsciousness as mass suicide. Hamlet instructs him to serve the collective as his active substitute in furthering the new political consciousness:

HAMLET: And in this harsh world draw thy breath in pain
    To tell my story. . .
    But I do prophesy th'election lights
    On Fortinbras, he has my dying voice. (V, ii, 353–61)

Prince Hamlet expires extolling two aspects of political discourse: the emotive, Eros-relational mode of his reputation, his-story, and the practical legitimating speech of rational government. The play ends with the arrival of Fortinbras and his army; an entrance far from the ritual display of the previous era of sacred monarchy. Fortinbras closes the play with a moving tribute to Hamlet. So the new, military style government sensibly creates an Eros link to the old:

FORTINBRAS: Bear Hamlet like a soldier to the stage,
    For he was likely had he been put on
    To have proved most royally: and for his passage,
    The soldiers music, and rites of war
    Speak loudly for him. (V, ii, 401–5)

Soldiers bearing Hamlet with rites of war enact *bodily* the complete transition of political forms. Just as Hamlet's absorption into Fortinbras's military rituals grant the new style rule Eros legitimacy, so Hamlet's final ambiguous status as political hero is sealed into a soldier's honourable death. War is the new political 'rite'.

Suggestively, however, alongside the triumph of military rule is a more egalitarian structure just visible in the *activation* of the friendship between Horatio and Hamlet. Before the soldiers re-ritualize Hamlet's body, he is cradled in Horatio's arms, just as the death of Laertes is one of reconciliation with his hated enemy. So here, perceptibly, is a fraternal mode of love between men, which might, in time, also yield a politics of brotherhood. Of sisterhood, the play offers fewer signs except the sympathy of Gertrude for dead Ophelia.

Crucially, of course, the most important transformation of consciousness is that of the audience. The play forges a new political form: the military state, alongside a new political actor: the politician with a new emphasis on ritual through words rather than articulation of power via the (sacred) body of the monarch. Behind and framing these new political forms is a numinous connection to death.

The rituals of sacrifice have mutated from the body of the king to the multiplicity of substitutes in soldiers going to war. A long way in the future, that multiplicity of the people will become the bearer of the numinous aspect of power itself, in the political forms now called democracy. In the play, Polonius's death is the literal prefiguring of the many deaths of a war in which the loosening of the signifier/signified means the elimination of kingship as a form of government can be brought to pass by means of his soldiers (infinite) substitutes.

So, if the play anticipates the bloody battles of the English Civil War, its fraternal ending also feeds the coming era's revolutionary attempts to establish egalitarian rule. The Levellers and the Diggers do not succeed, just as the very final seconds of *Hamlet* are of soldiers, not brothers. Nevertheless those democratizing ideals remained in the British political imagination, just as Hamlet and Horatio are presences in its culture. Although it must be remembered (and feminism has re-membered) that masculine fraternity has been built upon erosion of living bonds to the feminine. In *Hamlet*, the feminine 'other' frames the masculine action and is yet to find its political 'voice'.

Therefore, *Hamlet* the play is not so much a representation of politics as a reconstruction of collective consciousness that is part of the action of politics. Art such as *Hamlet* is a stage upon which political forms are mobilized, and in turn shape the collective psyche. Art is a crucible of changing political forms. And drama, for this historical period as others, is a political ritual through which society individuates.

Jungian literary criticism

In staying true to Jung's preoccupation with quaternities, it is worth revisiting the four key terms in his analysis of art. A work can be 'psychological' or 'visionary', in either recording the collective consciousness of its age, or by being profoundly traced by archetypal, sublime influences. It follows that visionary art brings into being the other two principles. It will be found to play a 'compensatory' role to the historical conditions of its time and to represent a 'teleological' movement towards future social processes.

Hamlet can be regarded in all four ways that fruitfully open up the work to understanding. First, it is a 'psychological' text in treating the transition between the 'magical' Virgin Queen and a male Stuart dynasty, and also by marking the invention of self-consciousness as the ground of ethical being. Symptomatically, it is hard to distinguish the psychological from the visionary acuity of this remarkable play. For instance, behind the thin screen of consciousness, and giving it tension, is a new awareness of death as a chaotic factor because existing religious narratives can no longer contain it. 'Death' becomes the carrier of the unknowablity of the unconscious, as that which exerts a fatal pressure on the rational grasp of the world:

HAMLET: To be or not to be, that is the question. . .
    But that the dread of something after death,
    The undiscovered country, from whose bourn
    No traveller returns, puzzles the will. (III, i, 56–80)

Today we call 'the undiscovered country' the unconscious, because it is the margin that undoes conscious being.

As a visionary work, *Hamlet* enacts the transition of the sacred state to its probable successor, one based on military might. It does so mainly by focusing on the evolution of a warrior prince into a politician. Optimistically, one could argue that it just hints at the possibility of feminine empowerment, not least because relational consciousness and ethics is no longer confined to the sphere of women: it becomes viable for recasting masculine social roles. Unfortunately, it takes the nearness of death exerting its numinous powers to effectively structure a fraternity. A sibling political form is some way distant.

As part of *Hamlet*'s compensatory properties, it provides a new relation to the sacred or self in developing away from imprisonment in archaic revenge tragedy (the dwindling power of the Ghost) to fate and death as numinous. Moreover it shows how this new relation may structure an ethical individuating consciousness. Given *Hamlet*'s own social context, the development of masculine kinship libido out of kingship libido may compensate the stress placed on the masculine relational network in the rule of ageing Queen Elizabeth. The Virgin Queen famously deployed an Eros relation to the masculine in her courtiers. In her final years her 'sacred' sexual potency inevitably declined.

Teleologically, of course, *Hamlet* is ominous for the prospects of the new Stuart dynasty with its determination to preserve the sacred dimension to kingly rule. Within the dynamics of the play can be discerned the fracturing of divine kin(g)ship, the threat of military rule and revolutionary fraternal forms of government.

Also perceptible is later modernity's painful loss of connection to the numinous in the confrontation with the brute matter of death in the grave-yard scene. It is just possible that Prince Hamlet's way through his immersion in materialism, his ability to embrace fate as something numinous that will bind him into the collective; that this may offer something to the twenty-first century citizen.

The only time the play specifies that Prince Hamlet wholeheartedly embraces a woman, she is dead. At this moment, with dead mad Ophelia in his arms, he announces himself not as a prince, but as, 'I, Hamlet, the Dane' (V, i, 250–1). As well as a warning that all is not well between masculine and feminine principles, this cry is also a restatement of identity shorn of the royal and asserting proximity. Hamlet is the Dane; Denmark is not Tudor England, but rather a Protestant state, nearby both geographically and politically. *Hamlet* is therefore a cultural space in which political possibilities are rehearsed for an English audience. The play occupies a liminal position in the collective consciousness.

A Jungian literary criticism of *Hamlet* has described what Andrew Samuels has identified as 'political forms' drawing on kinship libido. It has looked at the framing work of the myths of goddess rule and the goddess devouring god as making visible new forms of ethical consciousness emerging within the space of the play. In anticipating some of the turmoil of seventeenth century English politics, the play is a rehearsal for the future. Jung believed that the psyche was incarnated in a time and place, yet reached forward into future possibilities, personal, cultural and historical. For him, art was the crucible of collective modes of consciousness; *Hamlet* is a ritual construction of politics for its audiences, then and now.

Therefore Jungian literary criticism itself is more than a secondary treatment of material sealed in the past. Rather, it too, is a reformation of understanding. Such criticism draws the past into the present as an excursion of ego consciousness into the unknown. Art is a pathway into the other, where the 'other' is the act of creation, and, by extension, the past of which the art forms a constituent part. To Jung, art is where the psyche extends through time and history.

So by bringing past forms of consciousness into the present, Jungian reading of literature might provide opportunities to reframe the conflicts of our age. Just as, it is my contention, literary approaches to Jung's own writings have lasting value. For within Jung as a writer we find epistemo-logical and aesthetic tools for redesigning the ethical consciousness of the world not yet known, not yet brought into being.

References

Adams, M. V. (1996) *The Multicultural Imagination: 'Race', Colour and the Unconscious*, London and New York: Routledge.

Bair, D. (2004) *Jung: A Biography*, New York: Little Brown.

Bakhtin, M. M. (1981) *The Dialogic Imagination: Four Essays*, ed. M. Holquist, trans. C. Emerson and M. Holquist, Austin: University of Texas Press.

Barthes, R. (2001) 'Death of the author', in P. Rice and P. Waugh (eds) *Modern Literary Theory: A Reader*, London: Arnold, pp. 185–9.

Barton, E. L. (1993) 'Evidentials, argumentation, and epistemological stance', *College English* 55, 7: 745–69.

Baumlin, J. S., Baumlin, T. F. and Jensen, G. H. (eds) (2004) *Post-Jungian Criticism: Theory and Practice*, New York: State University of New York Press.

Berleant, A. (1992) *The Aesthetics of Environment*, Philadelphia, PA: Temple University Press.

Bishop, P. (ed.) (1999) *Jung in Contexts: A Reader*, London and New York: Routledge.

Bishop, P. (2002) *Jung's Answer to Job: A Commentary*, London and New York: Brunner-Routledge.

Bright, G. (1997) 'Synchronicity as a basis of analytic attitude', *Journal of Analytical Psychology* 42, 4: 613–35.

Brooke, R. (2000) 'Jung's recollection of the life-world' in R. Brooke (ed.) *Pathways into the Jungian World: Phenomenology and Analytical Psychology*, London and New York: Routledge, pp. 13–24.

Brooke, R. (ed.) (2000) *Pathways into the Jungian World: Phenomenology and Analytical Psychology*, London and New York: Routledge.

Burke, E. (1757/1990) *A Philosophical Enquiry into the Origin of our Ideas of the Sublime and the Beautiful*, ed. A. Philips, Oxford: Oxford University Press.

Butler, J. (1990) *Gender Trouble: Feminism and the Subversion of Identity*, London and New York: Routledge.

Charet, F. X. (1993) *Spiritualism and the Foundations of C.G. Jung's Psychology*, New York: State University of New York Press.

Charet, F. X. (2000) 'Understanding Jung: recent biographies and scholarship', *Journal of Analytical Psychology* 45: 195–216.

Coupe, L. (1997) *Myth*, London and New York: Routledge.

Coupe, L. (ed.) (2000) *The Green Studies Reader: From Romanticism to Ecocriticism*, London and New York: Routledge.

Davis, O. (2004) 'Theorizing writerly creativity: Jung with Lacan?', in J. S. Baumlin, T. F. Baumlin and G. H. Jensen (eds) *Post-Jungian Criticism: Theory and Practice*, New York: State University of New York Press, pp. 55–74.

Derrida, J. (1977) *Of Grammatology*, trans. G. C. Spivak, Baltimore, MD: Johns Hopkins University Press.

Derrida, J. (1978) *Writing and Difference*, trans. A. Blass, London: Routledge.

Derrida, J. (1989) 'The ghost dance: an interview with Jacques Derrida', trans. J.-L. Svoboda, *Public* 2: 60–73.

Derrida, J. (1997) 'Marx c'est quelqu'un', in J. Derrida, M. Guillaume and J.-P. Vincent, *Marx en Jeu*, Paris: Descartes, pp. 9–28.

Eagleton, T. (2003) *After Theory*, Harmondsworth: Penguin.

Edinger, E. F. (1996) *The Aion Lectures: Exploring the Self in C.G. Jung's Aion*, ed. D. A. Wesley, Toronto: Inner City Books.

Elms, A. C. (1994) *Uncovering Lives: The Uneasy Alliance of Biography and Psychology*, New York and Oxford: Oxford University Press.

Evernden, N. (1996) 'Beyond ecology: self, place and the pathetic fallacy', in C. Glotfelty and H. Fromm (eds) *The Ecocriticism Reader: Landmarks in Literary Ecology*, Athens and London: University of Georgia Press, pp. 92–104.

Freud, S. (1899/1976) *The Interpretation of Dreams*, trans. J. Strachey, Harmondsworth: Penguin.

Glotfelty, C. and H. Fromm. (eds) (1996) *The Ecocriticism Reader: Landmarks in Literary Ecology*, Athens and London: University of Georgia Press.

Hauke, C. (2000) *Jung and the Postmodern: The Interpretation of Realities*, London and New York: Routledge.

Hauke, C. and Alister, I. (eds) (2001) *Jung and Film: Post-Jungian Takes on the Moving Image*, London and New York: Brunner-Routledge.

Hillman, J. (1983) *Healing Fiction*, Barrytown, NY: Station Hill Press.

Hillman, J. (1989) *The Essential James Hillman: A Blue Fire*, ed. T. Moore, London and New York: Routledge.

Hockley, L. (2001) 'Film noir: archetypes or stereotypes', in C. Hauke and I. Alister (eds) *Jung and Film: Post-Jungian Takes on the Moving Image*, London and New York: Brunner-Routledge, pp. 177–93.

Holderness, G. and Loughrey, B. (eds) (1992) *The Tragicall History of Hamlet Prince of Denmarke*, New York and London: Harvester Wheatsheaf.

Hughes, T. (1992) *Shakespeare and the Goddess of Complete Being*, London: Faber and Faber.

Jones, R. A. (2002) 'The necessity of the unconscious', *Journal for the Theory of Social Behaviour* 32: 345–66.

Jones, R. A. (2003) 'Mixed metaphors and narrative shifts: archetypes', *Theory & Psychology* 13, 5: 651–72.

Joyce, J. (1922/1992) *Ulysses*, Harmondsworh: Penguin.

Jung, C. G. Except where a different publication is noted below, all references are, by volume and paragraph number, to the edition of *The Collected Works of C.G. Jung (1953–91)* (CW), eds H. Read, M. Fordham and G. Adler, trans. by R. F. C. Hull, London: Routledge/Princeton, NJ: Princeton University Press. The final date of the citation is the date of the English text.

Jung, C. G. (1963/1983) *Memories, Dreams, Reflections*, London: Fontana.

Jung, C. G. (1967/1984) 'Introduction' to "Psychology and Literature"', *The Spirit in Man, Art and Literature*, London: Routledge.

Le Guin, U. (1996) 'The carrier bag theory of fiction', in C. Glotfelty and H. Fromm (eds) *The Ecocriticism Reader: Landmarks in Literary Ecology*, Athens and London: University of Georgia Press, pp. 149–54.

Main, R. (ed.) (1997) *Jung on Synchronicity and the Paranormal*, London: Routledge/Princeton, NJ: Princeton University Press.

Main, R. (2000) 'Religion, science and synchronicity', *Harvest: Journal for Jungian Studies* 46, 2: 89–107.

Main, R. (2004) *The Rupture of Time: Synchronicity and Jung's Critique of Modern Western Culture*, London and New York: Brunner-Routledge.

Manes, C. (1996) 'Nature and silence', in C. Glotfelty and H. Fromm (eds) *The Ecocriticism Reader: Landmarks in Literary Ecology*, Athens and London: University of Georgia Press, pp. 15–29.

Marcus, L. (1994) *Auto/Biographical Discourses: Theory, Criticism, Practice*, Manchester and New York: Manchester University Press.

Meeker, J. W. (1996) 'The comic mode', in C. Glotfelty and H. Fromm (eds) *The Ecocriticism Reader: Landmarks in Literary Ecology*, Athens and London: University of Georgia Press, pp. 155–69.

Miller, D. L. (2002) 'The word/image problem'. Online. Available. HTTP: <http://www.rubedo.psc.br/artingle/wordima.htm> (accessed 6 May 2004).

Mitchell, S. (1996) *Improving the Quality of Argument in Higher Education*, London: University of Middlesex.

Murphy, P. D. (2000) 'Ecofeminist dialogics', in L. Coupe (ed.) *The Green Studies Reader: From Romanticism to Ecocriticism*, London and New York: Routledge, pp. 193–7.

Nashe, T. (1578/1994) *Hamlet* by William Shakespeare, G. B. Harrison (ed.), Harmondsworth: Penguin.

Papadopoulos, R. K. (1991) 'Jung and the concept of the other', in R. K. Papadopoulos and G. S. Saayman (eds) *Jung in Modern Perspective: The Master and his Legacy*, London: Prism Press, pp. 54–88.

Papadopoulos, R. K. and Saayman, G. S. (eds) (1991) *Jung in Modern Perspective: The Master and his Legacy*, London: Prism Press.

Pietikanen, P. (1999) *C.G. Jung and the Psychology of Symbolic Forms*, Helsinki: Academia Scientiarum Fennica.

Rice, P. and Waugh, P. (eds) (2001) *Modern Literary Theory: A Reader*, London: Arnold.

Rowland, S. (1999) *C.G. Jung and Literary Theory: The Challenge from Fiction*, Basingstoke and New York: Palgrave.

Rowland, S. (2002) *Jung: A Feminist Revision*, Cambridge: Polity Press.

Roszak, B. and Roszak, T. (2000) 'Deep form in art and nature', in L. Coupe (ed.) *The Green Studies Reader: From Romanticism to Ecocriticism*, London and New York: Routledge, pp. 223–6.

Rychlak, J. F. (1991) 'Jung as dialectician and teleologist', in R. K. Papadopoulos & G. S. Saayman (eds) *Jung in Modern Perspective: The Master and his Legacy*, London: Prism Press, pp. 34–53.

Samuels, A. (1985) *Jung and the Post-Jungians*, London: Routledge & Kegan Paul.

Samuels, A. (1993) *The Political Psyche*, London and New York: Routledge.

Samuels, A. (2001) *Politics on the Couch: Citizenship and the Internal Life*, London: Profile.

Samuels, A., Shorter, B. and Plaut, F. (eds) (1986) *A Critical Dictionary of Jungian Analysis*, London and New York: Routledge.

Segal, R. A. (ed.) (1992) *The Gnostic Jung*, Princeton, NJ: Princeton University Press/London: Routledge.

Segal, R. A. (ed.) (1998) *Jung on Mythology*, London and New York: Routledge.

Segal, R. A. (2003) 'Jung's very twentieth-century view of myth', *Journal of Analytical Psychology* 48, 5: 593–617.

Shamdasani, S. (1999) 'Memories, dreams, omissions', in P. Bishop (ed.) *Jung in Contexts: A Reader*, London and New York: Routledge.

Shamdasani, S. (2003) *Jung and the Making of Modern Psychology: The Dream of a Science*, Cambridge and New York: Cambridge University Press.

Snyder, G. (2000) 'Language goes two ways', in L. Coupe (ed.) *The Green Studies Reader: From Romanticism to Ecocriticism*, London and New York: Routledge, pp. 127–31.

Solomon, H. (1994) 'The transcendent function and Hegel's dialectical vision', *Journal of Analytical Psychology* 39: 77–100.

Soper, K. (2000) 'The idea of nature', in L. Coupe (ed.) *The Green Studies Reader: From Romanticism to Ecocriticism*, London and New York: Routledge, pp. 123–6.

Toulmin, S., Reike, R. and Janik, A. (1984) *An Introduction to Reasoning*, New York and London: Macmillan.

White Jr, L. (1996) 'The historical roots of our ecologic crisis', in C. Glotfelty and H. Fromm (eds) *The Ecocriticism Reader: Landmarks in Literary Ecology*, Athens and London: University of Georgia Press, pp. 3–14.

Wolfreys, J. (2002) *Victorian Hauntings: Spectrality, Gothic, the Uncanny and Literature*, Basingstoke and New York: Palgrave.

Index